T0283633

NEW PRIZE *for* THESE EYES

The Rise of America's Second Civil Rights Movement

JUAN WILLIAMS

SIMON & SCHUSTER

New York   Amsterdam/Antwerp   London
Toronto   Sydney   New Delhi

Simon & Schuster
1230 Avenue of the Americas
New York, NY 10020

First Simon & Schuster hardcover edition January 2025

SIMON & SCHUSTER and colophon are registered trademarks of Simon & Schuster, LLC

For information about special discounts for bulk purchases,
please contact Simon & Schuster Special Sales
at 1-866-506-1949 or business@simonandschuster.com.

The Simon & Schuster Speakers Bureau can bring authors to your live event.
For more information or to book an event, contact the
Simon & Schuster Speakers Bureau at 1-866-248-3049 or
visit our website at www.simonspeakers.com.

Interior design by Ruth Lee-Mui

Manufactured in the United States of America

1   3   5   7   9   10   8   6   4   2

Library of Congress Cataloging-in-Publication Data is available.

ISBN 978-1-6680-1235-2
ISBN 978-1-6680-1237-6 (ebook)

Dedicated to

CHRISTOPHER TEAL

and my generation beyond—

ELIAS, PEPPER, WESLEY,
MARGOT, *and* AUGUST

The previous generation, the Moses generation, pointed the way. They took us 90 percent of the way there.... So the question, I guess, that I have today is what's called of us in this Joshua generation? What do we do in order to fulfill that legacy; to fulfill the obligations and the debt that we owe to those who allowed us to be here today?

—Barack Obama, Selma Voting Rights
March Commemoration, 2007

Contents

NEW PRIZE *for* THESE EYES

INTRODUCTION

Birth of a Second Movement

Ferguson was burning.

It was the summer of 2014, and each night young Black people and white police violently faced off in this small, mostly working-class Black suburb outside St. Louis, Missouri. An unarmed Black teenager named Michael Brown had been shot in the street by a white cop. His body was left to lie in the August sun throughout the afternoon, infuriating people already distressed that Brown had been killed by police. By sunset, an angry crowd of young Black people began throwing rocks and lighting fires, furious with the shooting and the disrespect for Brown's lifeless body.

Ferguson was the latest incident in a recent series of white law enforcement killings of Black men. Two years earlier, in 2012, another unarmed Black teenager, Trayvon Martin, was shot to death in Florida by a vigilante community watchman. The gunman was found not guilty, sparking a national outpouring of rage and grief. Next, a forty-three-year-old unarmed Black man, Eric Garner, was jumped by New York police in July 2014 for selling single cigarettes on the street. He died while in a white policeman's chokehold. More protests followed. Now, a month later, the latest victim was eighteen-year-old Michael Brown. These stories of racial violence received front-page coverage in the daily papers and led the evening news on television. It also fed finger-pointing and blame around the clock on Black social media.

A new phrase and hashtag had entered the public discourse, calling attention to the insensitivity of the police—and of the broader society—to these deaths: Black Lives Matter.

The nation's first Black president, Barack Obama, watched on television as flames and tear gas became the lead story on every national news program for the next week. His senior advisers debated whether he should go to Ferguson. The idea of sending the president of the United States into a race riot had never come up at any other White House. All the previous presidents had been white men. With the first Black president the idea became relevant, however. Certainly he would have something unique to say to stop the rage and violence from spreading nationwide.

Obama was in an impossible situation—walking "between the raindrops" as one congressional ally would later put it—unable to deliver the justice that many protesters and online activists were demanding while failing to effectively counter the racist elements at the root of the problem.[1] He was unwilling to take the risk of speaking out against politicians and right-wing pundits who glamorized police to justify racist treatment of Blacks.

The difficulty Obama found himself in obscured the fact that he had started this new civil rights movement ten years earlier by raising expectations for a higher level of racial justice when he burst onto the national scene at the 2004 Democratic convention. He spoke to a national audience about an uplifting vision of America as a nation no longer defined by Black and white or red state and blue state. He was immediately hailed as christening a "post-racial" era.

This biracial man in so many ways was the fulfillment of the mid-twentieth-century civil rights movement's fight to end strict segregation between Black and white. His winning the presidency in 2008 was a dream come true, almost a fantasy of twentieth-century civil rights aspirations to enact voting rights protections that would increase Black elected officials. His intellect and character were widely appreciated as first-rate. He was handsome and spoke often of his love for his family. His speeches became celebrated events, a reminder of how earlier generations were stirred by words coming from Lincoln, Kennedy, or King. He was glorified by magazines, musicians, athletes, comedians, public figures of all colors as he built trust across the racial divide as the nation's leader.

But talk of the post-racial dream had turned into a cruel illusion. By 2014 and with smoke rising in Ferguson, Obama was his own man, trying to find his way in this new world but still chained by racial realities that he could not escape.

Obama was dealing with a nation radically different from what it was during the earlier civil rights era. The demographic mix was like nothing seen fifty years prior. For one, Hispanics had become the largest minority in twenty-first-century America. And although segregation was no longer legal, problems of racial injustice remained, especially when it came to police brutality in Black neighborhoods. It was also an America where politics and culture were being shaped by incredible advancements in technology. Instantaneous threads and memes were in everyone's pocket twenty-four hours a day, allowing events in a small town like Ferguson to become national fire.

Racial protests are nothing new in American history. In fact, much of the success of the First Civil Rights Movement in the 1950s and 1960s was precisely because of protests. But those protests had been conducted with precision by established civil rights organizations executing long-term strategies. Groups like the NAACP carefully planned picture-perfect marches of peaceful, well-dressed people. They condemned riots. They combined carefully planned protest with legal action in the courts, advancing lawsuits to outlaw discrimination as unconstitutional. Charismatic leaders like Dr. Martin Luther King Jr. arranged boycotts, sit-ins, and nonviolent marches, and accepted time in jail—all in the service of compelling white politicians to pass new laws protecting Black rights. And it worked. Congress enacted landmark legislation, including the Civil Rights Act of 1964 and the Voting Rights Act of 1965.

Nearly half a century later, Ferguson confounded Obama. His election in so many ways marked the culmination of decades of struggle to win Black Americans access to the halls of power, but it was clear to anyone watching the news that racial tensions in America hadn't gone away. Suddenly, the values and tactics of the First Civil Rights Movement seemed old and out of sync with the urgent racial issues of the new day. White cops were killing Black people, and Black people were rioting. History was shifting under the feet of the first Black president, driven by new realities, new goals, different players, and expanded possibilities. It reached beyond the compromises made by white-majority power, culture, and money in the last half of the twentieth century to keep race relations stable. New demographics of the twenty-first century had created new political coalitions that made Obama's election possible, planting the seeds of a new Second Movement. But as the fighting in Ferguson showed, this new movement was changing into something he had never expected.

As an author and journalist, I have been telling the story of the Civil Rights Movement my entire career. I'm seventy years old, so that is a long time.

More than thirty years ago, I wrote my first book, *Eyes on the Prize: America's Civil Rights Years, 1954–1965.* The book tells the story of America's great fight for racial equality—the dramatic, inspiring Civil Rights Movement of the twentieth century. The book was part of a collaboration with a celebrated television documentary series that aired on PBS.

My second book, *Thurgood Marshall: American Revolutionary*, was a prize-winning biography of the first Black person to serve on the U.S. Supreme Court, Justice Thurgood Marshall. When he was in his late eighties and near the end of his life, we talked for six months about all he had witnessed, his dive into the changing tides of race relations in America. Since then, I have written books and television documentaries on Black religion, historically Black colleges, and Black politics. And all along, as a working journalist, I have participated in the movement by writing books, magazine articles, columns, and speaking about injustice and the continuing drama of America's racial struggle.

Today I see a great fight for racial justice taking shape in the twenty-first century, a new civil rights movement. It is built on the achievements of the First Movement, but it's not an extension of the First Movement, and when we try to judge this new movement by comparing it to its predecessor of the twentieth century, we fail to see its true shape. Such comparisons are inevitable, but they are ultimately misleading. At my speaking engagements, I'm often asked, "Who is today's Dr. King?" There is no new Dr. King. The First Movement offers some context—a reference point—for what we are going through today. But this Second Movement is distinct. They cannot fairly be compared.

The First Civil Rights Movement was about getting Black people out of the back of the bus. It was about integration, breaking down segregation not just in busing, but in schools, housing, and voting. It put an end to "Whites" and "Colored" signs over water fountains. Its victories began in the courts in the 1950s. Later activists turned to the streets in the 1960s to demand that those constitutional rights be protected. In the 1970s politics became the main battlefield, with civil rights groups working to elect more diverse people to local government and Congress. Those elected politicians passed further protections in civil rights, including voting rights, housing, and affirmative action laws.

These victories formed the backdrop to the early days of the Second Movement. In the early 2000s, America's political leaders were more diverse than ever. Barack Obama, a Black man, had just become president. But a post-racial America continued to elude us. This Second Civil Rights Movement had to deal with persistent, deep-seated cultural issues that the First Movement had left unresolved and, in some cases, new issues that arose in the backlash to its legislative and political victories. The Second Civil Rights Movement was about police violence and reducing the number of Black people in prison. But it was also about standing up to persistent racism, such as daily intimidating experiences with police, lower achievement in schools that were no longer segregated by law but in practice, and widespread economic inequality as compared to the nation's white majority.

In some ways, it employed tactics used by the First Civil Rights Movement, but the context was radically different. The First Civil Rights Movement activists faced white segregationist violence led by government officials like Alabama's Bull Connor. The Second Civil Rights Movement saw Black people angrily taking to the streets in places like Ferguson to demand that police be held accountable for violence. No one even thought to protest Bull Connor's brutality. Their protests were against segregation at downtown stores and lunch counters. Connor's cruelty was a fact of life that no one dared to challenge. And where the First Civil Rights Movement simply called for desegregation, the Second Civil Rights Movement wants police officers jailed when they wrongly harass or kill Black people.

The First Civil Rights Movement's most successful tactics of nonviolent marches, and its strategy of filing lawsuits, was passed on like Moses's Ten Commandments to women's rights groups, LGBTQ groups, Latino rights groups, disability rights groups, Native American rights groups, and more through the latter half of the twentieth century and beyond. The movement's legacy served as the foundation of civil rights progress from affirmative action in schools, to increased racial diversity in corporate hiring, and the rise of political power with the election of more Blacks to local office, Congress, and eventually the presidency.

The Second Civil Rights Movement was born out of Obama's rise to the presidency and the hope that came with it. But frustration also came from still needing to confront the continuing reality of deeply rooted racism.

To be Black six decades after the passage of the Civil Rights Act is still to live in fear of police. The fury in Ferguson emerged from deep wells of anger and distrust between Black people and police across the years and across the nation. As a Black man, I am more likely than my neighbors of other races to be shot dead or mugged. To be Black today is still to feel less safe in your neighborhood. To be Black today is to live with the fear of being twice as likely to be killed by guns as whites—and tragically, most of the violence is Black-on-Black. More gun violence occurs in big-city Black and Latino neighborhoods. All neighborhoods need policing. But because of my race I don't expect officers to treat me fairly.

Despite the end of legally sanctioned segregation, racially segregated neighborhoods are still the unspoken rule today, even as America's population is now far more racially diverse than it was when the First Civil Rights Movement took flight. Looking out the car window in big cities I can tell when I'm in an affluent white neighborhood. It doesn't matter if I am in New York, Chicago, Los Angeles, Houston, or Atlanta. The differences are even starker in segregated small towns and rural areas, like Ferguson, Missouri. Race still matters.

Between 1950 and 2020 the U.S. population shifted from 90 percent white to 61 percent white.[2] One aspect of this transformation is that Black people are no longer the largest minority in this country. They are not even the fastest growing group—that's Asians. Latinos are now biggest. Meanwhile, the number of Black people in the nation has grown by about 30 percent in the last twenty years, even as the proportion of the total population remains at about 13 percent.[3] And Black people are more educated than ever. In the first two decades of the twenty-first century, the percentage of Black people with a college degree rose from 15 percent to more than 23 percent, with 9 percent of Black Americans having a master's degree or higher.[4] And while Black Americans remain far behind white Americans in family wealth—home ownership, stocks, and savings—more than 60 percent of Black Americans now classify as middle-class, according to a study by Brookings.[5] Even so, it's clear to any open eye that there are big socioeconomic differences, and big differences in social status, among races. These barriers continue to separate most white people, especially affluent whites, from minorities of all stripes, especially low-income Blacks.

In another surprising wrinkle, despite the remaining segregation, demographic changes have led to more Blacks, Latinos, and Asians living next door to one another. These working-class to middle-class neighborhoods remain separated by race and culture from the more affluent areas, which remain predominantly white. The same story holds in the suburbs, too. There is more racial diversity, but high-end houses, even gated suburban communities, separate most whites from people of color living in suburban apartment buildings and row houses in middle- and working-class neighborhoods.

Today's shifting racial composition in every corner of America does indeed create new incentives for more people to take an interest in improving race relations. But increased racial diversity is not a sure road to better race relations. Diversity can also inflame racial tensions, as elements of the majority group react to perceived loss of dominance. And it doesn't resolve ingrained racial stereotypes and fears. It doesn't create diverse neighborhoods by itself. And it doesn't solve the problem of police violence against minorities.

The line of division is strongest when it comes to education.

American public schools saw a gradual increase in Black and white students attending school together beginning in the 1970s. But since 1990, school segregation has increased. Today more than 40 percent of Black and Latino students go to public schools that are "hyper-segregated," or more than 90 percent Black and Latino.[6] Most of these schools have a high poverty level, astounding truancy rates, and lower academic achievement than white-majority schools.

There are shocking consequences to school segregation, such as Black children being more likely to end up in jail. As a father of two sons, it breaks my heart to know that one of every three Black boys will be incarcerated in his lifetime, and that 35 percent of the people executed in the last forty years have been Black, even though African Americans are only slightly more than a tenth of the population.[7] These are chilling realities seventy years after the Supreme Court's 1954 decision in *Brown v. Board of Education*, which promised to deliver equal education to Black and white children.

And where is the shining star of economic equality we hoped for in the First Civil Rights Movement? Stark disparities in income and wealth between Black and white households remain a fact of American life. Over the last seventy years, financial inequality between whites and racial minorities has grown starker as the economy has moved away from farm and industrial work to gleaming skyscrapers filled with college-educated workers in media, finance, health care, and technology.

This is the reality that Barack Obama faced as he took office as the first Black president of the United States in 2009, and it's a reality that persisted through the presidency of Donald Trump, who succeeded Obama and was viewed by many Americans as a racist. It is a reality that persists today.

In light of all this, it's not shocking that the new generation of civil rights activists has often felt deflated. They wondered why things didn't change more quickly after elevating Obama to the White House. Instead, they saw the Supreme Court gut the Voting Rights Act and affirmative action. They watched the rate of Black men in jail remain sky-high. They watched, appalled, as the government failed to protect racial, religious, and ethnic minorities from a rise in white supremacist violence. Their daily experience was that the First Civil Rights Movement and its hard-fought achievements were being battered, sometimes slipping away.

This new generation accustomed to seeing Black people like Obama in power expects real change. Previously, it was believed that the absence of Blacks and other minorities at these centers of American power led to acceptance of "systemic" or persistent gaps between whites and Blacks in wages and wealth. But now, with Black people at the table of American power, the younger generation wonders why more progress hasn't been made.

At its core the Second Civil Rights Movement is a daily, grassroots struggle to separate twenty-first-century American identity from nostalgia for white dominance of American life and culture. That nostalgia is full of winks and nods to negative stereotypes and damning assumptions about people who are not white.

The Second Civil Rights Movement's struggle against the new face of white dominance produced new tactics and a new type of leader.

In the First Civil Rights Movement, Martin Luther King Jr., Thurgood Marshall, and Malcolm X stood out as public leaders. And behind the scenes were leaders such as the NAACP's Clarence Mitchell, who lobbied Congress to promote civil rights goals, and local activists like Daisy Bates in Little Rock, Arkansas, who worked to organize students to integrate the schools there. Mitchell and Bates are not well known but both fit the traditional definition of civil rights leaders.

Barack Obama as a political leader may have started the Second Movement, but many of today's leading voices on race relations are different from Obama and past political leaders. The churning of the Second Civil Rights Movement's revolution can be seen on television, where corporate advertising and prime-time programming shows more doors opening to more people, with more women, Blacks, Latinos, and other minorities competing in the upper ranks of American business as well as in fashion, art, and philanthropy. Often their power to create change, primarily in the cultural sphere, comes from celebrity in entertainment, sports, and politics: Oprah Winfrey, Jay-Z,

LeBron James, Shonda Rhimes, George Takei, Jennifer Lopez, Tyler Perry, Margaret Cho, Lin-Manuel Miranda.

The Second Civil Rights Movement is Colin Kaepernick taking a knee during the National Anthem at NFL games to protest police killing Black people, challenging the culture of wealth and power exercised by the white owners of the nation's largest sports league. Faces and voices of influence in the news media are creating another kind of black leader, too. You see Lester Holt as the anchor of *NBC Nightly News*. There is Van Jones on CNN, Stephen A. Smith on ESPN, Charles Barkley on *Inside the NBA*. You see me doing political analysis on Fox News. Whoopi Goldberg is on *The View*, Steve Harvey hosts *Family Feud*, and Wayne Brady hosts *Let's Make a Deal*. Black people are in white American living rooms daily, exposing white audiences to Black perspectives on news and history.

The Second Civil Rights Movement is also about the millions of people taking to the internet to share their own experiences, thoughts, and analysis, not to mention activists on social media who eschew the older institutions and the old way of doing things. If the movement were only on the streets in Black neighborhoods, it would not have the political and cultural reach and resonance to reshape race relations in a country that is more racially diverse than ever. The faces and voices of people of color reach Americans all day every day, on cell phones, on social media, on the internet, as well as on television and radio. They are telling their lived experiences, their version of history—a story once solely guided by the perspective of white America.

White people remain the largest racial group in the United States. The number of white people as a percentage of the total population is declining, but there is no denying that whites remain the largest, best educated, wealthiest, and most powerful racial group in the nation.

Without a buy-in from white progressives willing to play a central role, the movement would not be growing. These are most often younger, college-educated white people who grew up with unprecedented racial mixing—at the playground, on television, in school, and at work. They have come to know Blacks, Latinos, and Asians as friends, co-workers, romantic partners. They are willing to speak up for racial diversity as a matter of their own belief

in advancing social justice and being on the right side of history, though critics have pointed out that there is room for improvement, as even young, white
progressives remain generally reluctant to buy homes in Black neighborhoods
or to send their children to Black-majority schools.

Progressive whites play another important role: as consumers who use
their dollars to reward racially sensitive, socially aware values. They are the
hand behind the accelerating consensus among America's corporate leaders
that it is good for the bottom line to embrace racial justice, gender equality,
and care for the environment. U.S. corporations have learned that the drive to
generate wealth includes consciously avoiding racial division inside the company, or having racism tarnish the company's brand.

Even so, the rainbow of races backing progressive policies to move the
country toward racial equality has produced a right-wing backlash, which has
become one of the defining characteristics of contemporary politics.

The backlash is fueled by grievance. Some whites claim to be victims of
what they label "politically correct" posturing by big companies, the media,
universities, and celebrities, arguing that they and their children have been
denied opportunities in favor of "undeserving" minorities. Today the far right
argues that promoting diversity is dividing Americans with "identity politics."
In fact, according to a 2021 survey by political scientists at the University
of Massachusetts-Amherst, fully two thirds of Republicans—a party that is
83 percent white—say that increasing attention to race and diversity "means
that America is in danger of losing its culture and identity." The survey also
found that among people who do not think that whites have an advantage living in America based on their skin color, only 21 percent agree that President
Joe Biden won the 2020 election.[8]

A majority of white voters have not supported a Democratic presidential
candidate since President Lyndon Johnson signed the 1965 Voting Rights
Act.[9] And in our own time, following the election of Barack Obama in 2008,
the Republican Party's opposition to his policies has taken on a racial coloration. For one early example, look no further than Trump's false claims that
the first Black president was not born in the United States and was therefore
ineligible to hold the high office. That lie, repeated for years on cable news,

propelled his run for the presidency. Once in the White House he advocated for a ban on Muslims entering the country and made insistent efforts to build a wall on the southern border.

In 2016 establishment Republicans found it politically expedient to look away from Donald Trump's racist and anti-immigrant talk as the party elevated his bigotry into the presidency. Since then, its elected leaders have seen no advantage in trying to win more Black voters at the polls; instead, they've opted for suppression, supporting measures that close polling stations in Black districts and that disproportionately purge Black voters from the rolls.

White evangelical voters, a key part of the Trump base, are comfortable with the concept of original sin, which took place in the Garden of Eden and extends across generations. But they reject the idea that slavery, the nation's original sin, extends its reach across time. Their resistance often adopts the same arguments, complete with the same bitterness, as the segregationists who battled against the First Civil Rights Movement in the 1950s and 1960s. As they trumpet their appeals to Southern pride and tradition, they repeat well-worn complaints about troublemakers from the North stirring up a previously complacent Black community.

Likewise, in the mid-twentieth century, segregationists complained about how schools taught the roots of the Civil War. They repeated the Confederate refrain that the war was a matter of Northern aggression and states' rights, an assault by industrialists against a rural farm economy—and not over slavery. Today many Republican leaders oppose allowing public schools to teach the history of slavery and discrimination. Addressing racial ugliness and racial realities has no place for them. They fear it is damaging to the nation's pride in its history.

Efforts to present an accurate portrait of American history have been recast by the right as a culture war centered on differences over the need to discomfort children by teaching about the history of race. Then there is the fight over school admission policies intended to repair the damage done by a long history of overt discrimination and to help more Blacks advance.

Similar arguments are made over diversity training for public and private sector employees, and over police reforms that would reduce the disproportionate number of Blacks and Latinos jailed by police and killed by police. There are arguments over bail laws and the high number of Black men in jail.

There is no real argument about the fact that a large percentage of Black and brown people continue to struggle to survive in twenty-first-century America.

But whites in Trump's Republican Party shun the history of America's racial oppression as well as stories of racial inequality today. Instead, they express fear of the government discriminating against white people. They blame high Black poverty rates on broken families and a lack of personal responsibility. They baselessly demonize immigrants as violent criminals, as rapists, as a threat to the white working class's jobs, and as minorities who commit voter fraud.

The extremes of racial politics can also be seen in the chilling rise of guns in the hands of violent white supremacist groups.

In 2015 nine Black people attending a Bible study at Emanuel African Methodist Episcopal Church in Charleston, South Carolina, were shot dead by a white supremacist. Similar shootings have taken place across the country, not just in the South, notably at a supermarket in Buffalo, New York, in 2022, where ten Black people were killed by a white man motivated by racism.

Most visibly, in 2017 white nationalist groups rallied in Charlottesville, Virginia, armed with guns and carrying Confederate battle flags and Nazi symbols. They chanted "Jews Will Not Replace Us," a slogan associated with "replacement theory," a racist and anti-Semitic belief that a cabal of wealthy Jews are secretly funding and masterminding a plot to replace white people as the dominant racial group in the U.S. The idea of whites being replaced is ridiculous at a time when whites continue to dominate the tables of power on Wall Street, in Washington, and in Hollywood. This is where decisions are made about money, politics, and institutions and culture that define daily American life. The leaders sitting at the head of those power centers remain overwhelmingly white, Christian, and male.

But more than at any time in U.S. history, there is a rising tide of Black people, people of color, immigrants, white progressives, and women demanding

to be heard and insisting on a seat at the table of power. Black people and
their allies are seeking to define racial progress on their own terms. Even as
it emerged and matured, the Second Civil Rights Movement has yet to come
into focus for many Americans. It is not always in the headlines, in the streets,
or on social media. But sometimes, like in Ferguson, it is.

With so much in our politics and culture coming back to race—and with
anger and moral arguments wielded by each side—it is important to understand where the Second Civil Rights Movement came from, how it developed,
and how it has reshaped our country for years to come. To understand it, you
first have to understand the most misunderstood president of recent times:
Barack Obama.

1

A POST-RACIAL AMERICA?

The First Civil Rights Movement ended and the Second Civil Rights Movement began in a seventeen-minute blowup at the 2004 Democratic National Convention in Boston.

No one saw it coming. The man scheduled to speak during those seventeen minutes, Barack Obama, was little known to anyone outside the state of Illinois. He was a total unknown to national civil rights leaders. A preview of convention speakers put a spotlight on the newcomer. It was headlined: "Who the Heck Is This Guy?"[1]

The blunt answer: he was a young Black man selected to help John Kerry, the party's nominee, win over Black voters.

The Kerry camp's first selection for the keynote address had been Governor Jennifer Granholm of Michigan. A former beauty queen and a Harvard Law graduate, she had upset a Republican favorite to become her state's first female governor. Kerry's advisers saw her presence on the convention stage helping Kerry with Midwestern voters, especially women. But two weeks before the convention, polls showed Kerry, a stiff New Englander born into a family fortune, in dire need of help connecting with Black voters, a crucial part of the Democratic coalition. That led Kerry's staff to try something different. They called on Obama.

The day Obama's selection was announced, the Kerry campaign also unveiled a record-setting, multimillion-dollar advertising buy in Black media for the week of the convention. It also issued a press release celebrating that nearly 40 percent of the delegates would be minorities, a first for any major party convention in American history.[2]

Racial considerations stood out about the choice of Obama, who had little to no recognition nationally. In fact, four years earlier Obama had lost a race for Congress from a mostly Black district. He had never run a statewide race in Illinois. His future campaign manager later defined him as "a candidate with no chance, no money, and the funny name."[3]

"Just think," said Senator John Edwards, the vice presidential candidate on the Kerry ticket, "the man is the keynote speaker at the Democratic National Convention, and he hasn't even been elected [to national office] yet."[4] Older Black politicians in Chicago dissed him by twisting his name from Obama to "Alabama." But Representative James Clyburn of South Carolina, the highest-ranking Black official in Congress, said that the point of Obama's presence on the big stage was to send a message "to young, upwardly mobile African Americans that this party is inclusive, that this party is not afraid of new thoughts and is not afraid of young Blacks."[5]

In the back rooms of the Kerry campaign, what went without saying was that Black voter turnout in the November general election would be key to a Kerry victory. And Kerry's campaign had polling showing that Black voters were not particularly excited by Kerry. Black voter turnout had steadily declined over the past four decades, after the excitement following the passage of the 1965 Voting Rights Act. Already depressed Black voter participation in presidential races hit new lows after the dispiriting riots following Dr. King's assassination. The exception had been when Rev. Jesse Jackson had run for the Democratic presidential nomination in 1984 and more strongly and seriously in 1988. After Jackson's second run, Black political energy on the national scene once again was at low tide. Between the 1992 and 2004 presidential races, no black Democrat won even one presidential primary.

In 1992 the Democrats won the presidency with a Southern, white governor, Bill Clinton of Arkansas. Clinton's victory was tailored to appeal to the kitchen-table, budgeting concerns of white suburbanites. His campaign

strategy was boiled down to a comment from James Carville, one of his strategists: "It's the economy, stupid." Clinton did business with Jackson but also
sent signals that he was a suburban-friendly political moderate. He took conservative positions on welfare reform, criminal sentencing, and even culture.
He staked a claim to moderate racial politics by denouncing a Black rapper,
Sister Souljah, who had told an interviewer that violence by Blacks against
whites could be "wise . . . if Black people kill Black people every day, why not
have a week and kill white people."[6] Clinton's response created a new entry in
the political lexicon: a "Sister Souljah moment." Speaking before a primarily
Black audience at Jackson's Rainbow Coalition, he said that the entertainer's
comment was not only wrongheaded but could have come from the murderous Ku Klux Klan. The front-page coverage put space between Clinton and
the Black left. It also put a stiff arm in Jackson's chest.

Nevertheless, Clinton did not lose Jackson's support and remained pop-
ular with African American voters, but Black turnout sagged in 2000 when
Vice President Al Gore, another white Southerner, lost a close election to
Governor George W. Bush of Texas. Like Clinton, Gore had focused his campaigns on pulling white middle-class voters away from Republicans. And like
Clinton, Gore knew it was in his interest to keep Jackson happy. As a matter of hardball politics, however, Clinton and Gore kept their distance from
Jackson's platform, specifically his left-of-center push for more spending on
social-safety-net programs. They spoke reverently about early civil rights triumphs but wanted nothing to do with Jackson and his fellow activists, who
insisted on talking about the current state of race relations and about the
racial gaps that remained since the 1960s—in unemployment, income, and
high school graduation rates, while federal prisons held more and more Black
people.

In the 2004 campaign, Kerry's team understood the need to reach Black
voters. But they faced a difficult racial calculus. They felt the need to move
beyond Jackson's increasingly limited appeal to whites as well as Blacks as an
old-guard civil rights leader. Obama was definitely not in the Jackson mold.
Whereas Jackson personified the Black experience of the mid-twentieth
century—he had roots in the South, had attended a Black college, and worked

with Dr. Martin Luther King Jr.—Obama was a biracial man from Hawaii, had gone to white schools, and earned an Ivy League law degree. He had no ties to the South or the history of slavery. He had no ties to King or any of the work of the Civil Rights Movement.

Barack Obama was born in 1961 to a white mother and a visiting African scholar from Kenya, whose union crossed deep racial lines in the United States. For most of American history even the hint of an interracial sexual relationship could trigger violence, lynching, murder. But Obama grew up physically and emotionally distant from that painful history. He was born in Hawaii, a state largely populated by a mix of whites, Asians, and Pacific Islanders, along with a tiny Black population. Then, after his parents' divorce, his mother took him to live in Indonesia.

After attending elite, mostly white colleges, Obama made the choice in his twenties to identify with Black Americans and their historic struggle for equal rights. His future in graduate school or corporate America was on a steady path. But he risked it all by taking a low-paying job as a community organizer in Chicago. He lived in racially diverse neighborhoods like Kenwood and Hyde Park but worked in Roseland, a Black, low-income section of the city.

That's when he came face-to-face with generations of Black American poverty, people living with high rates of crime. He was in and out of community groups and churches supporting families that had so many men in jail. He confronted the damage still inflicted on Black people by America's ugly past. It was hard for him, as it would be for anyone, to escape the legacy of slavery, legal segregation, bad schools, and high poverty rates.

Obama later wrote that his political ambitions led him to Chicago, a center of Black life, music, civil rights, and politics. The city was racially segregated, but the large Black population created opportunity for Black businesses, and Black economic power helped Black people step into the voting booth. Chicago was at the forefront of electing Black politicians to City Hall and Congress. Seeking to follow this emerging path to Black political power, Obama returned to the city after attending Harvard Law School (and serving as the first Black president of the *Harvard Law Review*). He won election to the Illinois State Senate in 1996, representing Chicago's racially diverse Thirteenth District, which covers the South Side of the city along the lakefront. He was elected to a four-year term in 1998 and reelected in 2002. In between, he lost his first campaign for federal office, in 2000, when he tried to unseat the incumbent congressman, Bobby Rush, in the Democratic primary. Rush, an older Black candidate and veteran of the Black Panther movement, defeated him handily.

Despite losing to an icon of the First Movement, in his speeches and writings, Obama said that he admired the Civil Rights Movement, envied its heroes, and saw himself in the brave young people, Black and white, who had faced down firebomb attacks, beatings, and murder to join the Freedom Rides and register voters during Freedom Summer. Their example had led him to his job as a community organizer.

All this was true, but Obama was never part of the civil rights establishment. When he graduated from Columbia, he wrote to several national civil rights groups looking for work, but none responded. Instead, it was white ministers at a local Chicago nonprofit who hired Obama. As one publication later delicately put it, they came out of far-left politics with past ties to communists and were viewed with suspicion by the local Black clergy. They needed a young Black man with no connection to their past to become their tie to the Black community.[7]

In practice, that meant that when Obama arrived in Chicago, his primary political sponsors were white progressives, people in line with union organizers and the liberal legacy of two iconic Illinois senators, Adlai Stevenson III and Paul Simon, and not Jackson's political machine. Later, as Obama went into politics, his financial support and voter base grew out of connections he made with the liberal whites he met through the church group. Obama's experience of civil rights activism was very different from the First Movement that inspired him.

That leads to another distinction between Jackson and Obama. Unlike Jackson, Obama was not a regular in Black church pulpits. Raised by his white mother and white grandparents in Hawaii, he never sat in the pews of a Black church until college. To this day Black churches remain an engine for organizing Black voters and getting them to the polls. Obama was outside the political alliances and deals that are part of Black church history. This background set him far apart from Jackson, who was deeply connected to Black ministers and local Black politicians across the country.

When Jackson ran for president in 1984 and 1988, he forced the party to change its nominating process. He did it by putting the party on the spot by claiming it had too few Black delegates relative to the percentage of Black Democratic voters. Jackson's point was a good one, based in fact: a racially diverse group of delegates might do a better job of selecting a presidential candidate—white or Black—able to turn out the Black vote. The party eventually reformed the delegate selection process. Then they paid for Jackson's travel to speak for the winning candidates and allowed him to have a say in campaign staff and operations, including outreach to Black churches and spending on advertising. Jackson's demands on the party came out of the First Civil Rights Movement's playbook. His campaign rallies did, too. They often felt to me, as a reporter covering him, like civil rights rallies.

It was no surprise that Jackson had a speaking role at the 2004 convention. Jackson's unquestionable political clout with Black voters commanded respect. But he was privately derided by the party's donors and elected officials for constantly pressuring them to put more money into jobs and contracts for Black people, often beginning with checks to the Rainbow Coalition, Jackson's organization. A lot of top Democrats considered Jackson less a civil rights player and Democrat and more like an arm-twisting extortionist. Jackson made similar demands on major corporations and Republicans. But he was most threatening to Democrats because they relied on Black votes. They lived in fear of being politically ruined if they angered Jackson to the point that he openly attacked the Democratic Party for taking Black people for granted. This fear was not unfounded, as Jackson had threatened to launch a third party for Black voters.

The surprise was that Kerry's advisers decided to go beyond Jackson in hopes of energizing Black turnout. By giving a prime-time television slot to Obama, they doubled down on their bet. The number-one added factor with Obama, the young biracial Senate candidate, was that unlike Jackson he seemed likely to appeal to the moderate, middle-of-the-road, white voters who had proved to be the winning difference for Bill Clinton, the first two-term Democratic president since Franklin D. Roosevelt.

In his Senate campaign, Obama had presented himself to Illinois voters as a reasonable, thoughtful politician, a refreshing new look for American politics. He'd approached the polarizing politics of race from new angles to create an advantage for his campaign. His campaign rallies were upbeat celebrations of common-ground approaches to lift everyone, Black and white, and his avoidance of the old racial arguments proved surprisingly effective with voters. He later admitted to a reporter that he thought Black politicians too often felt compelled to prove themselves to Black voters by having to "offend white people."[8]

Obama's political calling card was as the open face—not the angry face—of a Black man. He regularly spoke of being ready to bridge racial divisions, the divide between rich and poor, and global and religious division. His speeches challenged people to see beyond stereotypes, pushing white people to take responsibility for their bias and asking Black people to acknowledge behavior that had nothing to do with race that might be holding them back—like being an absent father. It all seemed like a sensible appeal from a rational, handsome young man. He targeted the broad middle of the political spectrum, promising to repair the racial wreckage by welcoming all racial groups—whites, Blacks, Latinos—as well as all religious groups into a common, post-racial identity as Americans.

Obama personified a brilliant idea: leave behind the pressure tactics of guilt and shame and replace them with a new sense of common purpose in resolving racial injustice. Blacks and whites, Latinos and Asians, as well as liberals, conservatives, and radicals, would be brought together to give new life to a civil rights movement growing gray. Obama did not directly propose the new path. But his speeches celebrated a road on which people of all colors walked together, took responsibility for racial pain and disparities, and worked side by side in the spirit of Dr. King's dream in which the "sons of former slaves and the sons of former slave owners will be able to sit down together at the table of brotherhood."[9]

Though Obama was not initially on Kerry's radar, and Kerry was unsure about Obama, once they met it became clear that Obama's vision filled
a need for the campaign. When Kerry came to Illinois to campaign in the
late spring of 2004, he agreed to make joint appearances with Obama, the
party's U.S. Senate candidate. They attracted television cameras for a tour
of a job training site and a visit to a local bakery in a Black Chicago neighborhood. After a successful fundraiser for the Kerry presidential campaign,
Kerry said what impressed him about Obama was the forty-two-year-old
politician's "charisma," especially his easy, yet strong presence in the or-
nate Hyatt Regency ballroom filled with wealthy donors, mostly white busi-
nessmen.

After Kerry's visit to Illinois, Obama's U.S. Senate campaign pushed
hard for a speaking slot at the convention, submitting an eight-minute video
of Obama's recent speeches with background music taken from a Muhammad Ali documentary. When Kerry's campaign called Obama with the news
that he would be delivering the keynote speech, Obama immediately told his
aides, "This is pretty big." He told reporters that his plan for the speech was
to give voice to all "who want to see us move past the politics of division toward the politics of hope."[10] There was no mention of race, no reference to
the Civil Rights Movement.

On the stage at Boston's Fleet Center, Obama began his speech describing
himself as the beneficiary of past civil rights activists and politicians, Black
and white. He said he owed a "debt to all of those who came before me. . . .
In no other country on earth is my story even possible." Later he simply described himself as the beneficiary of the movement, a member of the "Joshua
Generation," the people who inherited the Bible's promised land from the
generation of Moses and Aaron.

As a journalist, I was in the convention hall awaiting Obama's speech. His
introduction by Senator Dick Durbin was lackluster. And instead of Obama's
usual walk-up music, U2's "City of Blinding Lights," this time he entered to
soul music from the 1960s—Curtis Mayfield's high voice singing "Keep on
Pushing." People around me kept talking as he came onstage. He thanked

Durbin and praised the "great state of Illinois." In another deft move, the young Black politician also referred to the state as "Land of Lincoln," putting himself in line with the Great Emancipator.

Obama was unknown to most of the nation watching on television. Even I, a national political reporter, only knew of him as someone to keep an eye on, an up-and-coming Black politician from Illinois. No one told me to keep an eye on Obama as a leading man in a new civil rights movement.

But as his speech progressed, the energy in the room rose. Obama's power to connect with people was instantly apparent as he opened by confiding in the spirit of an inside joke, "Let's face it, my presence on this stage is pretty unlikely."

Then with gratitude for America as a land of opportunity not usually heard from Black Americans, he told his story, beginning with how his father came to the United States as a student from Africa, a village in Kenya. "He grew up herding goats, went to school in a tin-roofed shack. His father—my grandfather—was a cook, a domestic servant to the British. But my grandfather had larger dreams for his son. Through hard work and perseverance my father got a scholarship to study in a magical place, America, that shone as a beacon of freedom and opportunity to so many who had come before."

Next he spoke to his roots in Midwestern small-town Kansas. His other grandfather, he said, without explicitly identifying him as a white guy, worked on farms before joining the Army and marching "across Europe" with General Patton.

By now he was connecting with white and Black people in the crowd by pointing, chopping, and waving his hands. Then he revealed a personal detail by explaining that the name given him by his Black African father and his white Kansas mother, Barack, means "blessed." One reason they believed he was blessed, he said without a trace of irony, was that in "a tolerant America your name is no barrier to success. They imagined me going to the best schools in the land, even though they weren't rich, because in a generous America you don't have to be rich to achieve your potential." Next he quoted Thomas Jefferson, a Founding Father most often spoken of by Black people as having illicitly shared his bed with an enslaved Black woman. It is also true that Jefferson wrote in the Declaration of Independence that "all men are created equal" and have a right to "life, liberty and the pursuit of happiness."

As Obama spoke, a quiet buzz took hold of the room. Something was happening onstage. This young Black politician was expressing gratitude to America. It began when he said that "in no other country on earth is my story even possible."

He didn't mention race or civil rights directly, but he sent a message to white voters by knocking down stereotypes about Black politicians as only representing Black people, only loyal to the tragic elements of the Black experience. Obama was up to something different. He was talking to everyone in the audience. He wanted the vote of all Americans listening or watching. And in a peroration that became instantly famous, he proclaimed, "There is not a liberal America and a conservative America: There is the United States of America. There is not a Black America and a White America and Latino America and Asian America: There's the United States of America."[11]

This was a breakout speech. Obama was immediately celebrated for opening a door to a more inclusive racial vision. In that moment he revealed himself as the man, the vehicle, the vessel carrying hope for a new chapter, a new beginning in American politics—a new optimism about race relations. His Black face did not prompt anger or fear, calling up a past of slavery and racial hate with sadness and regret. He spoke with awareness of poverty, crime, and bad schools, but he projected optimism that didn't just look at the negatives of the Black past. Obama chose to take a positive view based on how far Black people had come and where they could go. He was heralded as a racial prophet.

The speech launched Barack Obama on his way to becoming the first Black president. It also opened a new era in American politics, a new era in Black politics, and launched a Second Civil Rights Movement.

America in 2004 was a different time for civil rights and politics. It was different from 1954. It was different from 1968. In many ways, the strategies and hard-fought changes achieved by the First Civil Rights Movement had run their course.

When Obama spoke in 2004, racial tensions remained, but there had also been real progress, notably in the growth of the Black middle class; the marches and sit-ins of the 1950s and 1960s were present only as celebrated history. It had been fifty years since the Supreme Court's historic decision in *Brown v. Board of Education*, the ruling that rang the bell to start the First Civil Rights Movement. A half century later, the high court's call to end segregated schools had become a messy proposition, often unfulfilled, with most Black children still in de facto segregated schools, producing test scores inferior to those of white children.

Standing before the convention, Obama did not harp on the First Movement's loss of direction, or the fraying of the consensus about a strategy for achieving more racial progress. He did not stick a knife in the glorious First Civil Rights Movement by identifying his emergence as the end of the road for the old civil rights era. He never labeled his seventeen-minute speech or himself as post-racial, although they were widely viewed as just that.

But Obama's presence on the national stage signified racial progress. He made it acceptable to dream and to talk about a post-racial era. The biracial young man, so classy and so distant from the time of slavery, segregation, sit-ins, and sad sermons on separatism, ignited a rush of news stories, essays, columns, academic conferences, and public debates on a post-racial America. And it did not matter if people saw Obama through white eyes or Black eyes. In either case they saw something new.

He was seen as rising above the same old exhausting racial arguments. He held mythic potential as a new Dr. King come to lead a wandering generation. Black and white Americans alike seemed to agree on Obama as the flesh-and-blood reality of the First Civil Rights Movement's pledge to produce exemplary Black people who would shame racists by demonstrating their intellect, integrity, and patriotism equal to any other American. People delighted in seeing Obama as that hero blazing a new frontier, taking them into a better world of race relations.

This collective sensation was taking place even though Obama never presented himself as post-racial or as a "race man," a description embraced by Frederick Douglass, W. E. B. Du Bois, and Dr. King. Those leaders earned that honorary title by standing up for Black people against their enemies. That was not Obama. He had a different frame of thinking. He wanted to make enemies into friends and then into votes that would put him in office. He didn't directly confront racial injustice because it would not help him win votes. In part, that's because racial arguments were background noise—not a hot topic for debate—during the 2004 campaign cycle.

The major event for all Americans, but especially Black Americans, that had put talk about racial justice on the back burner was the terrorist attacks of September 11, 2001. More than 2,900 Americans died, most of them in the towers of New York's World Trade Center. Alarm and outrage mixed with constant anxiety over the possibility of more attacks inspired fear that sank deep into every region of the nation. It led the federal government to reorganize itself to improve homeland security. It also led the country into two wars, in Afghanistan and Iraq.

The 9/11 attacks did ignite new arguments over civil rights, but they were about the violation of Muslim Americans' civil liberties. By the time of Obama's speech, the country had spent nearly three years searching for hidden terrorist cells, anxious about the prospect of another attack. FBI surveillance of Muslims extended to all recent immigrants, and any dark-skinned person, anyone with an accent, risked being seen as a potential terrorist. Racial justice and civil rights groups put their energy into standing up to bias against Muslims and Middle Easterners.

In his speech, Obama picked up on this concern. "If there's an Arab American family being rounded up without benefit of an attorney or due process, that threatens my civil liberties," he said, generating one of the biggest roars to come from the crowd.

As he neared the end of his convention speech Obama had to speak over chants of "Obama, Obama, Obama" from the delegates. Near closing, he delivered a line that would follow him far beyond politics: "The audacity of hope."

"In the end that is God's greatest gift to us, the bedrock of this nation . . . a belief that there are better days ahead . . . America! Tonight, if you feel the same energy that I do, if you feel the same urgency I do, if you feel the same passion that I do . . . then I have no doubt that . . . out of this long political darkness, a brighter day will come."[12]

Michelle, his wife, dressed in white, flowed onstage to hug him. Senator Durbin and his wife followed. The crowd roared and the arena vibrated. It was upbeat, inspiring to so many who sought a break from the negative, cynical politics of the day and a new window on racial politics.

One intriguing result of the success of Obama's speech was that his ongoing campaign for the U.S. Senate took a backseat nationally to talk about him as a future president. He had been a strong favorite to win the Senate race before the convention. A sex scandal had eliminated his Republican opponent, Jack Ryan, a former investment banker who reportedly had pressed his former wife, an actress, to go to "sex clubs and . . . engage in sexual activity in front of other patrons."[13] With Ryan out of the race, the Illinois Republican Party had reached out for a celebrity to run against Obama. But Mike Ditka, the former coach of the Chicago Bears, said no. Republicans then went out of state, courting a Black conservative radio talk show host. Alan Keyes, who lived in Maryland, transferred his residence to Illinois and registered as a candidate. He made headlines by saying that Jesus and every good Catholic in Illinois couldn't vote for Obama because the Democrat supported a woman's right to abortion.

Mary Mitchell, a Black *Chicago Sun-Times* columnist, called out the Republicans for turning the Senate race into a fight between two Black men. "So, what happened to all the white lambs?" she wrote. "Why aren't they being sacrificed." Again, Obama was being identified as Black, countered by a Black candidate, and celebrated as a singular Black politician. Political conversation had reverted to predictable patterns.[14]

But after the convention speech that seemed to transcend race, Obama's Blackness proved a positive by calling attention to him as a "cool" politician, a unique political entity with newfound potential to go all the way to the White House. In November he won with the biggest margin of victory for anyone—Black or white—in state history, taking 70 percent of the vote. At the victory party his fans chanted, "Yes, We Can," a slogan full of racial context that would follow him the rest of his political career.

Despite his emphasis on diversity, when he arrived in the Senate in January 2005 most of the media coverage focused on the fact that he was the only Black U.S. senator. He was only the fifth African American ever to serve in the Senate (and only the third to get there via a popular election). On his office walls he hung portraits of John F. Kennedy, Martin Luther King Jr., Abraham Lincoln, and South Africa's iconic racial healer and president, Nelson Mandela.

Senate Democratic leadership gave the newcomer with no seniority a prized seat on the Foreign Relations Committee, where he worked well with Republicans. He traveled to Russia with Richard Lugar, a senior Republican senator from Indiana. He co-sponsored an immigration reform bill with John McCain, the nationally known Arizona Republican. Lots of photos appeared of Obama and another Republican senator, Tom Coburn of Oklahoma. The attention to their partnership sent a political message that might have been staged but was certainly strategic. There was a good vibe, a mutually politically advantageous message, in promoting partnerships between the older white men and the young Black guy.

To fit into the Senate, Obama stayed away from cameras in his first months in Washington. The big exception came in August 2005, after Hurricane Katrina devastated New Orleans and the heavily Black population in the flood zone. Still, Obama tried to stay above the racial static, even as it gathered into lightning bolts of anger. "There's been much attention in the press about the fact that those who were left behind in New Orleans were disproportionately poor and African American," he said, coolly distancing himself from that perspective. The only heated comment from him was to characterize the ineffective federal response: "The ineptitude was colorblind." He also called attention to the poverty, not the race, of those in crisis, people unable to "load up their family in an SUV, fill it up with $100 worth of gasoline, stick some bottled water in the trunk, and use a credit card to check into a hotel on safe ground."[15]

When Obama announced in February 2007 that he was running for president, speaking from the top of the steps leading to the Old State Capitol in Springfield, Illinois, he quoted Lincoln as having declared from the same location in 1858 that slavery was evil and that "a house divided against itself cannot stand." He was beginning his campaign to be the first Black president by presenting himself as a modern-day Abraham Lincoln, a man looking to heal the current divide in the nation. He spoke about the "smallness of our politics" and identified America's biggest problem as a surfeit of skepticism and cynicism; people no longer believed in talking about hope.[16]

Whereas Jesse Jackson's campaign events in the 1980s had the feel of an old civil rights rally, with lots of reminiscing about the old days, the Obama events felt like rock concerts, attracting a younger, racially diverse crowd. The rhetoric invited people to try something new, to get a new movement started to deal with reality in the new century.

Obama knew his rhetoric signaled a change for Black listeners. "In the history of African American politics in this country there has always been some tension between speaking in universal [human rights] terms and speaking in very race-specific terms about the plight of the African American community. By virtue of my background, you know, I am more likely to speak in universal terms."[17]

Obama was a surprise winner in the first contest of the race for the 2008 Democratic presidential nomination, the Iowa caucuses. I was in Iowa the night of his victory to do television commentary, and I cried on the air. I explained to viewers that it was incredible for me as a Black man to realize that a Black candidate had won Iowa, a state with nearly all white voters. It was the start of Obama's run through the Democratic primaries.

The key contest would be in South Carolina, a state where most of the Democratic primary voters were Black. The state's leading Black political leaders had initially backed Senator Hillary Clinton, but Obama's success in Iowa had created the potential for a Black president, a new movement for social change.

Most civil rights veterans and Black politicians remained distant from Obama. They strongly supported Senator Hillary Clinton as the campaign got going. The Reverend Al Sharpton, after meeting with Obama in January 2008, said that he "left the meeting a little curious, feeling that he was noticing

our civil rights agenda, but I didn't understand what his civil rights agenda is."
Sharpton said that Clinton had "more of a civil rights program laid out. . . . I
always know where I stand with her."[18] But the old guard soon began to feel
pressure from Black voters' excitement about Obama.

At that point, Jesse Jackson and Al Sharpton had not endorsed Obama.
"People don't know who he is," said Ron Walters, a top adviser to Jackson
and a former dean of political science at Howard University who at the time
ran the African American Leadership Institute at the University of Maryland.
"They don't know his record. They don't know his background. . . . He has
to win their vote like anyone else."[19] As the campaign for the South Carolina primary heated up, Bill Clinton was frustrated by his wife's lack of traction with Black voters there. He pointed out, testily, that an Obama victory
in South Carolina, with its large Black population, would simply match the
success of an earlier Black candidate, Jesse Jackson, and did not reflect anything special about Obama. "Jesse Jackson won South Carolina twice," he
said dismissively.[20]

Obama's supporters took offense at the idea that he was attracting Black
voters simply because he was Black. Bill Clinton then accused Obama's campaign of having "played the race card on me."[21]

Andrew Young, a former top aide to Dr. King, was among the veterans
of the First Civil Rights Movement who were slow to back the Obama campaign. He took President Clinton's side when it was suggested that Clinton
was being dismissive of a Black man. "Bill is every bit as Black as Barack,"
Young said at a public political forum. "He's probably gone with more Black
women than Barack."[22]

This in turn stirred more arguments about Obama's racial identity. Did
he represent a new generation of Black people in American life, with ties beyond the history and life of the Civil Rights Movement, Black culture, and
climbing the ladder of success as a Black political leader?

"We claim him, and we are proud of him," Young later said. "But the fact
is that he has not had the experiences of deprivation, humiliation, and racism that I had to grow up with—which is good. He has the label without the
scars."[23]

During the South Carolina primary campaign, Jackson criticized Obama for not speaking out in support of Black high school students in Jena, Louisiana, who had been charged with assault and attempted murder after a fight with a white student. Civil rights activists described the "Jena Six" case as symbolizing how Black teenagers faced harsh criminal penalties that their white counterparts generally avoided. Obama's failure to be "bold" about the Jena case led Jackson to say publicly that Obama was "acting like he's white."

"If I were a candidate, I'd be all over Jena," Jackson said in a speech to a Black audience in South Carolina before the primary. Jackson said Jena was a "defining moment, just like Selma was a defining moment."[24]

In another sharp contrast with older civil rights leaders like Jackson, Obama described the tense situation in the small Southern town in racially neutral language. "Outrage over an injustice like the Jena Six isn't a matter of Black and white," Obama said. "It is a matter of right and wrong." This was a clear illustration of Obama's break from the First Movement.[25]

In Jackson's world, Obama was a sweet-hearted, childish political figure, feebly floating above racial realities, ignoring the tension between Black and white on the ground. Jackson set Obama further adrift when he added that Hurricane Katrina and the Jena Six case made "America's unresolved moral dilemma of race unavoidable."[26]

It may well have been unavoidable for Jackson and his old-school Black politics—but not so for Obama, whose idealism on race led him to see the uproar in Jena as a reason for people of all colors to come together to help each other heal by being fair to all sides. Obama's assertion of a common American identity across racial lines managed to survive the crisis and became a hallmark of his campaign. When a charge of aggravated assault was dismissed by a state appeals court, Obama said he was glad to see the court recognize that the charge was "inappropriate." He expressed "hope that the judicial process will move deliberately to ensure that all of the defendants will receive a fair trial and equal justice under law."[27]

In February, the Georgia primary saw 90 percent of Black voters backing Obama. By late February, Representative John Lewis, the civil rights activist celebrated for having stood up in Selma, Alabama, to a bloody attack from state troopers while marching for voting rights, announced he was dropping his support for Clinton and joining Obama's campaign. Lewis released a statement that praised Obama as "the beginning of a new movement in American political history," and he now realized he wanted to be a part of it and "on the side of the people."[28] That meant that Lewis, a superdelegate with a vote independent of the outcome of the caucus or primary in any state, would vote for Obama at the Democratic Party's national nominating convention.

John Lewis was upset about these divisions among Black politicians over the young Black man from Hawaii. He told his fellow congressman South Carolina's Jim Clyburn that there was a chance to see the fruit of all they had worked for if Obama won the White House. Following Obama's victory in South Carolina and Georgia, Jesse Jackson finally endorsed the Illinois senator at the end of March, but he did it in a telephone interview with the Associated Press, not in a public appearance. The old guard was still wary of the new champion.

In a revealing wrinkle, Reverend Jackson's son, Jesse Jackson Jr., a congressman from Illinois, became an Obama supporter before his father did. The younger Jackson put Obama's relationship to Black voters in the context of a next generation of Black leaders. He described Obama as an "inheritor" of his father's Rainbow Coalition, implying that Obama had to deal with the politics of a more diverse, less segregated America. Obama, he said, was talking to white people about doing better by Black people and talking to Black people about the need to expand Black political identity. That meant Obama needed support from Black politicians to "not limit him to a segment of the population," by attacking him when he spoke critically of Black people.

The difference between the younger Jackson and his father was evidence of the friction between young and old in Black America—the First and Second Movements. "When my father ran for president in '84 and '88, it was all for the legacy and a history from 1960 to the time he announced his candidacy in 1984 on speaking to issues of civil rights and social justice for African Americans primarily," Jesse Jackson Jr. said, pointing out that his father "started with an African American base."[29]

The senior Jackson expressed discontent with Obama's tendency to distinguish himself from older Black politicians—specifically by being willing to discuss high out-of-wedlock birth rates and absent Black fathers as pervasive problems in the Black community. Despite Jackson Sr.'s endorsement, he later, in unguarded comments captured by a live microphone on a cable television set, let loose. "I want to cut his nuts out," he said. "Barack is talking down to Black people." A day later, Jackson issued a forced apology.[30]

Obama's defining moment before a Black audience came in Selma, where he linked himself to the heroic effort of civil rights activists (like John Lewis) who marched for voting rights but were beaten by state troopers in 1965. It is because they marched, Obama said, that he "got a law degree, a seat in the Illinois Senate, and ultimately in the United States Senate." He told the story of people at a breakfast meeting that morning. They asked him if he saw himself as a Black American. They pointed to his father being African and his mother white, neither coming from slavery nor living through the U.S. history of legal racial segregation.

Obama's response reset the terms of the question. What happened in Selma, Birmingham, and other sites of civil rights history, he explained, opened the door for his father to come to America and for his mother to identify with people standing for racial justice. "So don't tell me I don't have a claim on Selma.... Don't tell me I'm not coming home to Selma, Alabama.... I'm here because you all sacrificed for me." He made an analogy between the leaders of the earlier civil rights era and Moses, the biblical figure, who led his people to freedom. "The previous generation, the Moses generation, pointed the way. They took us 90 percent of the way there. We still got that 10 percent to cross over to the other side.... So the question ... is what is called of us in this Joshua generation?" In that moment, Obama paid homage and respect to the First Movement but also separated himself from that past.[31]

As he held the lead through the primaries, Obama tactfully avoided debates on current racial issues. Then a past relationship with a Black minister became public, setting off a firestorm. Videotapes showed Obama's Chicago minister, the Reverend Jeremiah Wright, lambasting America as a nation built on racist lies. The fiery Wright was seen in his pulpit calling the Founding

Fathers liars. He said their real belief was only that "all white men were created equal." He added that white America continued to treat Blacks unfairly and emphasized that the federal government had an ongoing role in holding Black people down. "The government gives them the drugs," he said. "Builds bigger prisons . . . and then wants us to sing 'God Bless America.' No, no, no, not God Bless America. God damn America . . . for treating our citizens as less than human."[32]

Critics said that Obama had sat in Wright's church for years and never objected to his minister shouting out such racial anger. Obama claimed he never heard it. Inside the Democratic Party and among Black political leaders there was real fear that Obama's campaign had suffered a fatal blow. Hillary Clinton surged ahead of him in the polls. The damning question for Obama was whether he would stay loyal to the church or turn his back on his minister and, by association, turn his back on Black people.

To regain his balance on the high wire of racial controversies, Obama went to the National Constitution Center in Philadelphia, near the iconic imagery of Independence Hall and the Liberty Bell, to speak on the topic. He began by reminding his audience that voters are "hungry . . . for this message of unity."

He noted that some people saw him as "too Black" or "not Black enough." Recounting his personal experience, he said that his white grandmother, who raised him, had spoken of her fear of Black men. Similarly, he said that Reverend Wright had condemned all whites. He then said that he loved both the man who introduced him to his Christian faith and the woman who lovingly raised him. His goal was to bring them to see each other honestly. He pointed to the cynicism of white conservatives who saw his campaign as "based solely on the desire of wide-eyed liberals to purchase racial reconciliation on the cheap."

Only then did he speak directly to Wright's most controversial comments. He said his minister's call to damn America was "profoundly distorted." Wright sees "white racism as endemic, and that elevates what is wrong with America above all that we know is right with America . . . as if no progress had been made; as if this country, a country that made it possible for one of his own members to run for the highest office in the land and build a coalition of white and Black, Latino and Asian, rich and poor, young and old, is still irrevocably bound to its tragic past."

He concluded by saying, "Not this time." This moment, his campaign, he said, was a time to celebrate "every color and creed who serve together and fight together and bleed together under the same proud flag."[33]

Obama's poll numbers immediately rebounded. "Barack Obama's March 18th speech on race and politics is arguably the biggest political event of the campaign so far," Pew Research reported. "Fully 85 percent of Americans say they heard at least a little about Obama's speech, and most (54 percent) say they heard a lot about it."[34]

Black voters overwhelmingly stayed with him, and while moderate white voters came back more slowly, a significant percentage said that the episode gave them a more favorable impression of Obama, the speech having indicated that he would not carry the burden of racial hate.

Obama went on to win the Democratic nomination. The unknown young man who was a surprise hit at the 2004 convention was now the party's celebrated nominee, a hero poised to open new, positive dimensions in American race relations. But at his own convention in 2008, race was not at the center of his acceptance speech. Instead, he spoke about average people trying to pay their bills, get health care, and take care of their children in an unsteady economy. Obama painted himself as a man in touch with "Main Street" concerns, the antithesis of the powerful players on Wall Street or in Washington. He briefly acknowledged that he was delivering this speech on the forty-fifth anniversary of Martin Luther King's "I Have a Dream" speech at the 1963 March on Washington, recalling "Americans from every corner of this land" crowding together before the Lincoln Memorial, and the common embrace they had experienced. He repeated King's words: "We cannot walk alone."[35]

In November 2008, Obama won a clear victory in the general election, and the Black turnout set a record; for the first time in history, a higher percentage of Black voters went to the polls than white voters. Appearing before a massive crowd in Chicago's Grant Park, Obama became the center of a sea of emotion. Jesse Jackson, a longtime critic of the younger man, was seen crying as he listened to the nation's first Black president-elect. But once again Obama had nothing to say with regard to racial problems in the country or a new era in race relations. Rather, he deftly pointed to the history of past racial struggles as inspiration. "If there is anyone out there who still doubts that America is a place where all things are possible; who still wonders if the dream of our founders is alive in our time; who still questions the power of our democracy, tonight is your answer."[36]

Obama never said he would be a post-racial president. But his victory, with its roots in his celebrated 2004 convention speech, signaled that a new era of race relations had begun. In his inaugural address he said: "For we know that our patchwork heritage is a strength, not a weakness. . . . We are shaped by every language and culture, drawn from every end of this earth; and because we have tasted the bitter swill of civil war and segregation, and emerged from that dark chapter stronger and more united, we cannot help but believe that the old hatreds shall someday pass."[37]

2

BURSTING THE BUBBLE

In his first two years in the White House, Barack Obama was handed the greatest economic recession since the Great Depression. He carefully avoided talking about ongoing economic injustice, including racial disparities evident in financial pain suffered by poor people. Instead, the new president went to Congress to ask for money to bail out Wall Street and large corporations, which disproportionately helped white and upper-income Americans, the "too big to fail" crowd. In his administration's fight for federal funding to bail out failing companies, he never defined the battle in racial terms. Saving the economy fit his profile as a president who was post-partisan and post-racial.

As a matter of political calculation, Republicans saw Obama's election as a threat. Most white Americans had not voted for Obama—they had voted Republican. Obama was the leader of an emerging multiracial coalition that threatened to dwarf their voting bloc for years to come. Their criticism of Obama's policies took on a racial tint, especially when the president proposed health care reform, which became an immediate partisan lightning rod.

The almost all-white party's leaders insinuated that the Black president was advancing economic policies in favor of Blacks and other minorities, and at the expense of their white voters. The opposition to health care reform was that Blacks, Hispanics, immigrants, and young people, the Obama base, would disproportionately benefit from the new government-backed insurance marketplace while whites would pay a bigger tax bill. The plan had originated in a conservative think tank, but it didn't matter. Nor did it matter that the data showed white Americans would be the biggest beneficiaries of health care reform; Republican opposition and racial animus defined the debate.

This right-wing anger against Obama's plan was organized under the name "the Tea Party." Rick Santelli, a reporter for CNBC, created a national sensation calling for "Tea Parties" in the tradition of the Boston Tea Party that protested the British crown and began the American Revolution.

Rolling Stone magazine described the Tea Party as "millions of pissed-off white people sent chasing after Mexicans on Medicaid by the handful of banks and investment firms who advertise on Fox and MSNBC.... They are shockingly willing to believe the appalling horseshit fantasy about how white people in the age of Obama are some kind of oppressed minority."[1]

Obama never responded to the racial—often racist—attacks on him or his economic plans. When conservatives spread rumors that Obama had not been born in the United States, he seemed unfazed until he finally said he could not recall "any other president who was challenged about where he was born despite having a birth certificate."[2]

But Republicans in Congress opened new avenues of attack. Most of them had had no issues with deficit spending under Republican presidents, but they criticized Obama for driving up the deficit to prevent a national economic collapse.

Later in 2009, a white congressman interrupted the president's speech to Congress about the health care plan by shouting out, "You lie!" Mitt Romney, an unsuccessful contender for the 2008 Republican presidential nomination, said he feared that Obama was not in line with "Anglo-Saxon values." Newt Gingrich called him a "food stamp president."[3] Then came attacks for giving a fist bump to his wife—it was suggested it was a terrorist gesture. Glenn Beck, a cable television host, said openly that Obama held "a deep-seated hatred for white people."[4]

On radio, the top political talk show host, conservative Rush Limbaugh, mocked Obama with a song called "Barack the Magic Negro," set to the tune of the 1960s pop song "Puff, the Magic Dragon."[5] On cable news, New York businessman Donald Trump regularly claimed that Obama was not an American. Soon half of the nation's whites told pollsters that they had doubts about whether Obama had been born in the United States and therefore might be a fraudulent president. The attacks all fit with a long, historical line of doubt from racists about whether Blacks, having been brought here as slaves and not originally granted equal citizenship or a vote, were truly Americans.

The constant hectoring, with its explicit racial tenor, led most Black Americans to line up in defense of Obama. White support held until June 2009, when the Harvard professor Henry Louis Gates, a Black man, had a confrontation with a white police officer in Cambridge, Massachusetts. Gates was returning to his home after a trip, when a neighbor called police to report suspicious activity. When the police arrived and questioned Gates, he angrily responded that he was entering his own house. The policeman said that he knew that Gates owned the house but arrested him anyway, for disorderly conduct.

This seemingly small incident got surprising attention nationally, initially because Gates was so well known, but also because it opened a seldom-seen window on tense relations between Blacks and police. Gates, an older, prominent, wealthy Black man, claimed he was treated badly because of his race. He refused to dismiss the incident as a mere misunderstanding. Instead, he assailed the police for a lack of respect and lack of common sense in thinking that a man would break into his own house.

This was in line with young Black men complaining about "Stop and Frisk," and "Driving While Black," as harassment from white police. Beginning in the 1990s the New York City Police Department notoriously began wide use of a search tactic called "Stop and Frisk." The practice of randomly stopping people and subjecting them to a pat-down search disproportionately targeted young Black and Latino men. "Stop and Frisk" reflected an aggressive attitude among police that was rooted in stereotypes of minorities as criminals.

President Obama was asked about the Gates incident and said that "the Cambridge police acted stupidly." He also cited the "long history in this country of African Americans and Latinos being stopped by law enforcement disproportionately."[6]

Obama's support among whites immediately dropped. His 53 percent job approval with whites before the Gates incident immediately fell to 46 percent according to Pew polling in July. Obama's approval from whites never again went above 50 percent.[7]

"In that moment, any notion that Obama's election had transformed America into some kind of post-racial society was shattered," wrote *The Washington Post*. "In general, blacks agreed with him, and whites thought he played the race card."[8] Writing of that time in *Slate*, Jamelle Bouie, a Black writer, said that Obama's comments ended the "heady daydream of 'post-racial' America sustained by a president who was black, but who wasn't quite a black president.... Obama's observation—those black lives still faced unfair treatment—was an abrupt challenge to that idea, and it brought a backlash."[9]

Likewise, Blacks in Congress complained bitterly about Obama's lack of attention to them and their concerns. So, too, did leaders of civil rights groups. In 2010 Shirley Sherrod, a Black employee at the Department of Agriculture, was falsely accused of giving a white farmer racist treatment. Obama's aides ordered her fired before realizing their error and reversing course. Once again Obama was caught off guard by race-based attacks from conservatives aimed at him. He was also thrown off balance by Black leaders who accused him of a knee-jerk abandonment of a Black woman. The whole incident was telling, another indication of Obama's naive belief that reason rather than race should carry the day.

In the 2010 midterm elections, the Democrats lost sixty-three seats in the House and seven in the Senate. Obama described it as a "shellacking." Indeed, it was the biggest midterm defeat for a president since the 1940s. Afterward, the number of Obama's Black critics grew, but few were willing to speak out publicly. Negative appraisals among Black people were treated as traitorous. But that firewall steadily showed signs of breach. "With 14 percent [Black] unemployment, if we had a white president we'd be marching around the White House," said Emanuel Cleaver, the chairman of the Congressional Black Caucus.[10]

The next year, 2011, saw Obama's poll numbers rise after he oversaw the military operation that killed Osama bin Laden, the terrorist leader behind the 9/11 attacks ten years earlier. He also released his birth certificate to prove that he had indeed been born in the United States. Soon thereafter, he made humorous comments at the White House Correspondents' Dinner mocking the main promoter of that libel, Donald Trump.

The president also tried to boost his standing with Black voters by speaking at a Congressional Black Caucus gala. But at the event, Obama's gloves came off. He said that he expected "all of you to march with me and press on. Take off your bedroom slippers, put on your marching shoes. Shake it off. Stop complaining, stop grumbling, stop crying. We are going to press on. We've got work to do, CBC."[11]

Black critics came from all directions to ask why Obama was scolding Black people instead of reprimanding white racism and setting an agenda to dismantle the structure of racism in America.

"Symbolically," said the left-wing academic Cornel West, "Barack Obama will forever go down in the annals of time as having this great symbolic status, but the struggle for freedom and justice is not just about symbols. You have got to be able to seize the moment and let the world know you are a fighter for those who have been spit on, subjugated, dominated, exploited. They can't live vicariously through your symbolic success."[12]

The president saw the negative political response and became even more reluctant to address racial issues. His silence brewed discontent among Black Americans. *The Chicago Defender*, a Black newspaper, captured a noticeable mood shift taking place among some in Black America in 2012. "Maybe it is time for President Obama to have a conversation with black America about the state of black America, and what he is doing [if anything] about it," the paper wrote. "He can't forget where he came from, and when his communities call, 'answer the phone, dammit.' Don't tell us who else you represent."[13]

For a man defined for all time by being the first Black person to break into the most exclusive, all-white club in the nation, Obama's avoidance of race has made him one of America's most misunderstood presidents. Despite the incredible accomplishment of ushering in a new era in civil rights, Obama seemed unsteady in dealing with people who continued to argue over race. He had underestimated the depth of the nation's racial divide. Despite widespread talk of the post-racial era his election had supposedly ushered in, race continued to have an enduring impact in shaping American politics, debates on economics, health care, gun control, and crime. It was impossible for Obama to bridge that chasm.

With little attention from the mainstream press, a turning point for the emerging Second Movement came in September 2011, when the call came to stop the execution of a Black man in the South.

The White House press secretary said that President Obama agreed with the people protesting outside the Georgia jail, where a forty-two-year-old Black man named Troy Davis was scheduled to be executed in hours, that the death penalty did not prevent crime. But the press secretary also told reporters that Obama believed that some crimes deserve the death penalty, which he termed "the ultimate punishment."

The case went back to August 19, 1989, when twenty-seven-year-old Savannah policeman Mark Allen MacPhail, moonlighting as a security guard at a Burger King, heard cries for help just after 1 a.m. Men in the parking lot were fighting over a bottle of beer. MacPhail came running as a homeless man screamed while being pistol-whipped. The police officer was shot in the face and the heart. He died at the scene.

Two years later, seven witnesses testified that Troy Davis, who had been at a nearby pool hall before heading over to the Burger King, had killed MacPhail. Davis was convicted by a mostly Black jury and sentenced to die.

But there was no hard evidence. Though the bullets matched the ammunition found at another shooting where Davis had been charged, the murder weapon was never found. Nonetheless, after seven hours of deliberation, the jury found him guilty.

Davis denied he pulled the trigger that night. Several witnesses later recanted their testimony. His death sentence was delayed several times by appeals. Lawyers, civil rights groups, and social media posts focused on the fact that Davis was convicted on the basis of eyewitness testimony by mostly Black people to a mostly Black jury in the mostly Black city of Savannah. But the guilty verdict came without DNA evidence, without a murder weapon, and with witnesses who had recanted. One who claimed he could not read said the police had forced him to sign a damning statement against Davis.

All this uncertainty left a basis for more appeals, which unfolded over the course of two decades. He was ninety minutes from the death chamber in 2009 when the Supreme Court issued a rare stay, allowing time to hear a petition for another review. A federal appeals court then reviewed the trial transcript and heard new evidence but denied Davis's petition. He was back on death row. The Georgia Board of Pardons and Paroles, which had initially denied clemency, reopened the case, but the second hearing ended with the same ruling—no clemency for Davis. Calls for the president to get involved started slowly after Obama's election; by summer 2011, they had reached a crescendo among Black activists.

Across from the White House, in Lafayette Square, dozens of protesters held signs with Davis's face. Twelve students from Howard University chanted: "I am Troy Davis!" They and their professor were arrested after defying police orders to move away from the iron fence in front of the presidential mansion. They wanted the first Black president to stop the execution. Benjamin Jealous, the president of the NAACP, asked Obama for a reprieve for Davis. He got no response.

In Georgia there was a large protest outside the prison. About seven hundred people, almost all Black, listened to radios and checked their cell phones to see if Obama or the Supreme Court would move to prevent Davis's execution. They held a candlelight vigil and broke out in singing anthems from the Civil Rights Movement. And they spoke to reporters about their desire for a Black president to act to save another Black man.

Days before the scheduled execution, the activist political group Change .org and Amnesty International USA's Death Penalty abolition campaign presented 633,000 petitions to the local parole board in front of the television cameras. Activists also wrote to Obama, asking him to stop the execution.[14]

Long-standing opposition to the death penalty from the NAACP and other civil rights groups fueled questions about the morality of the punishment—especially in a case involving a Black man and overt uncertainty.

A stay of execution, they argued, would not render a judgment that Davis was innocent. But it would mean the president saw a life—a Black life—worth sparing; it would afford a convicted man who'd maintained his innocence for years the dignity to take another breath, even if he lived the rest of his days behind bars in the land of the free.

Pope Benedict XVI joined in calls for clemency for Davis. So, too, did former president Jimmy Carter, as well as the Nobel Peace Prize laureate Archbishop Desmond Tutu. A surprising call to stop the execution also came from former FBI director William Sessions. The hip-hop star Sean "P. Diddy" Combs said it was wrong to execute Davis. So did the rapper Big Boi, of the Atlanta group Outkast. Speaking at a church near the prison, he said there "is too much doubt," before explaining that he wanted to use his celebrity to "bring the word to the young people."[15]

The night of the execution, a crowd gathered outside the prison, many bent over in grief, crying in frustration, giving in to the heartbreak of being helpless to achieve what they saw as justice. Occasionally, someone shouted angrily at the dozen riot-gear-clad Georgia state troopers aligned on the other side of the highway to keep protesters away from the prison. Some people took more aggressive action, posting a local judge's phone number online and sending threatening messages to prison guards telling them to stay home.

"It harkens back to some ugly days in the history of this state," said the Reverend Raphael Warnock, the pastor of Ebenezer Baptist Church in Atlanta, once the home church of Dr. Martin Luther King Jr., following a visit with Davis as he waited to hear the outcome of his appeal. The day before, Warnock, who was later elected to the U.S. Senate, had led a rally of one thousand of his parishioners in support of Davis.[16]

As Davis's life-or-death watch continued, a disproportionate number of the U.S. death row population was Black, more than 40 percent. Most of these Black men, uneducated and poor, sat locked in jails of the Deep South, the former Confederate slaveholding states. This was a long-standing inequity in American history. "Racial disparities are present at every stage of a capital case and get magnified as a case moves through the legal process," observed Robert Dunham, the executive director of the Death Penalty Information Center. "If you don't understand the history—that the modern death penalty is the direct descendant of slavery, lynching, and Jim Crow segregation—you won't understand why."[17]

In 1972 the U.S. Supreme Court had halted use of the death penalty in the case *Furman v. Georgia*, with the first Black Supreme Court justice, Thurgood Marshall, writing that execution violated the Constitution's protection against "cruel and unusual" punishment. Marshall also called out white racism's role in sentencing. He noted that more than half of the people executed since 1930 were Black, making it "immediately apparent that Negroes were executed far more often than whites in proportion to their percentage in the population."[18]

Marshall's position barely carried the day in a 5–4 decision. Four years later, in another case from the same state, *Gregg v. Georgia*, the high court reinstated the death penalty, this time with new rules to protect against all-white juries sending Black people to death row.

More than forty years later, another Black man, Justice Clarence Thomas, handled emergency appeals from the federal courts in most of the South, where Davis now sat on death row. But Justice Thomas supported the death penalty.

With no Thurgood Marshall at the Supreme Court, President Obama became the focus of attention among Black activists trying to save Davis's life. Picking up on the growing popularity of social media to call attention to wrongs and to express public outrage, Black people took to Twitter to call for Davis's release. One person tweeted a quote from Dr. King: "#DearGeorgia: He who passively accepts evil is as much involved in it as he who helps perpetrate it."[19]

The White House Press Office told reporters that the president had no authority to stop the execution because he had no power to grant clemency in a case tried in state courts.[20] But Davis's supporters argued that Obama could pull the levers of power by asking Attorney General Eric Holder (himself the first Black person to hold that office) to announce a Justice Department investigation into the case, which would force a delay in the execution.

Obama was being challenged to do something for Black people that no white president had done—get a Black man off death row. But as the days ticked on, optimism waned.

In the lead-up to Troy Davis's execution, a Black civil rights lawyer named Joy Freeman-Coulbary wrote in *The Washington Post*, "The question for many African Americans, and for me, is why the deafening silence. . . . Is he afraid of appearing sympathetic to Black issues? Or is Obama agnostic towards issues of concern to Black people?"[21]

John Lewis, the legendary civil rights activist, told *The Atlanta Journal-Constitution* that he was considering a direct appeal to Obama. But Al Sharpton remembers counseling against a direct appeal. "I've always told people Barack Obama was a politician . . . not an activist," Sharpton said. "First of all, the Supreme Court would have to stop Troy Davis's [execution]. . . . Obama making a statement may or may not help. And I'm not going to attack Obama for not doing it."

Sharpton lived in the racially polarized world of the older Black activists. But he viewed Obama differently. "I'll never forget, Nelson Mandela, when he won election," Sharpton later recalled, "said the biggest challenge is that we have to learn to come together and transition people from fighting the government to being in the government, to being [in support] of a political figure." In the historical mold of Mandela, Barack Obama was not just another person looking at the case. He was the most powerful leader in the world, and Black. Yet he did not speak or act on behalf of the condemned man.[22]

A White House statement said that President Obama's work was to "ensure accuracy and fairness in the criminal justice system." But it was inappropriate for him "to weigh in on specific cases like this one, which is a state prosecution."[23]

To the activists standing outside the jailhouse, hoping for a miracle to save Davis's life, Obama's inaction screamed indifference from someone they had voted for and saw as a political ally, an inspirational leader, a hero, a friend. Ben Jealous of the NAACP said that he was waiting for Obama to "just say something publicly." But "the most searing betrayals," Jealous said, came from local power players close to the case, Black members of the parole board and the African American district attorney, all of whom declined to act.[24]

In the crowd the sense of hopelessness grew intense as darkness fell. The Twitter hashtag "#TOOMUCHDOUBT" blew up with 7,671 tweets per second. That night it was the most active Twitter trend and later ranked second for the most active Twitter hashtag of the year.[25]

The Georgia Supreme Court refused another appeal just two hours before the scheduled execution at 7 p.m. So Davis's final legal appeal went to the U.S. Supreme Court, where it fell to Justice Thomas, Davis's fellow Georgian and the lone Black person on the court. The prison delayed the execution to wait for word from Washington on Thomas's ruling.

Three hours later the Supreme Court made the announcement. It was a single sentence long: "The application for stay of execution of sentence of death presented to Justice Thomas and by him referred to the Court is denied."[26]

And from the White House, only silence.

When word came from the Supreme Court that the plea to stop the execution had been denied, the scene outside the jail became churchlike, with people praying, wiping away tears while hugging.

As the clock approached 11 p.m., Davis was escorted into the death chamber. He was strapped to a gurney, made eye contact with his attorney, and said he was innocent. What "happened that night is not my fault," he stated. Then he asked his supporters to "continue to fight the fight." Speaking to his executioners, he said: "God have mercy on your souls." Then he blinked rapidly and "squeezed [his eyes] tight," according to a reporter present.[27]

The curtain drew shut and he was given a lethal injection to stop his heart.

The White House maintained that, while they did not intervene in Davis's case, the president "has worked to ensure accuracy and fairness in the criminal justice system."

Jordan Taylor, an eighteen-year-old Black student, had been glued to his computer screen as he followed the story. He learned of the protests against Davis's execution through social media. He called Obama's silence "heartbreaking."

"I didn't understand," he told Jen Marlowe and Keeanga-Yamahtta Taylor (no relation) of the magazine *In These Times* five years later. "He's the president. The president has this platform, and he's a Black man."

The article pointed to Jordan Taylor as one of "many Black folks [who] hoped Obama's election would help" deal with white supremacy, putting the nation to work on facing racial disparities, opening the road to talk of a post-racial era. There was no "illusion" that a Black president could "eradicate white supremacy," the reporters wrote, but a lot of people "hoped Obama's election would help."

They concluded, "Davis' execution delivered a painful but eye-opening message: Even under a Black president, Black lives still didn't matter."[28]

In 2012, a year later, President Obama was asked about "criticism that your administration hasn't done enough to support Black businesses." His reply touched on the same idea offered by his spokesman at the time of Davis's execution. He was Black. His predecessors had all been white, and several had been openly racist and acted against the equal rights protections guaranteed to Black people. But Obama felt he was not in the job to counter racist actions by his predecessors. He offered to compare his track record to others, noting his support of broad-based programs that benefited Black businesses.

"I'm not the president of Black America," the president responded to *Black Enterprise* magazine. "I'm the president of the United States of America."[29]

3

SKITTLES AND A HOODIE

The neighbors called him "Mouse" because he was such a quiet kid. To his mom, he was "Cupcake."

On the night of February 26, 2012, he was walking down the street, a lonely and bored seventeen-year-old.

His dad had gone out to dinner, leaving him at home to watch TV and play video games. He loved old sitcoms like *Martin*. He loved playing video games. But by 6 p.m. he was restless and wanted something to do.

Mouse occasionally got into trouble. He was suspended once for talking back to his teachers and another time he was suspended for spray-painting "WTF" on lockers. When his locker was opened after that incident, school officials found some jewelry inside, leading to suspicion that he had stolen it. But he was never charged with any crime.

For all the trouble at school, family and friends said that Mouse was one of the good kids in his Miami neighborhood, an awkward and often shy teenager. And his family knew him as a hero. When he was nine, he pulled his dad out of a kitchen fire after the older man had been burned by hot cooking oil and was unable to get himself up and out of danger.

In the neighborhood, Mouse liked to put on a tough front. He always wore a hooded sweatshirt and baggy jeans to cover his skinny, five-foot-eleven, 150-pound frame. He thought tattoos were cool, and his parents let him get ink

on his thin arms, a pair of praying hands and the names of his grandmother
(Cora Mae) and his great-grandmother (Nana). That was not very tough, but
he bought some fake gold teeth he could put in his mouth to look like one of
the hard guys in hip-hop music videos.

Three weeks earlier, shortly after he turned seventeen, Mouse had been
suspended for a third time, when a marijuana pipe was found in his backpack.
His dad wanted to send a strong message that the school suspensions had
to stop. To take Mouse away from any bad influences in his Miami neighborhood, his father decided to have him spend some time living with him
in Sanford, outside Orlando, four hours away. It was a strong punishment.
Mouse was isolated, alone, and bored in a gated community of town houses.
He couldn't wait to get back to his friends in Miami.

It was raining that Sunday night. At around 7 p.m., Mouse walked out of
a 7-Eleven, where he had bought a package of Skittles and an Arizona Iced
Tea. He was chatting on his cell phone, talking to a girlfriend, Rachel Jeantel.
He pulled up his hood to keep the rain off as he took his time walking home.

Parked in an SUV nearby, a volunteer community watch guard decided
that the Black youngster looked suspicious. George Zimmerman, a stocky
twenty-eight-year-old, five-foot-seven and about two hundred pounds, called
the Sanford police to report that a Black kid was walking around the neighborhood slowly and looked suspicious. "He's got his hand in his waistband.
And he's a Black male . . . these assholes, they always get away."

The 911 operator told him not to stop the youngster.

But Mouse noticed Zimmerman eyeing him from the SUV. As he walked
by, he told Rachel that the man in a nearby car was "creepy." Listening over
the phone, she later told lawyers she overheard him asking the man in the car
why he was watching him. The response was "What are you doing here?"

Rachel later said she thought Mouse told him off and kept walking. But
Zimmerman got out of the car and caught up with him on foot. This time the
phone call was cut off. A fight erupted and Mouse's earpiece fell out.

Later, a recording of another 911 call, this time from a neighbor, revealed
sounds of people screaming and crying and then a gunshot.

Mouse's dad was out at dinner and had no idea what had happened, even after coming home to sleep. To his surprise the next morning, his son wasn't around. He called the police to report his son missing. When officers arrived at the house, they showed the father a crime scene photo of the dead boy, the victim of a gunshot to the chest. It was his child, Trayvon Martin.

Zimmerman claimed he shot Martin in self-defense as they fought in the street. Unlike Zimmerman, Martin had no weapon. And Zimmerman admitted to the police that he had initiated the confrontation. His conversation with the 911 operator was evidence that he had pursued Martin on baseless suspicions and contrary to the operator's instruction. However, he said he got into a fight with Martin and used the gun to defend himself. Zimmerman had a bloody head wound and a broken nose.[1]

Police said there was nothing to refute Zimmerman's claim of self-defense. Martin was dead, but the police did not treat Zimmerman as a murder suspect. He wasn't handcuffed. He got first aid on the scene and went home. The next morning, he even returned to the crime scene to reenact the fight and the shooting. Did police know it was the shooter, not the Black teenager, who had the criminal record, an arrest for allegedly assaulting an undercover police officer?

A homicide detective, Christopher Serino, later said that he wanted Zimmerman charged with manslaughter. He noted that Zimmerman did not identify himself to police that night as a neighborhood watch volunteer. But Serino was apparently overruled. No charges were filed.[2]

Two weeks after the killing, in mid-March, the only news about the shooting remained small, initial reports. The 10 o'clock local news on WOFL television mentioned the shooting on the night after it occurred. But the station aired no videotape, no interviews with witnesses or neighbors.

A brief mention of the murder appeared in the online edition of the *Orlando Sentinel*, but the story did not make it into the print edition. An editor at the newspaper later explained that it seemed to be little more than a "fight gone bad."[3]

Trayvon Martin's grieving parents wanted the Sanford police to arrest the man who had shot their son. A relative put them in touch with Ben Crump, a personal injury lawyer known locally for using video footage to win a 2006 case involving the death of a fourteen-year-old Black boy named Martin Lee Anderson, who had died after being beaten by adult guards in a Florida youth reform camp.

In that case, Crump used grainy, dark surveillance video as the centerpiece of his argument that the state of Florida had put the child in danger. The video showed the boy being brutally beaten by camp guards. To settle the case, the state paid the family $5 million, with no further prosecutions made.

When Trayvon Martin's family contacted Crump, the lawyer told the father his services wouldn't be required. He later recalled, "I thought you got a dope with a 9-millimeter gun, a private citizen, and they shoot and kill an unarmed teenager who was on the phone, holding a bag of Skittles. . . . I believe the system is supposed to work . . . so I told him to take a couple of days" to see what happened.

The Martin family called back two days later, and Crump, still thinking the problem with the police could be easily corrected, agreed to help for free. His first move was to build public pressure for an arrest through a media campaign. This was the strategy he had used in the reform camp beating case. "The court of public opinion has a profound impact on the court of law," he said.[4]

The first national news article about the parents' dissatisfaction with the police was a Reuters wire-service story on March 7. The next day, CBS This Morning picked up the story. On camera, Tracy Martin, Trayvon's dad, asked how police could dismiss the incident as a matter of self-defense when a man with a gun killed an unarmed Black boy. His face sagging with anguish, he said he couldn't believe the man who killed his son had never been charged and had walked free.

"It was one of those stories that, when you hear the pitch, you just say 'Wow, this has to be told,'" said CBS producer Chris Licht. "We knew we'd hit on something significant."[5]

The story immediately became a sensation on social media, where minute-by-minute updates were available to a growing audience. Kevin Cunningham, a white lawyer in Washington, D.C., who had attended the historically Black

Howard University Law School, read about the case on a listserv called "Men of Howard." Cunningham started a petition calling for Zimmerman to be prosecuted.[6]

The petition collected ten thousand signatures. Soon the up-and-coming website Change.org asked Cunningham to transfer control of the petition drive to Martin's parents.[7]

Change.org's petition went viral when Black celebrities began tweeting about the murder. "Will you help spread the word about the petition #Trayvon Martin's parents started," wrote MC Hammer. Janelle Monae tweeted a link to the petition, adding, "Justice 4 #TrayvonMartin." The campaign became the fastest growing campaign in Change.org's history. Within days it received more than 250,000 signatures, eventually reaching over two million.[8]

Athletes jumped on, too. LeBron James and his Miami Heat teammates posed for a photograph wearing hoodies before a game against the Detroit Pistons to signal their support for Trayvon Martin and his family. Prince, the music superstar, called Rev. Al Sharpton and offered large donations to support both the family and the legal case.

Established civil rights groups now started to pick up on the growing national attention to Martin's killing. "Trayvon's murder mirrored hostility built into law enforcement from days of white supremacy," said Wade Henderson, the president of the Leadership Conference on Civil Rights. The legacy organizations were getting on board a protest train driven by social media.[9]

Crump and Martin's parents promoted a rally on March 21, 2013, in New York City, soon to be known as the "Million Hoodie March." Celebrities, including P. Diddy and Nellie, also threw their support to the march and calls to prosecute Zimmerman.

The Million Hoodie March brought hundreds to Union Square alongside people still taking part in the ongoing Occupy Wall Street protest and the groups formed in opposition to Troy Davis's execution.

At the march, Al Sharpton compared Martin's mother, Sybrina Fulton, to the mother of Emmett Till, the Black teenager killed by Mississippi segregationists in 1955. Sharpton recounted how Till's mother had refused to be silent about her son's death, even choosing an open casket funeral to show the horrific beating her son had suffered before dying. She wanted the world to see the physical damage done by the evil of racial hate.

Fulton then addressed the crowd. "My heart is in pain," she said, "but to see the support of all of you really makes a difference. This is not a Black and white thing—this is about a right and wrong thing."[10]

Crump and the boy's parents also organized a march in Florida. That day-long rally drew thousands to hear Martin's father, and civil rights leaders like Jesse Jackson, the NAACP's Ben Jealous, and Sharpton.

Though the story was boiling on social media, it was confined to a few paragraphs in most newspapers.

But shortly after the New York rally, President Obama put the story on mainstream media's front pages. In an unscheduled White House news conference, he said: "If I had a son, he would look like Trayvon, and I think [his parents] are right to expect that all of us as Americans are going to take this with the seriousness it deserves."[11]

Now it was clear that Trayvon Martin's murder had hit a nerve. Unlike the reaction to Troy Davis, which had been limited to civil rights activists and a few celebrities, something very different was now in motion with Trayvon's killing.

For the first time in history, the leader of the free world had called attention to the murder of a Black teenager. And this president of the United States spoke as a parent of Black teenagers. He also spoke knowledgeably about the threatening image of Black kids, implying that Martin had been targeted and killed by a neighborhood vigilante because he'd been wrongly suspected of being a criminal.

Nearly fifty years earlier, during the race riots and protests of the First Civil Rights Movement, President Lyndon Johnson had spoken out about racial violence. As a white man, Johnson could never have spoken about a Black boy's death in the same way that Obama could. It was personal for Obama, and that made his message unique for America, especially for Black Americans, who expected him finally to take action, using the power of the presidency to deal with this personal racial injustice in a way that no other president ever had.

But despite his very personal statement, Obama stood back and took no further action to address the injustice. Just as he had done with Troy Davis, Obama said it was a matter for local officials. He said it was up to them to decide whether to prosecute and convict the shooter. He did not ask the Justice Department to intervene, nor did he challenge the "stand your ground" laws in Florida that were being discussed as Zimmerman's possible defense.

The old Civil Rights Movement's dream was to have Black people in power, at the controls of politics and police. Obama was in power, yet he acted only as a referee. He said that because he was the president of all the American people, he wouldn't take any special level of response as a Black man.

The disconnect between the expectation that Obama would act as a savior and deliver justice and racial healing stood in contrast to political realities. Obama was focused on his 2012 reelection campaign. If he once again took sides in a racial fight, as he had done without popular success in the conflict between Henry Louis Gates and the white Cambridge police officer, it would cost him votes among white Americans and make him a one-term president. There was a disconnect between the president's thinking as a politician and the sense of urgency among young Black activists demanding attention to racial wrongs.

Older civil rights leaders still supported Obama and felt he deserved their loyalty because he was the first Black president. But this controversy about Trayvon Martin's death didn't fit with the experience those veterans had during the First Movement. The public fury and media attention in response to this killing were quite different from what the reaction had been in the 1960s. Trayvon Martin was just an average kid. He was no Medgar Evers, a civil rights leader whose murder generated national attention. Anger on the street in those days was channeled into established organizations, like the NAACP.

But Martin's parents had no ties to civil rights leaders. Their attorney, Crump, had no affiliation with activist groups. The young people rushing to demand justice for Martin's death did not belong to any of the civil rights groups and had no interest in joining such organizations; in fact, they felt estranged from the overwhelmingly older, male leadership of the First Movement.

The biggest theme in the social media posts from young Black people centered on the idea that Trayvon Martin had done nothing wrong. He was not a criminal. He was just walking down the street. They made no apology for stories reporting on his love of "gangsta" rap music, his hoodie, or reports that he had been suspended from school.

Their defiant perspective led to a backlash from conservative talk radio and news. Just as segregationist newspapers and radio existed in the mid-twentieth century, mostly in the South, now there existed a modern right-wing media ecosystem to take up the cause.

Bill O'Reilly, a top-rated conservative host on the Fox News channel, had called Trayvon Martin's death a sickening tragedy when it first happened. But as the movement built anger over the shooting and after Obama spoke out, O'Reilly shifted to defending Zimmerman. He played on the fears of his conservative, older, mostly white audience, particularly their fear of crime committed by young Black men, portraying Zimmerman as a law-and-order hero who was unfairly called a racist by a liberal press and the first Black president.

Zimmerman's father went on Fox to say that his son had shot Martin in self-defense. Then Zimmerman's brother also went on television to say that the fight had left Zimmerman with a broken nose. Finally, Zimmerman himself appeared on Fox's Sean Hannity show, a leading platform for conservatives, to say that Martin had threatened him and had beaten him bloody.[12] He would later sue NBC (unsuccessfully) for its editing of the 911 audio, claiming that the network had framed him as a racist who was "racially profiling Trayvon Martin."[13]

Right-wing media outlets and social media personalities chastised national newspaper coverage for reporting that Martin had been shot by a white man. They pointed out that Zimmerman had Hispanic heritage and argued that he should not be described as purely white. They also celebrated Zimmerman as a civic-minded volunteer crime fighter and reported that Martin's blood analysis had tested positive for marijuana. They also pointed out his numerous school suspensions.

Martin's package of Skittles even became a source of suspicion. To his supporters, the candy was an emblem of Martin's youth and innocence. But the right-wing media reported that Black teens often combined candies and sugary soft drinks with cough syrup to get high. Martin did not have any

cough syrup. He had never even opened the bag of Skittles. But the sugges-
tion conveyed the image of a thuggish, threatening, drug-addled Black teenager in a dark hoodie. Geraldo Rivera of Fox News made headlines when he
called hoodies "Thug Wear."[14]

Martin was no Mouse on right-wing talk shows.

Liberal media outlets told a different story. "Trayvon was the victim,"
Tracy Martin told NPR, but now his son was being transformed into the "villain in this case." NPR later reported that "white nationalists and the alt-right
adopted Zimmerman's cause, seeing in him a martyr being sacrificed on the
altar of political correctness."[15]

The white lawyers with whom Crump consulted were mystified. They
could not imagine their child "walking home from the store, being profiled,
pursued, and shot in the heart . . . they can't even fathom that." White parents,
he realized, "can't even believe that the police would ever kill their child—it
is not part of their reality." His team went to work, taking on a "yeoman's
job of trying to push back" on portrayals of Martin in right-wing media as a
"criminal menace."[16]

Because of Crump stirring public pressure, Zimmerman was finally
charged with second-degree murder in April. Conservative talk show hosts
and websites, led by Rush Limbaugh and Glenn Beck, launched fundraising
drives for Zimmerman, quickly raising $200,000. It was "an early example of
how social media activism reflects real-world partisan divides," *Washington
Post* reporter Reis Thebault would observe more than a decade later.

At the time of Martin's murder "social media activism was in its
infancy. . . . It wasn't default logic to use social media for activism and to
raise awareness," said Sarah J. Jackson, a University of Pennsylvania professor.[17]

The Second Civil Rights Movement's new style of activism was having an impact. One month after the shooting, rallies in support of Trayvon Martin were
being successfully organized online, from coast to coast, uncoordinated by
any larger, nationally established civil rights organization. Fifty years earlier,
the First Civil Rights Movement featured precisely timed marches with the

best-known leaders lined up in front. These marches were tightly controlled
by the NAACP, Black churches, and Dr. Martin Luther King Jr.'s Southern
Christian Leadership Conference. Now a movement was forming with no
widely recognized leaders and with no master plan for timing and execution.

Still, Crump was aware that the Second Movement began to coalesce
around issues of criminal justice around the time of Troy Davis's execution.
"Troy Davis is symbolic of hundreds of innocent people of color put to death
by a racist criminal justice system," he reflected, years later. He believed that
Troy Davis's case was a first step in changing the focus on the justice system. Whether it was complaints that the man who shot a Black kid was not
charged, or about police treating Black people unfairly, or Black people getting harsh sentences and jailed in disproportionate numbers, this was a new
frontier for civil rights activism.[18]

In the 1950s and 1960s, innumerable stories of brutal police and racist
judges, especially in small Southern towns, went ignored by local media. And
so one hallmark of the First Civil Rights Movement was its success in getting
a few national newspapers and television networks to pay attention to stories
of racial injustice.

To get national media to send reporters and cameras, the top civil rights
groups arranged for dignified, orderly marches in which everyone wore their
Sunday best. And when their protests ventured into segregated restaurants,
the activist groups informed reporters of the exact timing to ensure coverage
of the demeaning treatment endured by Black people in the segregated South.
The strategy paid off mightily when television began to show local whites
turning fire hoses and sharp-toothed dogs on peaceful, well-dressed people
trying to register to vote. For those who weren't around at the time, it's easy to
underestimate the amount of work and planning that went into attracting that
type of media attention.

Martin Luther King Jr. became the star of this kind of television coverage.
He was gifted in using it to its full potential. "We are here to say to the white
men that we no longer will let them use clubs on us in the dark corners," he
said in Alabama during protests in 1965. "We're going to make them do it in
the glaring light of television."[19]

King wrote to his aides during the Birmingham protests that even with him in jail, "we must have a sense of drama"[20] to capture media attention. The drama unfolded on-screen: police setting dogs on protests, powerful blasts of water from fire trucks knocking down demonstrators, and police using batons on people trying to register to vote. King and his deputy, Ralph Abernathy, "knew the country had never taken Black people's word for the horrors that they endured," the journalist Alexis C. Madrigal observed. "It would not be enough to talk about the Black experience of America. White Americans, through their televisions, would have to see, with their own eyes, some of those horrors enacted."[21]

Besides King and the established leaders of the NAACP, the National Urban League, and the churches, the only other voices allowed into that national news coverage were white politicians and public officials. It was an event if a leader from a more militant movement, like Malcolm X or Stokely Carmichael, got airtime. Uneducated, poor Black people from the rural South or from Northern ghettos existed only as background figures.

Newspaper front pages and television news programs preferred educated Black people with leadership titles who could be trusted to make reasoned appeals for fair treatment. They designated King a leading voice, comfortable with a man who spoke against violent tactics, making his claim to the American dream on behalf of patriotic, hardworking Americans who happened to be Black.

That history was quite a contrast to the hyperactive media-on-steroids, no-gatekeeper world of websites like Facebook and Twitter that were being leveraged by the new civil rights movement taking shape in the twenty-first century.

One thing hadn't changed all that much: major print and television news outlets were still reticent to pay close attention to the plight of Black Americans. But young Black people found the new social media platforms an open road. They could hear from one another without waiting for editors and producers to judge their stories worthy of attention. Their narratives were filled with their own hip-hop style, culture, and the political sensibility of Black neighborhoods.

Posting or tweeting required no entrance fee and followed no rules. All you needed was a cell phone or a laptop. It became an easy-access, online highway for sharing and receiving news more quickly and easily than ever before. Cell phones with cameras also created a world of people ready to record any encounter where they—or someone nearby—were treated badly.

By 2012, this new frontier in media had become an open door to a new civil rights movement. It embraced Black anger, encouraged radical thinking, and celebrated extreme stands by rewarding them with "likes" that further spread the message. One study that year found that more than 96 percent of Black people between the ages of eighteen and twenty-nine who had access to the internet were active on social media. These young Black people also represented a larger portion of Twitter users than their share of the U.S. population, according to audience metrics.[22]

Black political voices on social media had first come to the forefront after Hurricane Katrina devastated New Orleans back in 2005. People shared horrific stories and pictures of houses torn apart by high winds, whole streets flooded, as well as Blacks struggling to get out and being cut off from white areas by police. By 2008, "Black Twitter" had started to become a recognized phenomenon.

Funny memes circulating among Black people on social media, such as "#YOUKNOWYOUREBLACKWHEN," had enough power to become the topic of a 2009 article appearing on *The Root*, a website devoted to Black news stories.[23]

The next year Farhad Manjoo, writing in *Slate*, described Black Twitter users as a distinct group in social media. They formed "tighter clusters . . . they follow one another more readily, they retweet each other more often and more of their posts are . . . directed at other users who initiate hashtags [creating] . . . a high-density, influential network."[24]

All these voices were boiling over by the time George Zimmerman finally went on trial in June 2013, more than a year after Trayvon Martin's death. After three weeks of testimony, the six women who made up the jury—five whites and one Hispanic—ruled that he was not guilty of murder or manslaughter.

A racial split immediately spread across the country. Eighty-six percent of Black people were dissatisfied with the outcome, but only 30 percent of whites felt that way. The divide was far deeper on social media.[25] Among the five million tweets on the day after the verdict, a Pew study found that by four to one, the younger, more racially diverse people using social media condemned Zimmerman's acquittal.[26]

This finding highlighted a very real generational split with the younger, more racially mixed group of people at the forefront of outrage at the verdict. These young Black people shared first-person stories about repeated intimidation by police, from stop-and-frisks without cause to brutal beatings by officers who were never held accountable.

In the Trayvon Martin case, the not-guilty verdict led to more nationwide protest marches, most of them outside courthouses and police stations. Speakers called for the federal government—run by the first Black president and the first Black attorney general—to file new charges against Zimmerman. Notably, the most common request was for charges that Zimmerman had violated Martin's civil rights.

Days later, the president stepped into the White House Press Room to say that he had no problem with the judge or jury, observing that "reasonable doubt was relevant." He added that Holder was reviewing the case. But he distanced himself from any expectation that he might be a leading actor in the fight for justice for Trayvon Martin. He explained that the killing was subject to state and local criminal codes, not federal law, so there was no way he could take action to punish Zimmerman.

Still insisting that he wasn't the "Black president," Obama spoke across racial lines by acknowledging a common refrain of white conservatives: there is a high rate of crime among Black teenagers, and Martin was more likely to have been shot dead by another Black person his own age than by a white policeman. He acknowledged that young Black men are "disproportionately ... both victims and perpetrators of violence." Even so, he maintained that this was still no excuse for labeling young Black men as likely criminals.

Obama did take the Black perspective in one regard. He said that systemic racism in the criminal justice system was punishing Black people. This was the line of conversation that continued to dominate Black social media. "There is a history of racial disparities in the application of our criminal laws. A lot of African American boys are painted with a broad brush. If a white male teen was involved in the same kind of scenario . . . both the outcome and the aftermath might have been different."

He then ended his remarks by talking about the positives in race rela-tions. It was a strong rebuttal to the idea that Black-white relations were worse than they had been fifty years earlier, during the First Civil Rights Movement.

"I don't want us to lose sight that things are getting better," Obama said. "Each successive generation seems to be making progress in changing atti-tudes when it comes to race. It doesn't mean we're in a post-racial society. It doesn't mean racism is eliminated. But when I talk to Malia and Sasha [his daughters], and I listen to their friends . . . they're better than we were on these issues."[27]

Obama's remarks were deeply disappointing to younger Black people, especially those who were influential online. They wanted a more active, more zealous response against what they increasingly labeled as structural racism, systemic bias against Black people in criminal justice and other areas of life. Obama's pledge to put federal money into educating more young Black men did not excite passions among this group.

There was also a glaring divide on social media about Obama's claim that "things are getting better" in American race relations. On this question, white people divided from Black people, young people from old people, and, especially, young Black people from older Black people. The older genera-tion of civil rights leaders—men like Andrew Young, Jesse Jackson, and Al Sharpton—agreed with Obama that contemporary America was a "better" place than ever to be Black. But the younger generation saw the heroes of the First Civil Rights Movement losing touch with a changing reality, the twenty-first-century face of racism.

To the new generation, the height of the First Civil Rights Movement was upending laws enforcing racial segregation in schools, pools, housing, em-ployment, and at the voting booth. The new movement, launched by the rise of Obama, was propelled by social media and gave oxygen to discontent with the realities of the current Black experience in America, the persistence of double standards and de facto segregation. This generation was now looking beyond talk of Obama representing a post-racial nation and looked instead at everyday injustices in Black people's lives, like Black people being marginalized at work. But the stories that went viral online were of Black people being treated as criminals while shopping, while driving, or while running. Black voices now had an unprecedented online platform and called for the government to stop treating all Black people as criminals by allowing the police, the courts, the jails to abuse them.

There is data to support the charge that Black people confront abuse in the criminal justice system. While the high share of Black people in the country's prison population is well known, Latinos also are heavily represented. They make up 16 percent of the nation but make up 23 percent of the prison population.[28]

A report by the Pew Research Center found that Black men are "especially likely" to be imprisoned. In the U.S. they are incarcerated at twice the rate of Latinos and five times more than whites. "The rate was even high among Black men in certain age groups," Pew found. "Among those ages 35 to 39, for example, about one-in-twenty Black men were in state or federal prison in 2018."[29]

The conversation about Black people in the justice system inevitably circled back to talk about the high incidence of poverty among Black people, especially children from poor neighborhoods with failing schools. It extended to talk about "white privilege" and ongoing racist stereotypes in a culture that celebrated "gangsta" Black rappers.

This contrasted with white conservatives' focus on high crime rates among Blacks and lower levels of academic achievement. These conservatives argued they were being silenced by a "politically correct" culture. They argued it was "PC" to make a big deal out of white frat parties featuring college kids in blackface while ignoring threats from Black crime.

To Black people this line of argument was an ongoing insult. Black activists on social media didn't dispute these statistics about poverty, education, and crime, but they saw such data as evidence of the reach and tenacity of entrenched structural racism. While some racial progress had been made by the First Civil Rights Movement, implicit stereotypes still painted Black people as more violent, more criminal, and less educated than white people. White men still dominated executive office suites in big cities across the country.

The elevated outcry after the Davis execution exploded after Trayvon Martin's death and grew into discussions of ingrained racial disparities. New Black voices amplified their discontent. The emotional power of the moment was captured by Alicia Garza, a young Black woman living in Oakland, California.

She was sitting at a bar when word came of the Zimmerman verdict. Discouraged, even depressed, she went home and scrolled Facebook to see what people had to say. She noticed that Black people "were blaming Black people for our own conditions," she later told *USA Today*. She read comments about the need for Black boys to avoid wearing hoodies because they are associated with street gangs. Other people insisted that Black boys needed to pull up their pants to avoid being negatively stereotyped. Garza felt that these self-criticisms were misplaced. "It wasn't Trayvon Martin's fault that [George Zimmerman] stopped him and murdered him," she argued.[30]

Garza, who worked on special projects for the National Domestic Workers Alliance, said that it depressed her to see all the analysis, by Blacks and whites, focus on Martin's behavior while Zimmerman was essentially given a free pass for killing an unarmed Black teenager. Ever since news of the acquittal, she told *The Guardian*, she felt "incredibly vulnerable, incredibly exposed, incredibly enraged . . . it was a verdict that said: Black people are not safe in America."[31]

Garza grew weary of the pessimism among Black people on Facebook when she saw posts saying there was no reason to be surprised at a racist verdict. "Stop saying we are not surprised," she wrote on Facebook. "That's a damn shame, in itself.

"I continue to be surprised at how little Black lives matter . . . stop giving up on Black life." Then she added for her Facebook followers: "Black people. I love you. I love us. Our lives matter."

Patrisse Cullors, a friend of Garza's who was engaged in prison reform work, read this social media post and shared it to her own network. With the message, she tagged "#Blacklivesmatter."[32]

A third friend, Opal Tometi, an immigration rights activist, joined them to set up social media accounts for others to make statements affirming that "Black lives matter." The resulting social media traffic became an instant online sensation.

That night the racial tensions, the swelling frustrations, that had been bubbling beneath the surface of American life suddenly erupted into something entirely unexpected.

4

#BLACKLIVESMATTER

Exactly a year and a day after George Zimmerman was ruled not guilty, the next national fire alarm on race relations rang out. On July 17, 2014, police in New York City were videotaped using a chokehold that left an unarmed Black man begging for mercy.

Eric Garner, a 350-pound, forty-three-year-old man who suffered from asthma, began gasping, "I can't breathe!" He repeated the phrase eleven times, trying to get the police off him before he passed out.

The scene began on a busy commercial strip, Bay Street, in a working-class area of Staten Island. There was no chase, no guns drawn, no robbery, no drug deal. There was only Garner, in a white T-shirt, talking loudly to two policemen dressed in plain clothes. The police had approached Garner because they saw him involved in what looked like a sidewalk argument in front of a discount beauty supply store. When the incident was over, Daniel Pantaleo, a twenty-nine-year-old officer, accused Garner of illegally peddling single cigarettes from an open pack in his pants pocket. Garner had been arrested more than thirty times, including for selling single cigarettes, or "loosies," as well as for having marijuana on him, and for driving without a license. This time Garner, who was out of jail on bail, reacted defiantly, telling the cops to leave him alone, that he had a right to stand on the street.

"Every time you see me, you want to mess with me," he said. "I'm tired of it. It stops today. . . . I didn't sell nothing . . . every time you see me you want to harass me. . . . I'm minding my business. Please leave me alone."[1]

One of the policemen started pulling at his hands, trying to handcuff him. Garner, now angry, asked the officers not to touch him. That's when Pantaleo grabbed Garner around the neck, pushing his face against the beauty shop's window front. The big man fell to his knees. Then five other white policemen jumped on his back, pushing Garner flat on the sidewalk. He pleaded with them, saying he could not breathe. A Black uniformed police sergeant came on the scene and allowed the arrest to continue. Garner soon blacked out, and an ambulance was called. An hour later he made it to the hospital, but he had suffered a heart attack and was dead.

The Reverend Al Sharpton, responding to news reports, held a news conference in Staten Island two days later. He complained about the way the police had choked Garner. People held up signs reading "I Can't Breathe." The slogan instantly became a social media hashtag. Activists around the country, loosely organized under the new Black Lives Matter banner, picked up on it, and #ICantBreathe became a national slogan.

Days later, shouts of "I Can't Breathe" became a chorus for a Times Square protest featuring Broadway stars. "Arrests look more and more like modern-day lynching," rapped the Broadway musical star Daniel J. Watts, standing outside the NYPD booth on Times Square. "It's your job to bear arms but not to wrap your arms about and choke like a boa constrictor."[2]

This was followed by a march in Staten Island, organized by Sharpton; most of the 2,500 people present had connected online.

Three weeks later the city's medical examiner ruled that Garner had died because of the chokehold and "compression of chest" as the police held him on the ground. The police union also strongly defended the use of force against Garner, making the case that the big man had resisted arrest, even if he had been unarmed. They complained about the increasingly "slanderous, insulting, and unjust manner in which police officers are being portrayed."[3] And a grand jury did not indict the policeman.

But numbers don't lie: a study by the medical journal *The Lancet* later showed that in the period between 1980 and 2018, "Black Americans were estimated to be 3.5 times more likely to die from police violence than white Americans."[4] And millions who watched video of the police choking Garner saw visceral, disturbing evidence that the statistics on police violence against Blacks were true. In large numbers they took to the streets, joining protests against the police tactics that had led to Garner's death. More protests in New York followed the decision not to indict the police officers, though the city eventually paid a multimillion-dollar settlement to Garner's family. This had become a familiar script, repeated time and again across the nation as incidents of police violence against Black people resulted in civil suits but little systemic change.

Fifty years earlier, during the First Civil Rights Movement, the facts were worse, with more and more brutal violence. But the debate was ignored. Police violence against Black citizens almost never resulted in a civil-suit settlement for the victims. In that era, big-city newspaper editors and TV network executives constantly celebrated law enforcement. They ran upbeat stories about the heroic "boys in blue" making sacrifices and risking their lives to protect the public. The perspective of Black people rarely got past the white gatekeepers of the mainstream press. When police resorted to brutal treatment of Blacks, it got ink only when prompted by a lawsuit. But that was rare, because poor people lacked lawyers—and also because judges, who were often former prosecutors with ties to the police, were unsympathetic.

The bloody policeman's hand runs deep in American culture and history, going back to the pursuit of runaway slaves, lynching, post–Civil War chain gangs, and Black prisoners being put to work as cheap labor. In the 1950s and 1960s, small-town Southern sheriffs commonly resorted to violence in their interactions with Black people. Public display of explicit racist violence was less frequent in the North, but it was no less a fact of life. It was no secret that the nightstick kept Black people on the wrong side of the tracks, in their segregated, broken areas of town. It was accepted that Black people had to bend to the threatening, even vicious, presence of white police if they got near a white neighborhood.

All this remained true even as Dr. King spoke of his "dream" and successfully marched on Washington in 1963 for passage of the Civil Rights Bill.

As we've seen, the First Civil Rights Movement's priority was to end segregation as enforced under the power of local laws. That style of activism operated on the assumption that integrating voting booths was the path to racial justice. Dealing with violence by all-white police forces was a secondary concern.

In the 1960s only the Black Panthers and the Nation of Islam, commonly known as the Black Muslims, made a point of complaining about how the police treated Black people. They got nowhere. In fact, the big white-owned newspapers and television stations trashed them, dismissing them as militants. The white media also put Malcolm X in the category of a radical figure who simply hated America and white people.

The Black press largely treated the Panthers as extremists, too. While some members of the Black press offered a few articles about the Panthers as "Robin Hood"–type revolutionaries, protecting the interests of the poor, most Black papers, like the *New York Amsterdam News*, depicted them as far outside the organized protests led by established civil rights groups.

But the mainstream papers always portrayed the police, even when brutal with Black people, as standing in defense of the good life, manning the "Thin Blue Line" between chaos and peace. In July 1964, for example, *The New York Times* gave more coverage to rioting in Harlem than to the cause of the discontent—a policeman had killed a Black fifteen-year-old named James Powell. Front-page articles described six days of violence and protests in which "groups of Negroes [roamed] through the streets, attacking newsmen and others . . . standing on tenement roofs [and] shower[ing] policemen in steel helmets with bottles and bricks." Little attention was paid to how police used force against the crowds. An incredible number of people—five hundred, mostly Black—were arrested.[5]

Later that year, when both a grand jury and a police panel cleared the officer who had shot Powell, the *Times* wrote nothing about complaints of violence from the Black community against the overwhelmingly white New York Police Department. Instead, the newspaper's story emphasized that civil rights groups had "stepped up their demands for a civilian review board" and noted that the mayor had rejected the idea. The *Times* did report that "2000 complaints a year" had reached the police. But only 10 percent of those cases merited "departmental trials," which took place behind closed doors, with no public accountability.[6] This was a time when white power players were able to curb activism by pressuring white employers to fire Black protesters. They even had banks pull mortgages from Black activists.

But in the twenty-first century, firing activists, beating down, or killing Black people was suddenly more difficult to hide. The internet opened the door to these stories about rough, sadistic handling of Black individuals by police.

In 2006, twenty-three-year-old Sean Bell and a group of his friends were shot more than fifty times by New York City police officers as he left his bachelor party in Queens. Four shots hit Bell in the body and neck, killing him. Three of the policemen involved were indicted, but they were found not guilty by a racially mixed jury that was told about drug use and drunkenness at the club where the incident took place. After the acquittals, the protests were old-school, with Sharpton leading marches to block streets and bridges. But a new force was also at play, as people could now easily send emails to share stories popping up on the internet.

Three years later the internet was a much bigger force for protests when police in Oakland, California, shot twenty-two-year-old Oscar Grant at a train station. Grant was unarmed. Cell phone video of the killing became a national sensation on the internet. A policeman said he intended to tase Grant but mistakenly shot him with a gun, killing him. However, cell phone video showed Grant seated on the ground, hands in the air, before he was shot. The footage inspired hundreds of people to march in protests that resulted in looting and a police car being set on fire.

Like the videotape that captured the 1991 police beating of Rodney King, the Grant video was taken by a bystander. And now video technology was in everyone's pocket. The use of cell phone videos in the Grant case gave people an incredibly effective new tool to hold the police accountable. It led to cell phones popping up to record police stops coast to coast. Still, in spite of the shocking images, neither Grant's case, nor any other, started a national protest movement.

It's hard to say precisely why. But it's notable that these incidents happened before there was a Black president. They also took place just as new technology in the form of social media applications became available on cell phones. Previously, websites had been gathering places for people to share information, and they were much faster than printed papers and scheduled TV programs. But the integration of social media into smartphones kicked the nascent media revolution into hyper-speed. Suddenly people could be easily and instantly alerted, at any time of day or night, to reports and videos of police violence.

The use of social media apps to expose police violence pushed the stories into mainstream media, increasing coverage of such violence in Black communities. This in turn prompted politicians to speak out on the issue as they never had before.

The impact of social media was particularly evident in generating attention and protest after the murder of Trayvon Martin. The protests around the Eric Garner case mirrored the tactics and strategy that had developed after the Martin case. The difference this time was that smartphones had become universal and even Black people living on the lowest economic level had immediate access to social media. It gave everyone a way to tell their stories of abuse by police, prosecutors, and the courts.

Additionally, there were more Black politicians in office, including at the highest level of power. Black activists online started asking why these politicians did nothing about the bad police. And they wanted to know why the major civil rights groups didn't do more.

Within weeks of Eric Garner being choked to death in New York, the rising tide of attention to police violence became a flood. The tipping point was an encounter between white police and a Black teenager in the small St. Louis suburb of Ferguson, Missouri.

There was a lot of resentment among Black residents against the white establishment in Ferguson, but the town had no history of big racial protests and was home to no major civil rights leaders. Yet the police shooting of a young Black man there in the summer of 2014 attracted national attention far beyond Eric Garner's death in the biggest media market in the country. And the difference in the response was the result of seeds planted the year before in the wake of Trayvon Martin's killing.

The basic elements of what happened were similar to other cases of police violence against young Black men. The Ferguson police got a call about a Black teenager stealing a box of Swisher Sweets cigars from a corner store called Ferguson Market and Liquor. The teenager also pushed an older man, the store's owner, into a display rack. After he left, the owner called the police, reporting a robbery.

The first response was a radio alert for two suspects, young Black men. A few minutes later, without hearing the radio report, a white police officer happened to see two young Black men walking the yellow line along a twisting street. The policeman, Darren Wilson, put down his car window and shouted at the men to get on the sidewalk. Eighteen-year-old Michael Brown and his friend, twenty-two-year-old Dorian Johnson, ignored him.

Despite his large size, Brown was an adolescent, and he was struggling. He didn't live with either of his parents and had recently been put out of his grandmother's house. He was staying at a friend's crowded apartment and his highest hope was to go to a technical college to learn how to repair air conditioners.

Several years after the fact, a documentary by Jason Pollock, *Stranger Fruit*, showed Ferguson Market's security video from the night before the shooting. The video shows Brown handing what looked to be a bag of marijuana to the store clerks, who appear to offer cigars in exchange for the bag. Brown, smiling on the video, hands the cigars back. It is not clear if there was a deal made—there is no audio. He may have intended to pick up the cigars the next day.

But when Brown returned the next day, it was a different shift, with different people working, none of whom appeared to know about any deal. They refused to hand over the cigars to Brown, who appeared angry, grabbed the cigars, and walked out. That, and shoving the old man, led to the call to the police.[7]

Now as the police confronted him for walking in the middle of the street, Brown turned and defiantly told Officer Wilson to get lost. The cop had already driven past the men when he realized that Brown was cursing at him. He put the car in reverse, backing up to come face-to-face with them.

Brown, at six feet four inches and weighing nearly three hundred pounds, began pushing the door to keep Wilson from getting out and brashly telling the cop to mind his own business.

According to a police report on the incident (which fit with a later review by the U.S. Justice Department), as Brown pushed on the door, he reached through the car window and punched Officer Wilson, also a big man at six feet four inches and 210 pounds. At that point, according to testimony, Wilson reacted by reaching for his gun. As Wilson pulled out the weapon, Brown grabbed it. The gun went off, shooting Brown in the hand. Bleeding, Brown pulled his arm out of the car and began running away. That was when Wilson got out of the police car, holding his gun.[8]

The worst of the confrontation seemed to be over. But as Brown continued to run, Wilson shouted for him to get on the ground.

At this point there are two versions of the story. In the first, the young man, enraged, turned and charged at the police officer, who was standing in the street with his gun drawn. The police officer again yelled for Brown to get on the ground before firing his gun. In the other version, Wilson got out of the police car and fired at the fleeing Brown.

In either version of the story, Wilson fired ten shots, missing with several but hitting Brown in his chest, his arm, through his right eye, and at the top of his head, killing him.

The whole episode was over in about ninety seconds. It took place on a residential street, bordered by green lawns and low-rise apartments. It was noon on a Saturday, and the two-way street was busy with traffic. Wilson's police car was stopped at an angle, near an intersection, blocking all traffic. People from the neighborhood began walking close to the scene, gawking at the police and the dead body.

An ambulance arrived, and the paramedics declared Brown dead at the scene, at 12:05 p.m. Traffic began backing up. A crowd gathered as more police arrived, followed by crime investigators. Brown's body remained on the street the whole time, uncovered, for hours. Finally, the police set up orange screens to block public view of the body, but it was four hours before Brown's body was finally taken away.

Pictures of Brown's dead body on the hot, midday August street began showing up immediately on social media. People in the neighborhood rushed to the scene with their phones out to video the police activity as well. One of them, Emanuel Freeman, lived in a garden apartment just feet from where Brown's body lay, and tweeted (under the handle @theepharoah), "I JUST SAW SOMEONE DIE OMFG."[9]

Twitter also began spreading reports from Brown's friend, Dorian Johnson, who said that the police had shot his friend in the back. Johnson, who hid behind a car during the gunfire, said that Brown had yelled at Wilson, "Hands up, don't shoot!"

Soon, Brown's mother, Lezley McSpadden, arrived, demanding to see if it was her son who had been shot. The police refused her request, saying that it was an ongoing investigation. Social media accounts showed the desperate mother, crying and unable to reach her child, and the indifference of the police.

That night, the rapper Tef Poe got national attention for tweets that went viral, including a post of Brown's dead body in the street. These were heavily retweeted by young Black people who got their news from Black Twitter. Soon the story spread nationwide, and the mainstream media began to pick it up. The AP ran a story with the headline "Ferguson, Missouri Crowd After Fatal Shooting of Unarmed Teen: 'Kill the Police.'"[10] Other major TV and newspaper outlets began running their own stories that night, based on social media accounts on Twitter, Instagram, and Facebook.

By the next night, the overwhelmingly white police and the younger Black protesters engaged violently, in what became a riot. Police dogs and a police team with the SWAT designation—Special Weapons and Tactics—were also brought in to deal with the crowd. Some of the 150 officers arrived with military surplus weapons, many riding in armored, tank-like vehicles built for war.

The military-style look of the police fed tensions, not only in Ferguson but also around the country. The David-and-Goliath contrast between the

two sides led reporters to investigate the source of this new military equipment. Federal and local officials around the country revealed that a stream
of surplus military gear, left over from the wars in Iraq and Afghanistan, had
been sent to local police departments. The militarization of the police led
to still more outrage online and the hashtag #Ferguson immediately began
trending as the confrontation grew.

As the riots and overwhelming police response turned into a nightly
event, Governor Jay Nixon set a curfew and declared a state of emergency. He
called in the National Guard. Clergy and older Black leaders tried to calm the
conflict. At one point, hundreds of Black teenagers pushed into a police line,
but Black ministers intervened to prevent another bloody scene. The nightly
duels between police and young people with rocks and firebombs continued
for two weeks. There was also a counter-protest in support of the police, featuring fifty people carrying a banner that read: "I Am Darren Wilson."[11]

Obama's initial response was to send Attorney General Eric Holder to
Ferguson. The elegant, tall Holder met with both sides, talking with police
and holding hands with the grieving Brown family. But the biggest impact
of his visit was to open a new wave of ugly recriminations on Black media
about feckless Black political leadership. Eddie Glaude Jr., a professor of African American studies at Princeton University, pointed out that "the hell that
Black communities are catching has happened on Black people's watch."[12] As
Obama sought to lower the heat, his words satisfied neither the supporters of
the police nor the growing number of Black young people who were involved
in the protests and gaining nationwide support on social media.

Ebony magazine, long a champion of Obama's, published an October
edition that signaled disappointment among older, more middle-class Black
Americans, noting the "tone-deaf response of the Obama Administration" to
the events in Ferguson. The magazine scolded the president as part of Black
leadership practicing "respectability politics instead of [voicing] the visceral
pain and rage so eloquently articulated on the streets of Ferguson." In harsh
language, the magazine pointed out that "the Ferguson rebellion has exposed
deep-seated racism, hyper-militarized state forces, unabashed police brutality
and the soul-crushing poverty that will come to define the 'Age of Obama.'"[13]

Ebony's comments were surprising because the president remained widely admired—a beloved icon in Black America. After he won the presidency in 2008, the magazine's cover featured a beaming Obama and the headline: "In Our Lifetime." But now polls showed a drop in Obama's personal approval rating among Black people due to his handling of the riots. The president—rightly acting as president of all Americans and not as the president of Black America—continued to urge calm and respect for the rule of law even as the protests continued.

In November, a grand jury declined to bring charges against the white police officer for Brown's killing. Riots again broke out. The president delivered the same message he gave after a jury cleared Trayvon Martin's murderer. Both Black and white people, he said, must accept that "the decision was the grand jury's to make." He called for the violence and rioting to stop. Then, doing his best to give voice to Black discontent, he shifted his persona to speak as a Black president. Noting that he had witnessed "enormous progress in race relations over the course of the past several decades," he nevertheless pointed out "that in too many parts of this country, a deep distrust exists between law enforcement and communities of color . . . result of the legacy of racial discrimination in this country. . . . We need to recognize that this is not just an issue for Ferguson, this is an issue for America."[14]

The question still haunting the president was why he didn't go to Ferguson or make a major speech from the White House. Remaining noncommittal, he told reporters: "Well, let's take a look and see how things are going."

The president never went to Ferguson. Instead, he created a "Task Force on 21st Century Policing." Its mandate was to report to him in ninety days on ways to improve law enforcement, with an emphasis on better relations between the police and Black people. He arranged for some of the young people in the protests to join older civil rights leaders in Washington as he unveiled the task force. Obama's initiative also included more money for body cameras on police and improvements in law enforcement training, along with a presidential order to federal agencies to review procedures for sending military equipment to police departments and to assess whether the United States was "militarizing domestic law enforcement unnecessarily."

"And in the two years I have remaining as president," Obama said, "I'm going to make sure that we follow through—not to solve every problem, not tear down every barrier of mistrust . . . but to make things better."[15]

But many of the young Black protest leaders present at the meeting didn't think it was enough. They said they were heading back to the streets to lead more protests. "We appreciate that the president wanted to meet with us, but now he must deliver. . . . We are calling on everyone who believes that Black Lives Matter to continue taking to the streets until we get real change for our communities," said James Hayes, the head of the Ohio Student Association, who attended the meeting.[16]

How people viewed Brown's death reflected a deep racial split across the nation. Less than a week after the shooting, Pew Research reported that only 37 percent of white people believed the shooting raised "important issues about race." But 80 percent of Black Americans said it did.[17]

Politics compounded the racial split. Most Democrats, including most white Democrats, said the shooting was an important racial issue. But only 22 percent of Republicans agreed. When television cameras showed young Black people shouting insults and threats at police, the divide got worse. Chris Christie, the Republican governor of New Jersey, said that the antagonism toward the police revealed the protests to be a fraud, arguing that such protests "can't be justified when they are calling for the murder of police officers."[18]

At Brown's funeral, a huge crowd of 4,500 people came to mourn, including national figures. Martin Luther King III was in the audience, as was Jesse Jackson (in the front row), the movie director Spike Lee, the rapper Snoop Dogg, and the radio talk show host Tom Joyner. Trayvon Martin's parents also attended. Their presence highlighted the pattern of Black men being killed and the lack of faith in the legal system to deliver justice, whether in Florida, New York, or now Missouri.

Al Sharpton, in his eulogy, asked if the mourners could imagine what it felt like for a Black family to have "their son taken, discarded and marginalized," referring not only to Brown's body being left in the street for hours "like he didn't have any loved ones, like his life value didn't matter," but also stirring memories of Trayvon Martin's family going through a night without knowing that he had been shot dead. It provoked memories of Eric Garner's family suddenly being told one afternoon that he was dead. It was a different way of saying "Black Lives Matter."

Then Sharpton changed direction: "Michael Brown does not want to be remembered for a riot," he argued. "He wants to be remembered as the one that made a difference. . . . This is not about you! This is about justice!"

Sharpton's voice hit high when he said that Black America had to feel outraged at Brown's death but also when Black-on-Black gunfire killed a nine-year-old child in Chicago or when young Black people were "running around gun-toting, [shooting] each other so that [police] are justified in trying to come at us, because some of us act like the definition of Blackness is how low you can go."

Sharpton called on the young people taking to the streets to redirect their energy and improve life in the Black community: "We can't have a fit; we've got to have a movement. A fit you get mad and run out for a couple of nights. A movement is when you turn your chants into change, our demonstration into legislation. . . . We've got to clean up our community so we can clean up the United States of America."[19]

Outside the church some people didn't appreciate Sharpton chiding the young people marching in protest as having a "ghetto pity party."

"I just don't see the relationship between the discourse of Black personal responsibility and the set of actions that resulted in Michael Brown's death," said Eddie Glaude of Princeton University. More criticism came from Ta-Nehisi Coates, who later complained that Sharpton engaged in "moral hectoring of black people."[20] The Brown killing provoked a national conversation about both police violence toward Blacks and Black responsibility for criminal behavior. The amount of national attention this captured was a surprise given that it was initiated by a killing that took place in a small Midwestern town, far from political and mainstream media power. St. Louis seemed an unlikely setting for a major civil rights event, but the city was just north of large Black populations in Arkansas, Mississippi, and Louisiana. It was best known for its iconic arch, marking it as the gateway to the American West. But its reach into the Southern states had made it a center for slave traders before the Civil War.

The city on the Mississippi ranked as second only to Baltimore in Black population for most of the twentieth century. It was also one of the ten most segregated metropolitan areas in the nation. When the industries that powered the nation's economy began moving further south and even overseas in the 1970s, whites began leaving town.

St. Louis's population fell from close to a million in 1950 to 300,000 by 2014, and the city became nearly half Black. The wealth remained in white hands, however. So, too, did the political power and the media. By the 1980s working-class Black people began following whites escaping St. Louis. They pushed into cheap housing in the suburbs, like Ferguson, only to find white people reacting once again by moving away.[21]

By 2014, the northwest suburb of Ferguson was home to only about 21,000 people, two-thirds Black and mostly working-class. A quarter of the people in Ferguson lived below the U.S. poverty level.

In ten years, between 1990 and 2000, Ferguson's racial makeup went from 74 percent white to 52 percent Black. The politicians and the police in Ferguson, however, remained mostly white. And 93 percent of the arrests made by Ferguson police were of Black people. When it came to jailing Black men, the town was later revealed to lead the country in that category for cities with more than ten thousand people. It was also a town where tickets for illegal parking and driving violations provided much of its revenue. In three years, 2012 to 2014, 85 percent of the drivers stopped by police were Black.[22]

This was the heated mix in Ferguson waiting to ignite like a volcanic eruption before Michael Brown was killed. Given the persistently high level of segregation in communities across the country, the issues that came to the forefront in Ferguson exemplified the tensions that remained. These tensions had not been resolved by the First Movement. Now they were left squarely in the hands of the Second Movement.

Far away, in Los Angeles, Patrisse Cullors, one of the women who had founded #BlackLivesMatter a year earlier, watched the around-the-clock social media updates after Brown's killing, especially the dramatic images of armored police standing against young Black people.

"I stayed up all night trying to figure out how to support the brave and courageous community of Ferguson and St. Louis as they were being brutalized by law enforcement, criticized by media, tear gassed and pepper sprayed night after night," she said.[23]

Opal Tometi, who had purchased the website BlackLivesMatter.com and had started Facebook and Twitter accounts for Black Lives Matter, activated those platforms. She used the network from her job with Black Alliance for Just Immigration to send email blasts to "dozens and dozens of Black community organizers," inviting them to become part of a Black Lives Matter network.[24]

The first time this nascent network showed its power was in Ferguson, as Tometi, Cullors, and the third founding member, Alicia Garza, began organizing what they called a "Freedom Ride." They called on their social media followers to go to Ferguson and add their bodies to the protests. Their call to action was a reference to the First Civil Rights Movement's Freedom Rides in 1961, protesting segregation on buses traveling through the South.

The Black Lives Matter protests in Ferguson were scheduled for Labor Day weekend. "We understood Ferguson was not an aberration but, in fact, a clear point of reference for what was happening to Black communities everywhere," Cullors explained.[25] In a later speech, she said that Black Lives Matter became a "tool to reimagine a world where Black people are free, free to live."[26]

Looking back, Tometi told a Georgetown University podcast that in her mind Ferguson was an unprecedented social media event: "And so, with less than two weeks of organizing, there was a mobilization of over five hundred Black people to Ferguson, Missouri."[27] In the weeks leading up to the Labor Day protests, the hashtag #BlackLivesMatter peaked at 58,747 citations a day.[28]

The power of the protests was described by Tometi as "righteous rage." She said it was the first time activists had dared to counter a "militarized police force" that "brutalized" people.[29] And it was being done as "the entire world watched" via social media video streams, taking the racial conflict global. This was different from the First Civil Rights Movement's protests for voting rights in Selma, where the video of violence by the Alabama state police against the marchers could not be seen until the videotape made it back to newsrooms in New York, and then only if the networks decided to broadcast it on the evening news.

In this new era, the Second Civil Rights Movement did not have to wait for distant media gatekeepers to tell its story. Social media provided an immediate connection for people of all races to share details that never made the press. Now supporters around the world could follow simply by using #BlackLivesMatter, which was becoming increasingly widely used.

By November 24, the day when a grand jury declined to indict Wilson for killing Brown, the hashtag reached 170,000 uses. It kept growing in the days that followed, soon reaching 1.7 million. It grew even further two weeks later, when a New York grand jury refused to indict Daniel Pantaleo for choking Eric Garner.[30]

Athletes and celebrities used their public appearances to amplify the movement. LeBron James and other basketball stars wore warmup shirts at nationally televised games that read "I Can't Breathe." Members of the St. Louis Rams football team came onto the field in uniform with their hands held up, signaling their support to claims that Brown had said, "Hands up, don't shoot!" These acts of solidarity took #BlackLivesMatter to an even higher plane of visibility in American popular culture.

For the first time since the O. J. Simpson case and the Rodney King beating two decades earlier, the predominant national conversation was about race. Whereas before Ferguson, the Black Lives Matter banner had only been carried online, after Ferguson, local Black Lives Matter chapters began forming, including in St. Louis. It was a model followed by protesters who came to Ferguson from around the country. When they left, they went home to form chapters, more than eighteen in the month after Brown's death.

Years later in an interview with *The New Yorker*, Tometi and Garza said that their success in Ferguson led them to conclude: "Hey, Fergusons are everywhere, and we don't want to just go back home and act like this was a one-off act of solidarity. We want to do something. And that was essentially the beginning of our network." The Black Lives Matter founders decided that "power goes on in the local chapters because they know what is going on, and they are the ones familiar with the terrain."

Unlike the NAACP, which was a centralized structure overseeing local chapters, BLM was different. Most of BLM's free-form chapters did not have a legal charter. Nor did many register initially for 501(c)(3) status with the tax authorities. Some chapters just "come and go," in the words of Tometi and Garza.[31]

And while most people saw Black Lives Matter as a movement against police brutality, some of the chapters envisioned a more expansive mandate. They wanted Black Lives Matter to lead the fight against white supremacy in all forms, extending the idea of confronting racial injustice to fighting for a higher minimum wage, supporting sex workers, advocating for more support for Black studies programs in high schools and universities, or taking a stand with the LGBTQ community. There were also calls for the movement to identify racism in news coverage as well as in Hollywood. "So different chapters might take on different issues, but there is this throughline of valuing Black life and understanding that we are not a monolith but being radically inclusive in terms of chapter makeup," Tometi and Garza explained to *The New Yorker*.[32]

In contrast to the First Civil Rights Movement, this new movement had an absence of hierarchy. There was also an absence of commanding men in leadership, in the tradition of Martin Luther King or Thurgood Marshall. Instead, this movement had three female founders who did not position themselves as leading the group.

They also spoke openly about sexuality. This was a big contrast with the men leading the twentieth-century movement, who kept their distance from such topics. It was also a cultural break from older members of the Black community who still held disdain for expressions of homosexuality. Their views reflected a time when the country had no tolerance for public support for gay life. For example, Bayard Rustin, the key organizer of the 1963 March on Washington, always kept a low public profile as a closeted gay man.

The Second Movement's embrace of LGBTQ rights and turn away from male leadership did not undermine its effectiveness. By April 2015, Black Lives Matter was on the cover of *Time* magazine.[33] By the end of the year, the movement was on the shortlist of everyone's most significant developments of the year. The brand remained strong. "The prevalence of the Black Lives Matter hashtag prompted media outlets to seize the phrase as shorthand for the struggle writ large," *Time* wrote. "The new civil rights movement had its rallying cry."[34]

It had become a true force in American society; millions of Americans were using #BLM to discuss policing and race relations on social media. *Time* summed it up: "A new civil rights movement is turning a protest cry into a political force."

But the political pressure, just like any other force in nature, generated a reaction, a counterforce. And it was on the way.

5

WHITE BACKLASH

With the gun in his hands, the scruffy Latino man was seconds from killing the pretty, white girl. What the brown-skinned man didn't know was that he was also a target. He was on the verge of being forced into the storm of the Second Civil Rights Movement.

The fifty-six-year-old Mexican national, Jose Garcia Zarate, was just out of the San Francisco County jail, where he had arrived immediately after serving four years in a federal prison for having illegally entered the United States. He had been deported five times previously. His criminal record showed seven nonviolent felony drug convictions. When his time in federal prison ended, he was transferred to San Francisco to face a twenty-year-old charge for buying marijuana. The charge was so old it was immediately dismissed. Then he was released.

Zarate was scheduled to be deported again, but the San Francisco police failed to notify Immigration and Customs Enforcement, leaving him with nowhere to go, a homeless man, diagnosed as schizophrenic, wandering the city for several weeks.

On July 1, 2015, he swallowed some sleeping pills he'd dug out of a dumpster. By 6:30 p.m., he was groggy, sitting on a bench by the piers of San Francisco Bay. In front of him on that breezy summer evening were affluent tourists enjoying squawking seagulls, slow-moving tour boats, and honking sea lions.

While on the park bench, Zarate felt the back of his foot touch something. He looked down and saw a T-shirt wrapped around a bulky object. It turned out to be a hair-trigger gun stolen four days earlier from a parked car belonging to a ranger with the U.S. Bureau of Land Management.

As Zarate unwrapped the T-shirt, the gun went off. The bullet skipped off the ground and hit a young woman, Kate Steinle, who was about ninety feet away, tearing into her back and severing the artery leading to her heart. She fell to the ground and struggled to breathe. "Help me, Dad," she said to her father, who moments before had been posing with her for photos on the waterfront. He began pumping her chest, giving CPR.

Along the beautiful, historic Embarcadero area of shops and restaurants, tourists screamed at the sound of the gunshot; some began running in panic. Camera surveillance showed Zarate jump up and run from the scene, tossing the gun in the bay. Within an hour the police identified him. They arrested him less than a mile away.

The killing of the thirty-two-year-old Steinle, who was beginning her career at one of the city's glamourous high-tech companies, made the local news that Wednesday night in San Francisco. But days later it spread across the nation. Conservative talk radio hosts told the story of her murder as proof of the need to put more federal agents on the nation's southern border. They lashed out at the rising number of immigrants in the country, especially the "illegal" or undocumented immigrants coming from Mexico. More extreme voices even called for a wall to be built to stop the flow of drugs and criminals coming into the United States.

Two weeks earlier, Donald Trump had announced his candidacy for the Republican Party's presidential nomination. His opening appeal to voters was all about immigrants as criminals.

"When Mexico sends its people, they're not sending their best," he said in his announcement, after he rode down a gold-plated escalator in his Fifth Avenue high-rise in New York City. "They're not sending you. They're not sending you," he told his largely white audience, implying an influx of threatening people, non-English-speaking brown people.

"They're sending people that have lots of problems, and they're bringing those problems [to] us," Trump explained. "They're bringing drugs. They're bringing crime. They're rapists. And some, I assume, are good people . . . but I speak to border guards, and they tell us what we're getting. And it only makes common sense. . . . They're sending us not the right people."[1]

Trump's loaded words were a brutish appeal to racial anxiety in a Republican Party that was 80 percent white.

His comments made front-page headlines. And he had supporters, including the country's leading radio talk show host, Rush Limbaugh (who told his audience he worked with "talent on loan from God"). Limbaugh said that the "illegal immigrant" who murdered Steinle was "exactly the kind of guy Donald Trump was talking about."[2]

Trump was long known for the television reality show *The Apprentice*, where he played the show's big boss, the insolent honcho who famously told contestants, "You're fired!" And for decades before the television show, he was a regular in New York's fiery tabloid newspapers, famed for his playboy lifestyle and for never holding his tongue about any suspected wrong done by Black people.

Before running for president, he created controversy by questioning whether President Barack Obama was really an American. Trump held news conferences and appeared on conservative radio and television shows to argue that Obama had lied about being born in the United States, making him ineligible to serve as president. The "birther" claim led Obama to produce his long-form birth certificate. Trump then demanded to see Obama's college transcripts, questioning how he got into Harvard Law School, calling him an "affirmative action" president.

Trump also stoked racial anger on Twitter. He used social media in much the same way that social justice activists, including Black Lives Matter, had used Twitter and Facebook to provoke public outrage. Trump used his celebrity on social media to champion the police and oppose calls for racial justice. In other words, he positioned himself in direct opposition to the ideas animating the Second Civil Rights Movement.

The Washington Post described Trump as turning American race relations on its head by charging Blacks with racism against whites. "Trump's use of words like 'racist' and 'racism,'" the paper reported, "is perhaps best understood in the context of a modern conservative movement that has come to believe, against all evidence, that whites face more discrimination than Blacks." The *Post* cited several targets of Trump's rants, including fury at affirmative action in college admissions and disgust with preferential hiring by large corporations that sought to diversify their workforces.[3]

A lot of people dismissed Trump as a shameless, race-baiting self-promoter, but his message on race relations was heard steadily on conservative media. He succeeded by promoting the stereotype that Black people, with disproportionate arrests for crime and reliance on government assistance programs, were taking advantage of white people.

Trump's racism extended beyond Blacks. Having opened his presidential campaign by calling Mexicans criminals, drug dealers, and rapists, he saw a golden opportunity in stoking outrage over Kate Steinle's tragic death. According to Trump, Steinle's killing was prime evidence of how the rising number of illegal immigrants was damaging a once great country. Calling Zarate an "animal that shot this beautiful woman in San Francisco,"[4] Trump called the incident "yet another example of why we must secure our border immediately. . . . I am the only one who can fix it. Nobody else has the guts to even talk about it."[5]

Trump's telling of the story quickly went beyond the facts. Without any evidence he argued that the government of Mexico "pushes back people across the border that are criminals, that are drug dealers."[6] At a gathering of conservatives at Iowa's Family Leadership Summit, Trump noted that Zarate had been deported five times, adding: "Believe me, Mexico kept pushing him back because they didn't want him. Believe me, that's true."[7]

Trump's lies had impact, resonating with the older white audience for conservative talk shows. Those programs saw their ratings go up when they focused attention on Trump's anti-immigrant rage. The top-rated cable television program in the country, *The O'Reilly Factor* on Fox News, joined Trump's choir. Bill O'Reilly presented Trump as a truth-teller daring to speak about murderous illegal immigrants from Mexico and told his audience that most politicians had their tongues tied in knots for fear of being called racists.

"Mexican criminals," said O'Reilly, "represent a whopping 16 percent of all convicts serving time in federal penitentiaries. That's a huge burden on the American taxpayer and a dangerous situation for we the people, like thirty-two-year-old Kate Steinle."[8]

The statistics were misleading. Most of the Mexicans in jail were being held for illegally crossing the border, not for violent crime. But that truth was a minor distraction, unimportant to commentators attuned to the depth of white grievance against immigrants. Tapping into that discontent proved successful in driving up O'Reilly's audience. It also boosted Trump.

O'Reilly went on to blame Steinle's death on liberal politicians. The Democrats in San Francisco's city government, he noted, had established a "Sanctuary City" policy of not cooperating with federal agents to deport undocumented immigrants. In practice that meant they had no obligation to notify federal authorities when releasing prisoners lacking legal citizenship unless there was a warrant. There was no warrant for Zarate, and that's why he wound up homeless on the street and not in federal custody.

O'Reilly charged that President Obama neglected to deal with criminal immigrants "because racial politics drives the law these days, which is why Trump caught so much hell."[9] O'Reilly proposed "Kate's Law," a new federal bill to require a five-year jail sentence for anyone caught illegally crossing the border after having previously been deported. Within days, an online petition collected 400,000 signatures and Trump's support.[10]

The fevered anger following Steinle's death drowned out a key fact. Immigrants, both documented and undocumented, were less likely to commit crimes or to be jailed than people born in the United States.

The facts didn't matter to Trump, Limbaugh, or O'Reilly. With the Steinle story as their hook, they began telling other scary tales about the evil done by "illegal immigrants." They sensationalized stories of undocumented people driving while drunk and cheating to get government money that was intended for people legally in the country. The stream of stories made immigration into a central political fight defining the 2016 Republican primary.

"Something happened in July to send Trump's numbers soaring," wrote David Frum in *The Atlantic*. "That something may have been the murder of Kathryn Steinle."[11] At the time of his campaign announcement, polling showed Trump in seventh place among Republican candidates. By the end of July, he led the contest.

Trump embodied the backlash to the Second Civil Rights Movement. From his early opposition to Obama's rise and disparaging Blacks as criminals, it now extended to the idea that dangerous, brown-skinned immigrants were flooding the United States and wrecking his nostalgic vision of a mostly white nation.

Trump even used Steinle's death in political advertising aimed at his best-funded competitor, Jeb Bush, whose wife was Mexican. The advertisement featured a jailhouse mugshot of a disheveled Zarate. The ad was reminiscent of the notorious Willie Horton ad that George H. W. Bush's 1988 campaign had used against Governor Michael Dukakis of Massachusetts, the Democratic presidential nominee that year. Horton, a Black man with a long criminal record, had been convicted of raping a white woman while on a prison furlough program in place during Dukakis's time as governor. The ad was later described by CNN as "one of the most racially divisive in modern political history because it played into white fear and African American stereotypes."[12]

Trump's attack on Mexicans as rapists and criminals was as effective as the Horton ad. David Duke, the former grand wizard of the Ku Klux Klan, told his followers to "call Donald Trump's headquarters [and] volunteer." He promised his audience that at Trump's campaign they will "meet people who are going to have the same kind of mindset that you have."

Duke dismissed every other Republican running for the nomination. He said voting for anyone but Trump "at this point is really treason to your heritage."[13] Other white supremacists also began endorsing Trump, including the American Freedom Party, which had been established by racist skinheads. Then, Jared Taylor, who ran the white supremacist magazine *American Renaissance*, added his endorsement. In taped robocalls to potential voters, Taylor said: "We don't need Muslims. We need smart, well-educated white people who will assimilate to our culture," he said. "Vote Trump."[14]

When Trump was asked by CNN to disavow the KKK's explicit

endorsement, he responded, "I don't know what group you are talking about. You wouldn't want me to condemn a group that I know nothing about."[15] Later, confronted with his evasive answer, Trump said he had trouble hearing the question because of a broken earpiece. As difficult as it was to believe that a sixty-nine-year-old American wouldn't know who the KKK was, it was even more so in Trump's case, given his family history. His father, Fred Trump, had been arrested at a Klan rally in 1927 when the KKK was protesting the presence of Roman Catholics in the New York Police Department.[16]

With Trump on a path to win the Republican nomination in the spring of 2016, the nation's racial climate was rapidly fraying. This was different from any time in American history because of the historic demographic shifts taking place in America. Many Americans' frame of reference on immigration had been established in the early twentieth century, when immigrants were primarily European and white-skinned. Since the 1960s, there had been a growth of brown-skinned people, adding to the racial divide and shifting the racial composition of the country.

The changing population was especially apparent in California. In 2014, the year before Steinle was killed, Latinos became the state's largest ethnic group. Also in 2014, a surge of Central American immigrants crossed the U.S. border with Mexico. Gang violence was spiking in Honduras, Guatemala, and El Salvador as well as parts of Mexico, as a result of failing economies and public corruption linked to powerful drug cartels. Even though the immigrants were fleeing such social ills, they nonetheless were maligned by Trump and Limbaugh to their conservative supporters as a burden on American society and distorting the culture.

The "border crisis" became an explosive political fight. The growth of the Latino immigrant population was now an emotionally gripping story for white conservatives fearing a loss of country and culture. For others, it was a harrowing story about desperate people willing to risk it all to seek asylum. In 2014, nearly seventy thousand migrant children without parents, including infants and toddlers, tried to cross the border. The government reported a nearly 80 percent increase in one year's time in unaccompanied children seeking asylum.[17]

. . .

The immigrant population in the United States in the 1960s, prior to the Immigration and Nationality Act of 1965, and following four decades of severely restricted immigration, totaled less than 10 million people. Thirty-five years later, more than 31 million people living in the United States had been born in another country. Most of those immigrants were Hispanic.[18]

At the start of the twenty-first century, the Hispanic population had grown to the point that many small towns and rural areas had come to depend on migrant farm and factory laborers. They created ethnic neighborhoods in towns, cities, and rural areas that for generations had been nearly all-white. Suddenly, in addition to a few Black people around town, there were Latino churches, food markets, and taco trucks. Schools had to develop classes for children who spoke Spanish at home. Hospitals saw an increase in uninsured patients, many of them immigrants.

In a nation that had seen slow demographic change for much of the previous century, there was obvious discomfort with the racial, ethnic, and linguistic upheaval. For younger, non-college-educated whites, conservative voices portrayed these newcomers as posing a threat to take their jobs. Older whites were put off by even minor changes like pressing "two" on the phone to hear Spanish.

For decades, the conversation on race had been focused largely on relations between white and Black Americans. Suddenly it involved a cacophony of voices from different races, including Latinos, Asians, Africans, and more. Blacks and whites had volatile arguments over race stretching back to the founding of America, but at least they shared a common framework, which began with a shared history involving slavery, followed by Civil War and segregation.

With the increase in immigration, common references for talking about race began to fade. This was a disconnect from the 1960s, when the white population was more than 88 percent of the country.[19] By 2010, it was down to 72 percent.[20]

The Black population, while growing in absolute size, was also shrinking in terms of its share of the overall population. The 2010 U.S. census, the first done after Obama took office, also showed that there were more than 50 million Hispanics living in the United States, comprising about 16 percent of the population. In fact, by 2010 it had already been years since Hispanics overtook Blacks to become America's largest minority group.[21] That created some of the same cultural anxiety among Blacks that was troubling whites. They, too, feared losing political power, as well as jobs, to the newcomers, despite seeing a Black president.[22]

Even as their numbers grew, Latino immigrants were easy scapegoats. They lacked political influence because large numbers tended not to vote. Many also retained strong ties to their place of birth. And while most of them were properly documented, by 2010 there were almost 11 million people in the U.S. without proper legal authorization, living in fear of being deported if they were reported for breaking the law or angering a boss.[23]

There had been repeated efforts to gain control over the faulty immigration system. The last major immigration reform was enacted when Ronald Reagan was in the White House. George W. Bush and Barack Obama had tried and failed to get congressional support for an improved immigration system. The stumbling block was strong opposition from white conservatives to granting so-called amnesty to people who had already entered the country illegally, who were maligned on right-wing talk radio as criminals and "lawbreakers." Conservative pundits painted them as people who should not be "rewarded" for violating the rules of immigration. This led to calls for more deportations, more walls, and impassioned opposition to President Obama's 2012 executive action (called the Deferred Action for Childhood Arrivals, or DACA) to allow children who had entered the country illegally years earlier to stay in the United States.[24] These immigrant children, known as "Dreamers," had spent nearly their entire lives in the United States, going to school and in some cases even serving in the U.S. military.

With no congressional reform to deal with the issue, anti-immigrant activists in border states took it upon themselves to confront the challenges of immigration. Republican politicians and sheriffs in Arizona, a direct neighbor of Mexico, jumped to participate in the crackdown. SB 1070, known as the "show me your papers" law, required that Arizona law enforcement officials demand evidence of legal status from anyone they deemed "suspicious."[25]

As the 2016 presidential campaign heated up, polling showed that 71 percent of Republicans believed that immigrants were making the economy and crime worse. For Democrats it was exactly the opposite. Only 34 percent said immigrants were a problem.[26]

Donald Trump became the leading voice of opposition to any immigration reform. He called for more deportations and more guards on the border. He campaigned for building a two-thousand-mile wall to separate the United States from Mexico. Over three fourths of Republican voters favored the idea.[27]

The white backlash among Trump's supporters wasn't just a reaction to increasing immigration, there was also a growing sense of grievance among white conservatives in response to the Black Lives Matter protests over police violence. Following the death of Eric Garner in New York, some police around the nation reacted by promoting a new social media hashtag, #CopsLivesMatter. An Indiana cop even began selling T-shirts with the phrase "Breathe Easy. Don't Break the Law" inscribed across the chest.[28] Politically conservative talk shows dedicated days of coverage to Garner and the crime issue. They saw aggressive policing, even if it edged into brutality at times, as necessary to correct bad behavior, criminal acts, and "thug life" attitudes among Blacks and Latinos. They told their audiences that Black people were viewed as more threatening by the police for a good reason—they are more likely to be involved with crime.

This led to a deep divide on the issue of policing that was often portrayed as Black-versus-white. The reality was more nuanced. By 2015, an increasing number of whites, especially the college educated, were siding with Black people as a matter of social justice. According to Pew, the percentage among whites concerned about racism in American society had climbed from 17 to 44 percent.[29] Even so, a majority of whites still believed that too many protesting Blacks were "seeking an excuse to engage in looting and violence," according to a *Wall Street Journal*/NBC News poll.[30]

Bill Bratton, the New York police commissioner at the time of Garner's death, emphasized that last point to the press and even when speaking to a group of Black police officers. He told the National Organization of Black Law Enforcement Executives that his city's Black and Hispanic population "commit 95 percent of our shootings—and Blacks and Hispanics represent 96 percent of our shooting victims."

Bratton saw the online and activist movement against "racist police terror" as wrong. He opted not to confront racist attitudes within the police force, instead blaming the social and economic issues bedeviling "neighborhoods of color." He saw crime as a problem affecting "neighborhoods where poverty bites deepest, where jobs are most scarce, where schools are most challenged." Black communities needed more police protection, not less, he said, because most of the victims of crimes were Black people, and those crimes were committed by Blacks.[31]

The FBI director, James Comey, joined the debate when he made a speech that featured the line "Everyone's a Little Bit Racist," from the Broadway show *Avenue Q*, a satirical musical about race and sexuality in modern America. He used the line to acknowledge that the police did treat Black and white people differently, but went on to say it "may be rational by some lights" to do so because of the higher rate at which Black men are arrested. Like Bratton, Comey refused to deal with racist police officers and their long history of violence against Black people.[32]

Bolstering Bratton and Comey's claim, a report from a group of Black doctors found a "violence epidemic in the African American community." The National Medical Association reported that homicide was "the leading manner of death for African American males ages 10–35." The organization noted that African American men made up "only six percent of the population but make up greater than 50 percent of firearm related deaths."[33]

In a survey of Black people, fear of violence, especially violent crime, ranked as the most important issue, despite concerns about police brutality. "When asked in an open-ended question to identify the most important issue in the community they live in, the top issue was violence or crime," according to a later report by the Pew Research Center. "This includes Black Americans who listed specific issues such as drug activity, shootings, or theft; but also, those simply listed 'violence' or 'crime' as the most pressing issues in their communities."[34]

Black people remained in favor of strong police presence in their neighborhoods; they just didn't want police beating them up or harassing their children. As 2016 wore on, Black activists ramped up their protests against police violence. Black Lives Matter activists disrupted speeches by the leading Democratic candidates during the 2016 presidential primaries. Black Lives Matter cofounder Alicia Garza criticized Hillary Clinton in particular for her earlier support of the 1994 crime bill, passed under her husband's administration, and for her language back then, particularly her reference to young gang members as "super predators."

When Clinton was campaigning in New Hampshire, she agreed to meet with several Black Lives Matter activists to understand why they were there to protest. The young Black people insisted that she speak out more forcefully against racism. She said that her goal was not to change hearts, but to enact policies to help the Black community. "You can get lip service from as many white people as you can pack into Yankee Stadium and a million more like it, who are going to say, 'Oh, we get it, we get it. We're going to be nicer.' That's not enough—at least in my book. That's not how I see politics," she said.[35]

Clinton backtracked on her earlier language about "super predators," in a strategic effort to appease Black Lives Matter. At the same time, she still needed to appeal to moderate white voters concerned about crime.

Former president Bill Clinton pushed back, too. He got angry at a Black Lives Matter protest during a rally for his wife's presidential campaign. The protesters shouted that the 1994 crime bill signed by the former president had hurt Black people. Clinton fired back: "I don't know how you would characterize gang leaders who got thirteen-year-old kids hopped up on crack and sent them out on the street to murder other African American children," he said, adding, "You are defending the people who kill the lives you say matter."[36]

Then, as both Donald Trump and Hillary Clinton were about to accept their parties' nominations, a series of killings occurred that forced the whole country to dive deep into uncharted racial waters. On three consecutive days in July 2016, three Black men were killed by police in three different states— New York, Louisiana, and Minnesota. The last was the most famous of the cases. Thirty-two-year-old Philando Castile was driving his car when he was stopped just outside Minneapolis for a broken taillight. He informed the white policeman that he had a licensed gun in the car, and then, as he reached for his identification, the policeman fired seven shots, hitting him five times. Castile died in twenty minutes. For much of that time, his girlfriend, Diamond Reynolds, was on Facebook broadcasting live footage of her efforts to keep him alive while comforting her four-year-old daughter. "Stay with me," she told Castile, as his white T-shirt turned red with blood and life faded from his body.[37]

The day before Castile was killed, an unarmed Black man named Alton Sterling was killed by police while selling CDs outside a convenience store in Baton Rouge. White police officers tased Sterling and pulled him to the ground before shooting him to death. And the day before that, a road rage incident led an off-duty New York police officer to kill Delrawn Small, another unarmed Black man.

But it was the bloody, heart-wrenching Facebook video of the Castile shooting that went viral around the world. There was a frenzy of attention, as demonstrations and statements from public officials tried to explain away what people could plainly see on their phones.

Hillary Clinton tweeted for the first time after Castile's death with the term "Black Lives Matter." In a dramatic online response, she wrote: "America woke up to yet another tragedy of a life cut down too soon. Black Lives Matter. #PhilandoCastile –H."[38] Ending on the H indicated that Clinton had personally written the tweet. She then traveled to meet with Castile's family. "We cannot let this madness continue," she said after meeting with grieving relatives. "This violence cannot stand."[39]

Traveling in Poland at the time, President Obama broke away from international affairs to comment on the turmoil at home. Just as Black Lives Matter and Donald Trump found social media to be a direct line into the national debate, so did the president of the United States. Taking immediately to the White House Facebook page, Obama wrote that all Americans should be "deeply troubled," adding that the Department of Justice planned to open a full civil rights investigation.

Obama's post spoke about larger social issues that were "not isolated incidents" but "symptomatic of the broader challenges within our criminal justice system, the racial disparities that appear across the system year after year, and the resulting lack of trust that exist between law enforcement and too many of the communities they serve. . . . We've got a serious problem," he continued, though he also stated that the vast majority of police officers deserve respect.[40]

A generation earlier, this racial debate would have taken place at dining room tables. The newspapers and television broadcasts would have featured statements from spokesmen with established civil rights groups and politicians. In the age of social media, though, any American could join the conversation with their own posts and tweets.

Quickly, a stream of responses flowed on social media from thousands of Americans, directly engaging and judging Obama. "Mr. President, with the utmost respect for you . . . Americans should not be deeply troubled. We should be enraged," commented one woman, Lauren Onkeles-Klein. "The time for puzzlement, for furrowed brows, for sadness and comfort has passed. . . . [Action] comes from pain. From a roiling, earth-shattering sense of injustice. It comes from the kind of affront to our humanity that shifts the heavens and earth, rending our collective souls with a singular cry. 'This must change.'"[41]

Immigration, which had been at the forefront of the 2016 presidential race and debates over social activism, was now competing for attention with the social media response to fatal shootings of Blacks by police. The hashtag #BlackLivesMatter became the vehicle for organizing those protests as well as an outpouring of rage.

As the vitriol went up, so did the violence. This time it was Black men killing white police officers. The worst took place the day after Philando Castile's death.

In Dallas, a twenty-five-year-old Black Army reservist, Micah Johnson, drove downtown and used a high-powered rifle to assassinate police officers.

His shooting spree took place over several hours and was televised live to the nation; Johnson killed five white officers before police sent out a robot to shoot him. Johnson's motives were the earlier shootings of Black men at the hands of police. He had repeatedly watched the video of the Rodney King beating and regularly followed Black nationalist and Black separatist social media sites. A friend told CNN that Johnson "wanted justice and equality for Blacks."[42]

Ten days later more police were killed, this time in Baton Rouge, where Alton Sterling had been killed. Gavin Long, another Black veteran, ambushed police in a shopping center. He killed four, including Black police officers, before he was shot to death. Like Johnson, Long followed Black separatists on social media. He expressed anger at the police killing of Sterling and praised Johnson's Dallas shooting spree as an act of "justice."

Hillary Clinton now expressed sympathy for the policemen who had been murdered in Dallas and Baton Rouge. "Killing police officers is a crime against us all," she said at a teachers conference. "It can be true, both that we need law enforcement and that we need to improve law enforcement."[43] But her effort to be evenhanded failed to quiet protests, even among her supporters. Several people marched to the stage, interrupting her and chanting the words of Michael Brown: "Hands up, don't shoot!"

As the violence exploded, President Obama cut short his trip to Europe, finding himself once again caught in the quicksand of anger that had surrounded the deaths of Trayvon Martin, Michael Brown, Eric Garner, and others. He delivered half a dozen speeches, held news conferences, and appeared at a televised town hall, as well as speaking at a memorial in Dallas for the slain officers.

In Dallas, he was joined by former president George W. Bush, creating an image of national unity between a white man and a Black man, a Republican and a Democrat. At one point Michelle Obama, amid the grief, was seen holding hands with Bush. The former president, in brief remarks, offered powerful words of reconciliation. "Too often we judge other groups by their worst examples, while judging ourselves by our best intentions," he said to the packed hall in Dallas.[44]

Speaking about the tumultuous events of the past week, Obama said: "It's as if the deepest fault lines of our democracy have suddenly been exposed.... Faced with this violence, we wonder if the divides of race in America can ever be bridged.... We turn on the TV or surf the internet, and we can watch positions harden and lines drawn, and people retreat to their respective corners, and politicians calculate how to grab attention . . . and it's hard not to think sometimes that the center won't hold and that things might get worse."[45]

Donald Trump had not bothered to respond immediately after Castile and Sterling were killed. However, he quickly called the shooting of the Dallas police officers "an attack on our country." In a video statement he said, "We must stand in solidarity with law enforcement, which we must remember is the force between civilization and total chaos."

Trump crowned himself the "law and order" candidate for president. He changed the topic of the political conversation from systemic racism against minorities to victimization of the white majority and their mostly white police, saying that cops were "the most mistreated people in this country." After all the killing of Black men at the hands of police, Trump boldly announced that police violence was not a major issue, and that Black Lives Matter was a misguided slogan: "It's a very divisive term, because all lives matter."[46]

There was no way to resolve the political divide with data. The FBI did not keep track of police killings and many police departments did not publicly report them. That meant there was no way to see if law-abiding Black people were disproportionately victimized by the police.

The Washington Post stepped in by creating a database of police shootings. It found that Castile was at least the 506th person and 123rd Black American shot by the police in 2016. The *Post* found that more than 24 percent of the people who had died at the hands of the police were Black, close to twice their percentage in the population.[47]

Still, no amount of fact-finding could quiet the rage from conservative media and the daily fire coming from the Trump campaign. Clinton was caught off guard. As a white woman, she expected to capture the votes of white women with relative ease, but polls now showed her *losing* white women, who were responding to Trump's focus on crime. Meanwhile, Black Lives Matter activists, pointing to Black Americans as Clinton's most reliable voting base, pushed her to take a stronger stand against racist cops.

As summer turned to fall, a new twist in racial protests emerged to further divide the country. It began in preseason National Football League games, when San Francisco 49ers quarterback Colin Kaepernick began protesting police brutality by sitting during the national anthem. His action went unnoticed for several games until TV cameras turned it into a national spectacle. "There's a lot of things that need to change, one specifically is police brutality," Kaepernick told reporters. "Cops are getting paid leave for killing people. That's not right."[48]

Kaepernick was maligned for disrespecting the American flag and, by extension, the soldiers who had died protecting the country. After consulting with a friend who was a Green Beret, he stopped sitting during the Anthem, taking a knee instead to register his protest.

Kaepernick's support for Black Lives Matter fit with LeBron James's protests following the deaths of Trayvon Martin and Eric Garner. The difference was that the NFL had a bigger audience and Kaepernick's protests came in the middle of a presidential campaign and led to a heavy response from Trump and the conservative media.

"I think it's a terrible thing," Trump said about Kaepernick. "And you know, maybe he should find a country that works better for him. Let him try, it won't happen."[49]

Even as he was attacked by Trump, Kaepernick went on offense, not only against him, but also against Hillary Clinton. "Both are proven liars," he said. "It also seems like they are trying to debate who is less racist."[50]

Kaepernick's anger reflected far-left attitudes toward both presidential contenders. In fact, Black Lives Matter cofounder Alicia Garza refused to publicly endorse Clinton. In an interview with *Elle* magazine, she said, "Absolutely not. You know, I think one of the things that I have been struggling with in this electoral cycle is that our choices are not great."

Garza tied Hillary to her husband's years in the White House, specifically the 1994 crime bill: "Incarceration through the roof, the demonization of poor black women, the unraveling of the social safety [net]. . . . And I know sometimes people give a lot of criticism like, well, that was Hillary's husband's policies. And I am like no, no, it's not like she was sipping tea! She was also campaigning on those policies."

But when asked what would happen if Trump defeated Clinton, Garza said she believed it would make the Black Lives Matter movement "stronger, and it starts to get more strategic."

"Here's my last question," asked the interviewer. "If Donald Trump wins the American presidency, what shoes are you going to wear for the inauguration?"

"Running shoes!" said Garza.[51]

Garza would later explain her refusal to endorse Clinton by speaking to her disappointment with President Obama. She wanted Obama as well as older civil rights leaders like Sharpton and Jackson to address the structural racism that was locked in the foundation of the American system. "Sometimes you have to put a wrench in the gears to get people to listen," she said.[52]

For Black History Month in 2016, Obama's last in the White House, he invited a group of civil rights leaders, including the young people involved with Black Lives Matter, to discuss the nation's progress on racial issues. Even the framework put off some young activists. They felt the emphasis should not be on progress but on the work that remained to be done. Aislinn Pulley, a Black Lives Matter leader from Chicago, turned down the invitation. Instead, she wrote a critical article calling Obama's civil rights meeting "a sham."

She was unstinting in her disdain for the president's gesture. "As a radical, Black organizer, living and working in a city that is now widely recognized as a symbol of corruption and police violence, I do not feel that a handshake with the president is the best way for me to honor Black History Month or the Black freedom fighters. . . . What was arranged was basically a photo opportunity. . . . I could not with any integrity participate in such a sham that would only serve to legitimize the false narrative that the government is working to end police brutality and the institutional racism that fuels it."[53]

The prior generation of civil rights leaders continued to stand by Clinton and Obama. When Obama held meetings to deal with the shootings and racial tensions in the country, he had reliable support from the graying giants of the First Movement. Among the attendees to the White House meeting on race were Representative John Lewis and Cornell Brooks, the president of the NAACP. The most prominent civil rights leader of the moment, Al Sharpton, was also in the room.

Though many younger Black leaders were critical of the event, there were some Black Lives Matter members who saw an advantage in having access to the president. And the White House was careful to select those with less critical views for meetings. Brittany Packnett, a leading activist tied to Black Lives Matter in Ferguson, attended, as did DeRay Mckesson, who had been active nationally for the organization.

"The value of social movements and activism," the president later said, "is to get you at the table, get you in the room, and then start trying to figure out how is this problem going to be solved. You then have a responsibility to prepare an agenda that is achievable, that can institutionalize the changes you seek."[54] His perspective was not shared by a growing number of activists who did not want meetings and compromise—they wanted immediate action.

Across the country racial tensions continued to rise. A Gallup poll found that the percentage of Americans who worried a "great deal" about race relations had risen from 17 percent to 35 percent between 2014 and 2016. The biggest jump in concern about race relations came from Black people, Obama's political base and the people who had hoped that his election would signal a new era in race relations. According to the poll, 53 percent of Blacks, compared to only 27 percent of whites, were now worried about racial strife.[55] White criticism of Obama, largely coming from Republican opponents, rested on the idea he had a "fundamental misreading of American society as irremediably racist" in viewing the country through the eyes of an "aggrieved Black activist." But among actual Black activists, Obama was seen as an ineffective moderate.[56]

Through the racial crises during his presidency, Obama repeatedly called for calm, trying to be everyone's president, floating above the violence, the hatred, and the politics of the moment. This approach would come to define Obama on race relations. He was not the Black president; he was a Black man trying to be America's president. However, even eight years after his inauguration, he couldn't escape the racial politics or the expectations that he would bring new light and healing on issues of race.

The 2016 Democratic National Convention took place in a racially tense atmosphere, with Trump having already been chosen as the Republican nominee. The tension came not just from the police shootings and Black Lives Matter protests, but also from Trump's calls on the campaign trail to build a border wall, as a well his call for a ban on Muslims entering the country.

The tension came to a head at the convention when Khizr Khan, the father of a Muslim U.S. soldier killed in Iraq, was invited by Hillary Clinton to speak to a prime-time audience about the threat posed by Trump's racial hate. Khan told a hushed convention that Trump posed a danger to the country by inviting further racial division. With his wife standing next to him onstage, he warned, "Donald Trump consistently smears the character of Muslims. He disrespects other minorities—women, judges, even his own party leadership. He vows to build walls and ban us from this country. Donald Trump . . . Have you ever been to Arlington Cemetery? Go look at the graves of the brave patriots who died defending America—you will see all faiths, genders, and ethnicities. You have sacrificed nothing and no one."[57]

Trump immediately lambasted Khan and his wife. In a cynical statement, he asked if Clinton's speechwriters had taken advantage of an emotional, grieving father. He also pointed out that Khan's wife never spoke, suggesting that this was evidence of how Muslims treat women as inferior.[58]

Trump's final message in the closing months of the campaign was to promise uncritical support for the police and to promote anger at immigrants. The slogan for his campaign called for a return to an America where the demographic shifts had not occurred and where Blacks and other minorities did not challenge their inferior social status. It was called "Make America Great Again"—MAGA. He also spoke angrily about President Obama's policies as diminishing America at home by embracing Black Lives Matter and by turning America from its previous dominance into shrinking power on the world stage.

The message hit home with white working-class people without a college

degree. Fear of lower wages and job losses caused by globalization was compounded by the rise in immigrants and the prominence of the Black Lives
Matter protests.

Obama's two elections, which were once heralded as historic evidence of
a post-racial America, had in fact stirred a ferocious backlash among a sizable
number of white voters.

The Democratic Party had suffered a loss of enthusiasm among Blacks
and young people who had been disappointed in Obama. Such constituents
were also disillusioned by Hillary Clinton's past support for the war in Iraq
and for tough criminal policies that had put record numbers of Black people
in jail.

Trump would go on to win the white vote by 15 percentage points. He
even outpolled Clinton among white women by 2 percentage points.[59] There
was another dynamic at work as well. Without Obama on the ticket, and with
disillusionment tied to the increased racial tensions in the country, Black turnout slipped in 2016, enough to be a factor in an exceptionally close election.

Trump lost the popular vote to Clinton by 2.8 million votes but received
a majority in the Electoral College. It was only the fifth time a candidate had
won the presidency while losing the popular vote. It was also the most surprising upset of modern political history.

Two months later, in his inaugural address, Trump reiterated the white
grievance that had gotten him elected. He said that the political elites in Washington had prospered during the Obama years, while middle-class "jobs left,
and the factories closed."

"The establishment protected itself, but not the citizens of our country.
Their victories have not been your victories. Their triumphs have not been
your triumphs," he indignantly thundered, as President Obama, President
Bush, and Hillary Clinton sat behind him, looking stunned.

Speaking to his core supporters in the white working class, he said, "This
is your day. This is your celebration, and this, the United States of America, is your country." And in a racially loaded swipe, he vowed to get rid of
"the crime, and the gangs, and the drugs that have stolen too many lives and

robbed our country of so much unrealized potential. . . . This American car-
nage stops right here and stops right now."[60]

The man endorsed by the Klan, the man who had said that President
Obama was not really an American, the man who had demonized Mexicans by
exploiting the death of Kate Steinle, was now president of the United States.
And he made clear that unlike Obama, who had tried so hard to be racially
neutral, his priorities as president would be the priorities of white Americans.
That racial messaging went beyond Nixon's southern strategy and Reagan's
dogwhistles. The backlash to the Second Civil Rights Movement had arrived
in the Oval Office.

6

THE ALT-RIGHT WHITE HOUSE

As Donald Trump gave his inaugural address on the steps of the Capitol, Black Lives Matter was far from the scene. Black Lives Matter was also surprisingly far from the center of discussions of race in America.

The organization had grown from a website and a hashtag into more than two dozen chapters in cities around the country. But the founders—Alicia Garza, Opal Tometi, and Patrisse Cullors—were no longer media darlings. As Trump dominated the airwaves, there was less demand to hear their speeches, to see them on television, or to hear them on radio shows. It was a near-total eclipse of the attention that shined on them after the Ferguson protests in 2014.

Cullors was asked why Black Lives Matter's profile in American media had virtually disappeared since the election of Trump, having previously been on the cover of *Time* magazine and the front page of *The New York Times*, as well as dominating social media. "I don't think we fully understood that the attention to our movement would just literally end" with the election of Trump, she said in an interview.[1]

It did not help that Black Lives Matter had no centralized leadership structure. The organization had no headquarters, no easily recognizable face, no single spokesperson—and yet the founders bristled when others tried to speak for them in the press. They remained insistent that the First Civil Rights Movement's "great man" model of national leadership was out of touch with the new movement's reality of how people freely shared opinions on social media.

"Why are we holding on to a trope about leadership that is older than me?" Garza said. "People are still looking for the Reverend Dr. Martin Luther King Jr. when, actually, leadership of movements today looks more like Lena Waithe [a lesbian screenwriter, producer, and actress] and Laverne Cox [a transgender actress]."[2]

Instead of centralized male-dominated national leadership, the women of Black Lives Matter argued that a variety of new voices, including people from pop culture as well as grassroots organizers, had better instincts. They saw them as best able to face off with police departments and press city politicians in cases of police violence. The three founders remained reactive. They had no consistent set of responses and only an idealist agenda that called for utopian visions, such as "No More Jails" or "Defund the Police." The "Defund" slogan was first heard in Minneapolis from a female-led group, "Black Visions Collective," that had worked to cut the local police budget before George Floyd's death. Doing away with jails and police was idealistic. But the ideas had no real impact on the immediate problems in Black America. That often led to disillusionment and left a bad taste of disappointment among people who had been excited by the possibility of new approaches to real-world problems.

The Black Lives Matter leadership never had much traction in Republican circles, but now they also lacked political allies among top Democrats. This estrangement was especially glaring with regard to the number-one Democrat in the country, Barack Obama. During Hillary Clinton's losing presidential campaign, Obama constantly raised the alarm that Black Lives Matter was depressing voter turnout among young Black people with its refusal to back Clinton and energize its network to support voter registration efforts.

Obama showed his discontent during the spring of 2016. At an event in London, he gave credit to Black Lives Matter for bringing new attention to racial injustice. But pointing to his own work as a community organizer in Chicago, he argued that once the "spotlight" was on the problem, "you

can't just keep on yelling . . . you can't refuse to meet because that might compromise the purity of your position." Obama seemed disappointed by Black
Lives Matter's refusal to meet with him at the White House, as if he were the
problem.[3]

Here again was a split that had been evident a generation earlier in the First
Civil Rights Movement. The split then was between the nonviolent, compro-
mising strategies of Dr. King versus the militant, "by any means necessary" demands of leaders like Malcolm X, SNCC, and groups like the Black Panthers.
In the twenty-first-century's Second Movement, the split became a canyon
between Obama's gradualist approach and BLM's call for immediate action.

Obama kept up the criticism in a commencement speech a few weeks
later at Howard University: "It's thanks in large part to the activism of young
people like many of you, from 'Black Twitter' to Black Lives Matter, that America's eyes have been opened—white, black, Democrat, Republican—to the
real problems, for example, in our criminal justice system," Obama said. "But
to bring about structural change, lasting change, awareness is not enough. It
requires changes in law, changes in custom. Passion is vital, but you've got to
have a strategy. And your plan better include voting . . . all the time."[4]

But as far as Black Lives Matter was concerned, Clinton had never been
their candidate. What some viewed as a stark contrast between a moderate
Democrat and a racist Republican, they viewed as an insignificant distinction. In their eyes, it was a choice between an unappealing, white centrist version of Obama or excusing the explicit racism in Trump's appeal to "Make
America Great Again." Alicia Garza later wrote that many activists "simply
had no interest in getting involved in the election. Eight years of a Black president hadn't brought as much hope and change to Black America as had been
promised." Black Lives Matter mocked the idea that Obama's election was
evidence of racial progress and dismissed all talk of a post-racial America.[5]

Black voter turnout in 2016 sank from a record high 66.6 percent four
years earlier to just 59.6 percent. Young Black people between the ages of
twenty and thirty-five turned out in small numbers, dropping from 55 percent to just over 50 percent.[6] Garza accepted no blame for the weak turnout,
instead pointing her finger at Clinton. "No candidate was able to meet the

challenge of engaging and capturing the imagination of younger Black voters (and potential voters) who were in the midst of their own civil rights movement," she later wrote. "Even though the movement was in full swing, no candidate could seem to talk about Black Lives Matter, or any policy solutions associated with it, without being forced to do so."[7]

During the campaign, Black Lives Matter's focus was on dismantling what it viewed as a racist American system oppressing Black people. It wanted to hold every candidate for every office "accountable." That led many activists affiliated with the organization to disrupt political rallies. Even the most progressive white leaders in the Democratic Party came under attack. At a town hall on immigration in Phoenix featuring Senator Bernie Sanders, Black Lives Matter took over the stage. One member grabbed the microphone, demanding "concrete" policy proposals to address racial wrongs and to call out the names of Black people killed by police. Sanders became angry, saying: "I spent fifty years of my life fighting for civil rights."[8]

Cullors later told reporters that Sanders's claim to being a white "progressive is not enough—We need more."[9]

"Agitating a perceived political ally to the Black community is strategic," she later wrote in a *Washington Post* opinion column. "For far too long, the Democratic Party has milked the Black vote while creating policies that completely decimate Black communities. Once upon a time Bill Clinton was widely perceived as an ally and advocate for the needs of Black people. However, it is the Clinton administration's [crime bill] that set the stage for the massive racial injustice we struggle with in law enforcement today."

Cullors's motivation in confronting politicians came from personal pain. She blamed Democratic Party policies, which she said had "destroyed my family," as much as Republican policies. She said that her father had been repeatedly jailed on drug charges and her brother "inhumanely brutalized" by Los Angeles police. "The goal of Black Lives Matter," she wrote, "is to transform America's systemic hatred against Black people. . . . We are demanding . . . our right to life . . . dignity and respect."[10]

But there was pushback to the insistent pressure, even among Democrats who supported Black Lives Matter. The Congressional Black Caucus endorsed Hillary Clinton early in the primaries. Urging Black Lives Matter to get behind her, the chair of the caucus, Representative G. K. Butterfield, argued that Clinton understood their plight. He said with "Black lives being lost on the streets of America because of police misconduct and gang violence . . . we must have a president [who] understands the racial divide."[11]

Similarly, older civil rights activists and Black politicians did not have much use for Black Lives Matter if the organization was not helping them win votes or allies among white moderates. "So much is at stake, if not for them, for the masses of Black people," Joyce Ladner, a former leader of the Student Nonviolent Coordinating Committee, told *The Washington Post*. "What is the substitute for not voting? They need to put forth an alternative political, social, or economic structure that delivers some relief to Black people. . . . To whom are the BLM folks accountable when they remove the vote from Black people?"[12]

With all its agitation, criticism of political candidates, and failure to mobilize voters, Black Lives Matter now had no base of electoral support, and the organization also lost the media's attention with Trump in the White House. Garza's earlier comment about needing "running shoes" if Trump were elected was glib. It now seemed that Black Lives Matter was in fact running off course.

Instead, America's attention turned to the backlash, as the racist rhetoric of Trump's campaign unleashed actual racist attacks. In one year alone, the FBI reported that hate crimes jumped from about six thousand in 2016 to more than seven thousand by the end of 2017. The Southern Poverty Law Center, which tracks hate groups and their crimes around the nation, saw an immediate uptick in episodes of racial attacks the very day after Trump's election. One SPLC staffer told the story of coming into the office after election day to find "a flood of voicemail and emails from people who had been victims of hate incidents or had witnessed them."

"The calls came from all over the country," according to the SPLC, "and seemed to represent every population Trump had attacked during the campaign. . . . A wave of hate was breaking over the country and we started to collect as much information as we could."[13]

The prime platform for the white supremacist backlash was social media, the same internet that had bolstered Black Lives Matter's activism. But this was a parallel universe, a funhouse mirror in which the growing alt-right used social media to organize itself and spread hate. Their ranks were led by men such as David Duke, the former Klan leader, and Jared Taylor, who founded the racist magazine *American Renaissance*. Their vitriol led to the creation of newer groups, including the Oath Keepers and the Proud Boys, which soon became household names. Beyond organized groups there was a proliferation of individuals who remained anonymous online as they posted hateful, racist comments.

The one common theme they used to draw an audience was to claim that white people were being "replaced" by Blacks and immigrants in a process orchestrated by Jews operating behind the scenes. This "replacement theory" suggested that whites were the victims of minorities who were feeding at the so-called welfare trough at the expense of hardworking white Americans. Polls found that more than 50 percent of whites felt that they were more likely to face discrimination than Blacks. Two thirds of Trump voters agreed with this statement.[14]

The online power of this new wave of racism had long been evident. In June 2015, on the day after Trump launched his presidential campaign, a nineteen-year-old white South Carolinian named Dylann Roof walked into the Emanuel African Methodist Episcopal Church in Charleston. After sitting down with a Bible study group, he pulled out a gun and killed nine Black people.

Roof had spent most of his time immersed in online hate, and his social media history included posting comments on alt-right sites. He found support for his racial rage when in the aftermath of the Trayvon Martin murder, he typed in the term "black on White crime."

"I have never been the same since that day," Roof later wrote in a manifesto that was discovered after the shooting. "The first website I came to was the Council of Conservative Citizens. There were pages upon pages of these brutal black on White murders. I was in disbelief. At this moment I realized that something was very wrong." Roof's radicalization deepened, fueled by websites like the neo-Nazi site *Daily Stormer*, until he found himself with a gun in his hand at the Charleston church, trying to spark a race war.[15]

Roof's access to extremist, racist material online was now increasingly common among young white men. In the early age of the internet, the *Drudge Report* was a pioneering platform for the concerns of the radical fringes among conservatives. It was now eclipsed by openly racist websites, including VDARE, *Daily Stormer*, and *InfoWars*.

Young white men were also going onto Discord, a social media network created in 2015 and heavily used among the video gaming community. It was infamous for tolerating memes of vulgar and racist tropes. These young men turned to Discord to avoid scrutiny by coming together anonymously in chat rooms to discuss their views and grievances, including their opposition to removal of Confederate statues and monuments around the country.

Their most notorious effort became the "Unite the Right" rally planned for Charlottesville, Virginia, in August 2017. The alt-right's pretext for the march was to protest the Charlottesville City Council's decision to remove the statues of two Confederate generals, Robert E. Lee and Stonewall Jackson, from city parks near the University of Virginia. The statues were among some four hundred built in the first two decades of the twentieth century as part of a Jim Crow backlash to Black progress during Reconstruction. The City Council had acted out of concern that the statues celebrated slave owners, perpetuating racial divisions and hatred. But for the alt-right, the decision signaled a loss of "Southern tradition" and the rise of the political power of minorities.

The neo-Nazi leader Jason Kessler used Discord to bring together several different white nationalist groups, including David Duke and others among the alt-right, a term first used by Richard Spencer, the leader of a white supremacist organization called the National Policy Institute, to signify that it was distinct from mainstream conservatism. His group's priority was dedicated to white identity, the protection of white "western civilization," and other racist ideas.

On the night before the planned rally, young white men gathered on the campus of the University of Virginia. David Duke was there and told his supporters, "We're going to fulfill the promises of Donald Trump because he said he's going to take our country back."[16] As a multiracial group of counter-protesters, including local Black Lives Matter activists, surrounded the base of a statue of Thomas Jefferson (which was not being removed), the alt-right members began chanting "White Lives Matter!" and making monkey noises. Shoving and fighting broke out with limited law enforcement presence, but the groups eventually separated.

Later that night, the alt-right protesters marched past the city's lone syna-gogue with automatic rifles slung over their shoulders. The worshippers were forced to leave through the back door as the men paraded toward the statue of Robert E. Lee. They wore white polos and khaki pants; some also wore swas-tikas and chanted "Sieg Heil"—the Nazi salute. They bellowed in unison, "Blood and Soil!" and "Jews will not replace us!" as they marched.

The next morning, the scene became chaotic. To stop the alt-right ac-tivists from entering the park, counter-protesters threw bottles and rocks at the white supremacists, who were armed with clubs and shields. Even as the neo-Nazis dispersed, their presence provoked further confrontations. A Black woman yelled from her front porch: "Go the fuck home." They responded by shouting: "Go the fuck back to Africa." One man said, "Dylann Roof was a hero."[17]

News of the violence went viral on social media. At 1:14 p.m., the city of Charlottesville's Twitter account posted: "CPD & VSP [Charlottesville Police Department and Virginia State Police] response to a 3-vehicle crash at Water and 4th Streets. Several pedestrians struck. Multiple injuries."[18] A white nationalist had driven his car into a crowd, killing a counter-protester named Heather Heyer.

Heyer was a thirty-two-year-old paralegal who had been active on social media denouncing Trump. On Facebook she had expressed alarm at his elec-tion, posting, "If you're not outraged, you're not paying attention." The writer and activist Shaun King posted after her killing: "She was not murdered by an immigrant or refugee or Muslim or Black man, but by a white supremacist—A true domestic terrorist."[19]

President Trump initially responded to the violence with anodyne comments via Twitter: "We ALL must be united & condemn all that hate stands for. There is no place for this kind of violence in America. Lets come together as one!"[20]

The violence sparked heated, angry discussion on social media as to whether Trump's words and actions had instigated the deadly scene in Charlottesville. When reporters asked Trump if he felt responsible for what happened, the president blamed his predecessor, saying there had been similar racial tension under Obama. Then Trump said there was "blame on both sides." He argued that some people had joined the alt-right rally out of concern about "changing history . . . changing culture."

He continued: "I'm not talking about the neo-Nazis and the white nationalists because they should be condemned totally." Trying to make a distinction where none seemed to exist, Trump claimed to be talking about people who were "protesting very quietly" the removal of the Robert E. Lee statue, arguing that these were innocent, legal protests.

In fact, the march had been organized and led by white extremists. "They didn't put themselves down as neo-Nazis," Trump argued, contrary to the facts. "You had some very bad people in that group . . . you also had people that were very fine people on both sides."[21]

Trump's defense of the extremists drew furious responses, but many Republicans rallied to his defense. According to a *Washington Post*/ABC News poll after the incident, a surprising 35 percent of Americans believed Trump was not equating people opposed to the statues with neo-Nazis. Among his Republican base, over 60 percent approved of his response. Nonetheless, 42 percent of Americans said Trump was wrong to equate the white supremacists and the counter-protesters.[22]

Among the alt-right, Trump was unanimously cheered. "Thank you President Trump for your honesty & courage to tell the truth about #Charlottesville," David Duke tweeted. "We are determined to take our country back. We are going to fulfill the promises of Donald Trump. That's what we believed in. That's why we voted for Donald Trump, because he said he's going to take our country back."[23]

Richard Spencer was also gleeful when Trump initially avoided condemnation of white nationalists. On the *Daily Stormer* website, one commentator openly lauded the president's response: "No condemnation at all. When asked to condemn, [Trump] just walked out of the room. Really, really good. God bless him."[24]

The alt-right was not operating in isolation. The backlash against Black Lives Matter had tremendous support online and from a growing right-wing media that found it could generate profits from an audience attracted to depictions of people of color as the cause of crime and terrorism.

The biggest of these burgeoning alt-right sites was *Breitbart*, which featured conspiracies and white grievance, founded by the journalist Andrew Breitbart in 2005. After its founder's death in 2012, the site was taken over by Steve Bannon, a Hollywood producer and former Goldman Sachs executive who had gone into the business of online video gaming. Bannon was acutely aware of the market potential of appealing to young male gamers.

Taking the site to new extremes with its conspiracies and stories of white racial rage, Bannon used marketing lessons from Hollywood and gaming to generate more clicks for *Breitbart*, whose monthly average audience had jumped to more than 64 million by 2016. By comparison, one of the largest mainstream conservative publications, *National Review*, received only around 10 million hits per month.[25]

Bannon's use of extremist, right-wing political conspiracies had roots that stretched back to the John Birch Society in the 1950s. The Birch Society was founded on a strident "Anti" philosophy: Anti-communist, Anti-big government, Anti-Semitic, Anti-feminist, and Anti-immigration. Birchers were also a leading platform of opposition to the First Civil Rights Movement and supported Republican presidential candidate Barry Goldwater, who had voted against the 1964 Civil Rights Act.

Breitbart also tapped into right-wing political populism that flowed from Richard Nixon's "Southern strategy" through Ronald Reagan's focus on "states' rights" and Pat Buchanan's condemnation of racial diversity. Buchanan said in his 1992 presidential bid that diversity was diluting the nation's heritage and dumping it into a "landfill called multiculturalism." Buchanan was Trump before Trump, saying that Americans should "put the needs of Americans first"—meaning, of course, white Americans.[26]

Bannon pushed stories that painted white conservatives as the heirs to "western civilization" under assault from a multiracial liberal mob, and he increasingly promoted the Trump campaign. Both Bannon and Trump played to anxieties of their core audience—white men.

Trump was already a prominent part of this right-wing media chamber. He found great utility in rousing anger, particularly through his use of Twitter, trading in conspiracies, and spreading alarm over Barack Obama's depiction of working-class whites clinging to "guns or religion" or Hillary Clinton's description of Trump supporters as a "basket of deplorables." Hate groups, such as the Proud Boys and Oath Keepers, found *Breitbart*'s and Trump's messaging helpful to their recruiting efforts.

According to Ben Shapiro, until March 2016 the editor-at-large of *Breitbart*, "Under Bannon's leadership, Breitbart openly embraced the White Supremacist Alt-Right."[27] That summer of 2016, as Trump was being nominated by the Republican Party, Bannon did away with any pretext of neutrality, admitting about *Breitbart*: "We are the platform of the alt-right."[28]

The alt-right's online success got a boost from Russia. President Vladimir Putin saw the racial division in the United States as an opportunity for his effort to destabilize American democracy. Even before the 2016 election, Russian troll farms—internet manipulation groups linked to military and intelligence services—began twisting American social media users. They created fake accounts to spread lies, conspiracies, and inflammatory language. The Senate Intelligence Committee found that these trolls had been mimicking Black Lives Matter online. On Facebook, Instagram, and Twitter, with handles such as "Woke Blacks" and "Blacktivists," they created an "expansive cross-platform media mirage targeting the Black community." Then creating fake alt-right accounts, the trolls provoked clashes, both online and sometimes on the street, further dividing Americans by race.[29]

The alt-right shared with Putin a disdain for popular elections. They also had in common an opposition to racial diversity, gay rights, and feminism. Trump claimed that there had been no collusion between his campaign and Russian agents, even though the Mueller report documented scores of contacts.[30] In one famous campaign speech, Trump even openly asked the Russians to use their social media operation to uncover damaging information about Hillary Clinton.

Several of Trump's senior advisers had significant ties to Moscow and some also shared Putin's disdain for racial justice. Michael Flynn, for example, who served briefly as Trump's first national security adviser, was in frequent contact with the Russians during the 2016 campaign.

Stephen Miller was a senior adviser stoking racist fears. A former aide to Senator Jeff Sessions of Alabama, Miller had long promoted fears that immigrants were replacing white Americans. Miller sent emails to *Breitbart* and Bannon complaining that immigrants were hurting white Americans' job prospects and draining social welfare. He was particularly concerned about the increasing number of public schools that taught English as a second language. "White youth population disappearing," he wrote as a comment when sharing an article on increasing diversity in the country.[31]

Miller's former boss, Sessions, a far-right Southerner, was known for his anti–civil rights and anti-immigrant positions. In 1986, when he was serving as a U.S. attorney, the Senate denied him a federal judgeship after Department of Justice attorneys told senators that Sessions had made racist comments. One Black assistant U.S. attorney noted that Sessions thought the Ku Klux Klan was "OK until I found out they smoked pot."[32]

Despite this, Sessions was later elected as Alabama's attorney general and later to the U.S. Senate. Given his extremist views, he gravitated to Trump and was the first U.S. senator to endorse his candidacy. Untroubled by the senator's difficult racial past, Trump made Sessions an early cabinet selection as attorney general.

Another key player from the far right pulled into the Trump orbit was Mike Pompeo, who as a congressman was infamous for his anti-Muslim stances and conspiracy theories. He gained prominence in congressional hearings by attacking Secretary of State Hillary Clinton with charges that her neglect had allegedly led to the death of American diplomats in Benghazi, Libya. The charges went nowhere, but they produced sensational headlines and endless cable news show innuendo that dragged on for two years.

One of the strangest Trump advisers, Sebastian Gorka, was *Breitbart*'s national security editor. Even more unusual were the allegations concerning his long association with Hungarian far-right and anti-Semitic political groups. While he denied them, on the day of Trump's inauguration, rather than wearing an American flag pin, Gorka wore a medal from Vitézi Rend, a Hungarian extremist group that had collaborated with Nazi Germany during World War II.

The KKK's David Duke would call these Trump appointees "great." The founder of the *Daily Stormer*, Andrew Anglin, wrote: "It's like we're going to get absolutely everything we wanted. . . . Basically we are looking at a Daily Stormer Dream Team in the Trump Administration."[33]

Immediately, this alt-right "Dream Team" began pushing extremist policies on immigration and race. In Trump's first week in office, Miller drafted an executive order to ban people from seven Muslim-majority countries from entering the United States. The order prevented travel of all citizens from Iran, Libya, Somalia, Sudan, Syria, Yemen, and even a close U.S. ally, Iraq. In addition, it suspended the resettlement of Syrian refugees and lowered the number of all refugees eligible for admission to the United States.

The "Muslim ban," which Trump had promised on the campaign trail, was hastily thrown together with no consultation with the federal agencies that would have to enforce it. It was immediately challenged in federal court, which found the wording too broad and issued a restraining order preventing its implementation.

Trump's team tried again in March 2017, but once again the order was found to be unconstitutional and halted by the courts. It was not until the third version included a few non-Muslim-majority countries with ties to "terrorist activity" (North Korea and Venezuela) while dropping Iraq and replacing Somalia with Chad that the Supreme Court upheld limitations on travel.

At the same time, Trump was also pursuing tougher laws to stop the flow of people from Latin America into the country. In that first week of his presidency, Trump signed executive orders to build a border wall separating the United States from Mexico. He also ordered the hiring of five thousand additional Border Patrol officers and a tripling of immigration agents to speed deportations of unauthorized immigrants already in the country. "Beginning today, the United States of America gets back control of its borders," Trump said in a speech at the Department of Homeland Security.[34]

In addition to calling for the wall, he also proposed a cut in federal money for so-called sanctuary cities if they did not cooperate with his immigration efforts. Reaching back to the Kate Steinle case and his criticism of San Francisco, Trump lowered the standard for deportation to mere suspicion by immigration officials that a foreigner was "a risk to public safety or national security."[35]

Months later, a San Francisco jury found that the shooting of Steinle was an accident and acquitted Jose Garcia Zarate of murder. Trump immediately took to Twitter blasting the ruling: "A disgraceful verdict in the Kate Steinle case! No wonder the people of our Country are so angry with Illegal Immigration."[36] Attorney General Sessions joined with the president in blaming sanctuary city policies for the young woman's death. "San Francisco's decision to protect criminal aliens led to the preventable and heartbreaking death of Kate Steinle," he said in a statement.[37]

Sessions also reversed President Obama's efforts to rein in abusive police behavior. He directly blamed an increase in shootings and gun-related deaths on Black Lives Matter. "If you want more shootings, more death, then listen to the ACLU [American Civil Liberties Union], Antifa [antifascists], Black Lives Matter, and groups who do not know the reality of policing. If you want public safety, then listen to the police professionals who have been intensely studying this for decades," he said, dismissing any complaints against law enforcement as unwarranted.[38]

Sessions limited the Department of Justice's use of consent decrees to get local police departments to change their tactics. The Obama administration had used such agreements to gain greater oversight of policies on the use of force, as well as police hiring practices and training. Two of the most high-profile consent decree cases involved Ferguson and Baltimore, the latter of which was the site of Black Lives Matter protests in 2015 after another young Black man, Freddie Gray, died in police custody. Instead of issuing consent decrees, Sessions wanted to send this message to rank-and-file police: "We're on your side. We've got your back, you got our thanks."[39]

Sessions also wanted to reverse the Obama administration's efforts to limit jail sentences. In 2010, Obama signed the Fair Sentencing Act, which ended the disparity in jail time between those individuals convicted of possession of crack, a heavily minority population, and lighter sentences for the mostly white people found with powder cocaine. Obama's reform efforts had reduced the federal prison population for the first time since the mid-1970s.

Alicia Garza acknowledged that Obama had commuted the sentences of more than 1,700 people. "This makes him the only President in history to have granted as many second chances," she said. But that had not been enough for her and her fellow Black Lives Matter activists, who continued to berate the first Black president for not doing more. Even after Trump's election, she continued to criticize Obama. "The outcomes of the last eight years didn't come to realize Obama's promised vision of hope and change," she wrote in *Time* magazine, describing his administration as a "disappointment" and calling out his failure to address the reality that "race and racism negatively impacts our society, our democracy and our economy."[40] She dismissively said that Obama was delusional in telling people that there was "an even and level playing field between black communities and law enforcement."[41]

By sitting out the 2016 election and not seeing a difference between the Democrats and the Republicans on race, Black Lives Matter and Garza had helped open the door to Trump and an administration full of people diametrically opposed to police reform. While they carped on the sidelines about Obama, their absolutist ideology left them out of the conversation and gave them no relationship with the hardline conservatives now in the White House.

In retrospect, Garza acknowledged errors in not seeking opportunities to make progress through compromise with people in power. "It is hard to build a plane while you are flying it—while also under enemy fire," she later wrote. Black Lives Matter members, she went on, "hadn't learned to struggle together politically in ways that could help us get sharper and have more of a unified position. And as a result, we missed key opportunities to engage our communities and shift the balance of power."[42] Black Lives Matter had made the decision not to engage with Republicans because it was "faced with a new administration that is seemingly hell bent on rolling back nearly everything we've fought so hard for over the last forty years."[43]

With Black Lives Matter out of the picture, *The New York Times* reported, Sessions pressed federal prosecutors to "put more people in prison for longer periods, adopting the mass incarceration strategy that helped flood prisons during the war on drugs during the 1980s and 1990s."[44]

At the same time, and in spite of his social media support for white nationalists, Trump saw a political opportunity in the prison reform effort. He wanted the embrace of online influencers, celebrities like Kim Kardashian and Kanye West, who were advocating for people convicted of minor drug offenses, disproportionately minorities, to have their sentences reduced. Jared Kushner, Trump's son-in-law, a man whose own father had gone to prison for tax fraud, also took a personal interest in prison reform. He began working with Van Jones, a former Obama official and TV personality, to slash the prison population in all fifty states.

Jones had been a longtime prison reform advocate. After graduating from Yale Law School, he focused on prison reform at a center for human rights. And with Black Lives Matter muted after Trump's victory, Jones ironically found himself the leading Black voice heard inside the administration.

It was a surprise for many to see Jones working with Trump's people. On election night, as a commentator for CNN, a distressed Jones had called Trump's victory "a whitelash against a changing country." He added that it was also a "whitelash against a Black president in part, and that's the part where the pain comes." Jones observed that white voters' response to Obama was to back a candidate known for his unbridled harsh racial rhetoric.[45]

But Jones's prominence as a TV personality attracted Kushner, who was trying to moderate Trump's reputation as a racist. Jones's engagement with Trump officials led to social media criticism by people affiliated with Black Lives Matter. Jones dismissed these influencers as "not kind" and "not strategic." He felt that getting as many Black people as possible out of jail was a step forward, even if the precise method wasn't the ideal and the legislation would be signed by President Trump.

"Do we want to lead everybody into freedom. . . . Or do you just want to be mad at injustice," Jones said later of the widespread criticism from Black Lives Matter. He pointed out that there were 2.3 million African Americans behind bars and another 4.5 million on probation or parole. In total, more Blacks were part of the judicial system in the twenty-first century than had been enslaved in the nineteenth century.[46]

Patrisse Cullors disagreed with Jones's pragmatism. "Many of us agreed that we would not have any negotiations under this presidency," she stated, trashing these reform efforts as insufficient. "You don't try to save a few people, you try to save everybody," she pronounced.[47]

Online "cancel culture," a slogan referring to sudden waves of calls to shun and exclude voices deemed damaging to liberal causes, was a sensation at the time. Now it surrounded Jones with efforts to depict him as unworthy of being taken seriously, especially after he appeared in a photograph with Kushner, Trump, and the far-right Black media personality Candace Owens. "I will take a picture with Trump every day, twice on Sunday to get 25,000 people out of prison," Jones said four years later, offering a high-end projection of the number of prisoners that could be released under the administration's plan.[48]

Jones and Kushner got bipartisan support in Congress for the first prison reform effort in nearly a decade, while neutralizing opposition from Attorney General Sessions and right-wing Republicans in the Senate. Even the Republican majority leader, Mitch McConnell, supported the legislation, and in December 2018 Trump signed the First Step Act, which reduced sentences on low-level drug offenses and allowed for immediate release of some older prisoners. The Sentencing Project, a major reform group, estimated that more than three thousand inmates, more than 90 percent of whom were Black, were released that first year.

Jones cheered Trump on Twitter, writing: "Give the man his due: @realDonaldTrump is on his way to becoming the uniter-in-Chief on an issue that has divided America for generations. Congrats to everyone on both sides who fought for this. #FIRSTSTEPact #CriminalJusticeSummit #CriminalJusticeReform #justicereform #Trump."[49] Established civil rights groups from the First Movement, like the NAACP and the National Urban League, agreed that the bill was a help.

This further isolated Black Lives Matter. They viewed it as a trifling achievement. Cullors went so far as to say she felt betrayed by Jones, accusing him of a flawed strategy that led to a "profoundly insensitive lauding of President Trump."[50] A Black Lives Matter press release dismissed the First Step Act for failing "to address the systemic issues and driving forces behind mass incarceration and, more disturbingly, it further invests in structural racism." The organization claimed that the reform did nothing to repair "the decades of harm caused by their criminalization, and the irrevocable trauma caused to many Black families . . . the undocumented, and the refugee population."[51]

His success on prison reform notwithstanding, Trump was seen as a chaotic president, often tweeting in the middle of the night and bullying his critics. Much of the country saw him as a racist, and even those who approved of his most hateful views recognized that he had not succeeded in building the wall and his ban on Muslims faced constant court challenges and was unpopular. Trump's approval in polls, as the 2018 midterm elections approached, remained historically low, but he doubled down on the racial rhetoric as alt-right online conspiracy theories continued to flourish.

The hidden force behind these conspiracies was the contention that Jews, especially as political donors, but also as elites in Hollywood and on Wall Street, were diminishing the power of white Christians. Fringe websites pushing anti-Semitism proliferated. Message boards and apps like 4chan, 8chan, and Gab were among the leading purveyors of this hate speech. Even on mainstream platforms like Twitter and Instagram, white nationalist leaders such as David Duke and Andrew Anglin, and their trolls, used social media to belittle politicians, journalists, and academics as part of a Jewish conspiracy to replace white America with Blacks, immigrants, and other dark-skinned minorities.

According to the Anti-Defamation League, between July 2016 and January 2018 the use online of the terms *Jew* and *kike*, a slur for Jewish people, "more than doubled." Likewise, the ADL noted a sharp rise in the use of those terms after Trump's inauguration and the days surrounding the Unite the Right Rally in Charlottesville.[52] The United States also saw a precipitous rise in violence against Jews, mirroring the rise of hate crimes against Blacks and Hispanics. The ADL recorded an almost 60 percent spike of physical attacks in 2017, describing it as the "largest single-year increase on record."[53] The Southern Poverty Law Center, also tracking a rise in neo-Nazi hate groups, found a 20 percent growth between 2016 and 2017.[54]

The most prevalent conspiracy theory centered on the billionaire George Soros, who was portrayed as the mastermind behind the "replacement theory." Soros was one of the biggest Democratic Party fundraisers and had long been demonized by Republicans, who viewed him as a political rival. But now this partisan antagonism took on a new coloration, drawing on long-established anti-Semitic tropes.

The term "Soros-funded" became shorthand among far-right conservatives as a derisive dog whistle to describe anyone—or any program or group—who aided immigrants. Soros himself was an immigrant. He had survived the Holocaust, fled communist-controlled Hungary, and used his later wealth to promote democracy and support refugees around the world via his Open Society Foundations.

The antagonism to Soros, an international figure, created an unusual alliance of far-right groups in the U.S. and Europe. The American alt-right had noticed the early success of populist anti-immigrant voices in Europe, led by Hungarian president Viktor Orbán. He, too, made Soros a villain at a time of rising numbers of Muslims coming into Europe.

As the 2018 midterms approached, Trump escalated his own anti-immigrant remarks, warning of "migrant caravans" from Honduras that were about to invade the southern border. When asked if Soros was "funding" the caravans, Trump said he "wouldn't be surprised." His comments fed social media rumors, promoted on right-wing websites, about Soros encouraging "illegal" immigration to replace whites.[55]

One Republican congressman, Matt Gaetz, posted a video on Twitter of a hidden figure paying migrants to "storm the U.S. border." He then asked: "Soros?"[56]

These conspiracies quickly spread to conservative talk radio and conservative news shows. The rage inside the conservative echo chamber was all about immigrants crossing the border, with the theory that Jews, specifically Soros, were facilitating their arrival to help Democrats win the midterm election.

This was no dog whistle. It was hostile and powerful and led to one of the bloodiest days in Jewish American history—October 27, 2018.

Robert Bowers, a man who lived in a small town in western Pennsylvania, had consumed extremist media for months, reposting viral images and comments about what he called a "third world caravan" of approaching "invaders." He wrote that "Jews are the children of Satan" and demeaned Blacks as well, complaining that "Diversity means chasing down the last white person." He expressed his support of Gavin McInnes, the leader of the Proud Boys, and frequently took aim at Soros and Jewish charity work.

On the morning of October 27, Bowers posted a message on Gab that was a hate-filled screed against HIAS, the Hebrew Immigration Aid Society: "HIAS likes to bring invaders in that kill our people. I can't sit by and watch my people get slaughtered. Screw your optics, I'm going in."[57] HIAS, initially founded in 1881 to help Jewish refugees fleeing persecution in Europe, has become a leading agency supporting migrants. Working closely with the State Department, HIAS has been very active in supporting the resettlement of Muslim immigrants in the United States, especially those escaping persecution in Syria, Iraq, and Afghanistan.

After posting his final warning, Bowers drove half an hour on that rainy Saturday morning to Squirrel Hill, the neighborhood at the center of Jewish life in Pittsburgh. He entered the Tree of Life synagogue just before 10 a.m. as Shabbat services were beginning. Carrying three Glock pistols and an AR-15 semiautomatic rifle, he went from the basement to the upper floor, firing all four weapons. According to worshippers who hid in closets, under pews, and fled through the back door, Bowers shouted: "All Jews must die!" He killed eleven people and injured six others before he was subdued and arrested. Officers later reported that he told them that Jews were committing genocide against white people.[58]

The murders made international headlines and prompted widespread words of sorrow and regret. President Trump joined the condemnation of the killings, but his sentiment turned in a different direction when he was pressed about whether his inflammatory political appeals had paved the way to this anti-Semitic violence. His response was to call for an increased use of guns to secure synagogues: "If they had some kind of [armed] protection inside the temple, maybe it could have been a much different situation."[59]

A week later, when American voters went to the polls for the 2018 midterm election, it was clear that the white supremacist backlash to Black Lives Matter was facing a backlash of its own. In the highest voter turnout for any midterm election since 1914, the Democrats picked up forty-one congressional seats, with staggering losses for Trump's party. The House of Representatives flipped to a Democratic majority, which would be led by the fiery former speaker, Nancy Pelosi.

A record number of women were elected to Congress—117, an unprecedented 23 percent of the House and Senate. Included in that trailblazing group were Ilhan Omar of Minnesota and Rashida Tlaib of Michigan, the first Muslim women elected to the House. Among some of the other firsts were Ayanna Pressley, the first Black representative from Massachusetts, and the first Native American women, Kansas's Sharice Davids and New Mexico's Deb Haaland. A new generation of women of color also gained seats. Lauren Underwood of Illinois, thirty-two, became the youngest Black woman ever elected to Congress. Alexandria Ocasio-Cortez of New York, at twenty-nine years of age, became the youngest female member of the House. Together, the group's political identity was defined by their opposition to Trump. Ocasio-Cortez, Pressley, Tlaib, and Omar called themselves "the Squad," and were immediately vilified in the conservative press.

The midterm election was a repudiation for a man who had campaigned on white grievance and played to a white male base. Trump would now face a more diverse Congress than ever as he continued to fight demographic and political shifts by defiantly flying his banner "Make America Great Again."

7

STACEY AND THE SQUAD

The backlash against Donald Trump went beyond votes against him. It led to big victories for congressional Democrats in the 2018 midterm elections. New voices were emerging to escalate the backlash to Trump's right-wing, white supremacist extremism.

The leaders of this political backlash came from a new generation. They went beyond traditional media into heated online brawls with the far right. That drew far more attention from a wider, younger audience than had ever paid attention to the older, established congressional Democrats. The newcomers were twenty years younger than the average member of Congress. The youngest, Alexandria Ocasio-Cortez, had defeated a ten-term Democratic incumbent who had been in the congressional leadership. She became known simply as "AOC"—an instant media sensation.

The child of Puerto Rican parents, Ocasio-Cortez was elected from a liberal, working-class congressional district in New York City, covering parts of the Bronx and Queens. Before she was in Congress, she worked as a bartender and was an organizer for Senator Bernie Sanders's 2016 presidential campaign. She soon became the most frequently targeted Democrat on Fox News, even more than the new speaker of the House, Nancy Pelosi.

Ocasio-Cortez and the other members of "the Squad" came to represent, in the words of *The New York Times*, a "disruptive relationship to the status quo in Washington."[1] Their agenda spoke for young and minority Americans and provided a channel into national politics for the priorities of the Second Civil Rights Movement.

Though Black Lives Matter remained absent as an organizing political force for any of these campaigns, it did change the political discourse. Capitalizing on the sense of injustice and the passion whipped up by BLM, progressive candidates drew attention in the press and online to a left-wing political agenda. In this new world, the Squad celebrated expanding health care, canceling student debt, and rebutting the conservative denial of climate change. They branded their environmental agenda with the catchy phrase the Green New Deal. It called for cutting greenhouse gas emissions and creating jobs in "green" renewable energy. Picking up on BLM's primary issue, they echoed the movement's calls for reining in police tactics. They also opened the door to debate about allowing lawsuits against wrongdoing by individual police officers.

This agenda was the polar opposite of Trump's. He was soon tweeting that they should "go back"[2] to their countries, as if they were not real Americans and did not belong in Congress as part of the mainstream national political dialogue. He called them "hate-filled extremists who are constantly trying to tear our country down."[3] He wrote: "The 'Squad' is a very Racist group of troublemakers who are young, inexperienced, and not very smart. They are pulling the once great Democrat Party far left. . . . And are now against ICE and Homeland Security. So bad for our Country!"[4]

Ocasio-Cortez immediately fired back on Twitter: "You are angry because you can't conceive of an America that includes us."[5] Pressley tweeted: "THIS is what racism looks like."[6] Speaker Pelosi, who was not always in support of the Squad's agenda, immediately defended them. She remarked that Trump's "xenophobic comments" were intended to "divide our nation" and reaffirm the fact that "his plan to 'Make America Great Again' has always been about making America white again."[7]

But Trump's comments hit their mark among the president's supporters; soon people at Trump rallies regularly began to berate the New York congresswoman with crass chants of "AOC sucks." Ocasio-Cortez again countered: "He doesn't have another woman—Hillary Clinton or whoever else—to vilify anymore, so they need to find another woman to kind of prop up and become a lightning rod."[8]

Though Trump portrayed the four young congresswomen as "foreign," in fact only one member of the Squad, Ilhan Omar, had been born outside the United States. She was a refugee who had fled Somalia's civil war as an eight-year-old child and arrived in the U.S. at age twelve, after years in a refugee camp. She became an American citizen at seventeen and was known as a strident advocate on the issues of poverty and health care for the Somali community in Minneapolis. When she was thirty-four, she won a seat in the Minnesota House of Representatives, and at age thirty-six she was elected to Congress.

The other Muslim member of the Squad, Rashida Tlaib, was born in Detroit to Palestinian immigrant parents, the oldest of fourteen children. She won a seat in the Michigan legislature in 2008, becoming the first Muslim woman to serve in the statehouse. In 2018, she won a mostly Black and Hispanic congressional district, replacing the retiring John Conyers, the longest-serving Black member of Congress, who arrived on Capitol Hill in 1965, during the heart of the First Civil Rights Movement. On her first day in office, Tlaib made national news by telling an audience of progressive activists that she was not going to be bullied by Trump: "We're going to go in there, impeach the motherfucker."[9]

The final member of the Squad was Ayanna Pressley, who defeated a ten-term Democratic incumbent in Massachusetts. Pressley had been the first Black woman to serve on the Boston City Council and would now become the first Black woman to represent the state in Congress. Her campaign had faced opposition from traditional Black Democrats. John Lewis, the civil rights legend from Georgia and longtime congressman, campaigned for her white opponent, the incumbent Michael Capuano. Pressley said that the liberal district needed not just someone to vote against Trump policies, but a stronger voice to take on the president. *The New York Times* described her victory as being "in sync with a restless political climate that has fueled victories for underdogs, women and minorities."[10]

The Squad's rise was also fueled by a feminist backlash to Trump that had begun the day after his inauguration in 2017, when the Women's March saw half a million protesters fill the streets of Washington, D.C., supported by six hundred smaller marches around the country. Ironically most white women voted for Trump. But the left-wing women, mostly white, who showed up that day wearing pink "pussy hats," created what *Time* magazine called: "Perhaps the Largest Protest in U.S. History [and it] Was Brought to You by Trump."[11]

The Squad's political impact was just one reflection of the backlash to the rise of racial hate under Trump. It also extended to celebrity influencers and ordinary people on social media. It was felt in Hollywood, where the hashtag #OscarsSoWhite led to more Asian, Latino, and especially Black actors and directors being recognized in the motion picture industry. The superhero movie *Black Panther* broke barriers, becoming the number-one movie in America by the time of the 2018 midterms. With a heavily Black cast and a Black director, the film grossed $1.3 billion.

In the face of unleashed white supremacy, here was a popular culture counteroffensive featuring Black characters with superpowers, originating in a mythical African nation filled with wealth, technology, and highly educated people. The Electoral Justice Project, a small offshoot of Black Lives Matter, used the movie's unprecedented success, especially with young Black moviegoers, to begin a 2018 midterm voter registration effort called #Wakanda TheVote.[12]

Another counter to Trump's embrace of white rage was found in women's magazines. *The New York Times* reported that Black women appeared on the majority of fashion covers in September of 2018, the critical start to the fall fashion season.[13] This represented a significant break with a long history of top magazines largely promoting white beauty standards. A Nielsen study concluded that Black consumers now constituted an important role in shaping American style. This wasn't just a result of the rising purchasing power of Black women, however; Black taste in fashion created a "cool factor." Nielsen wrote that the result was a "halo effect, influencing not just consumers of color, but the mainstream as well."[14]

The cultural backlash to Trump went further. The *New York Times*'s list of best-selling books was filled with explorations of the nation's struggles with race, including *White Fragility* by Robin DiAngelo, Ibram X. Kendi's *How to Be an Antiracist*, and *The Hate U Give* by Angie Thomas, which also became a popular movie.

One high cathedral of American culture, the Pulitzer Prizes, embraced Black popular music by recognizing the work of the Black rapper Kendrick Lamar. Previously the award had only gone to classical musicians and, on rare occasions, jazz artists. This recognition seemed more about the Pulitzer committee making a statement than about Lamar's virtuosity. The award "shines a light on hip-hop in a completely different way. This is a big moment for hip-hop music and a big moment for the Pulitzers," said Dana Canedy, the administrator of the prize.[15]

Meanwhile, Black Lives Matter as an organization continued to struggle in finding its footing. It had never been a powerhouse in Washington, and now the organization's founders seemed burned out. Their magic had faded in the face of questions about a lack of achievable goals and about the organization's ineffectiveness. Where once they had been the chic newcomers to the scene noted for raising the issue of police violence, now there were more questions about their effectiveness and goals. This left them feeling more isolated.

Two of the founders left the group. Alicia Garza returned to the National Domestic Workers Alliance, which advocated for "dignity and fairness for the millions of domestic workers."[16] She also started the Black Futures Lab, launching a "Black Census," a poll to determine the top priorities of Black Americans. She gave particular attention in the survey to the opinions of Black women, an essential element of the base of the Democratic Party ahead of the 2020 presidential election. This survey also put a heavy emphasis on Black members of the LGBTQ community, people that were rarely heard by politicians.[17]

Opal Tometi also left Black Lives Matter's leadership. She put her energy into working as the executive director of the Black Alliance for Just Immigration, an organization fighting for immigrant rights. Tometi wrote that her responsibilities with Black Lives Matter "quickly became too much." She realized that she was depressed and overwhelmed by the pressure falling on her "at the intersection of Black Women Lead and Black Girl Magic."[18]

Patrisse Cullors co-wrote a best-selling book in 2018, *When They Call You a Terrorist: A Black Lives Matter Memoir*. She was the only one to remain involved in the day-to-day activities as executive director of the organization.

Even as the creative minds behind Black Lives Matter went in different directions, the police violence that had initially spurred their activism remained a major problem. According to the *Washington Post*'s "Police Shooting Database," the rate of police killings kept slowly rising, with 999 Americans dying at the hands of the police in 2019, compared to 962 police killings in 2016, the last year of Obama's presidency. Still, none of the steady stream of scattered incidents occurring during Trump's first two years had generated the massive street protests that had taken place during the Obama administration.

The data made clear that Black Americans continued to die at the hands of the police at a disproportionately high rate. By contrast, whites lost their lives in police interactions at a much lower rate. They made up 76 percent of the nation but were only 42 percent of police victims.[19]

Black Lives Matter seemed rudderless in the face of this continuing police violence. Most of the time when their leaders appeared in the news, it was to embrace Black actors and musicians. Suddenly, BLM's most notable public campaign was to rally support for a Grammy-nominated Black British musician, the rapper 21 Savage, when he was threatened with deportation.

21 Savage had been convicted in 2014 on a drug-possession charge. It was then discovered that he had overstayed a visa, and under President Trump there was a more aggressive attitude in favor of deporting people, even those who were not a major public threat.

The organization's preoccupation with celebrity causes and unrealistic goals like abolishing the Immigration and Customs Enforcement agency now overshadowed its groundbreaking work on police violence. "Black Lives Matter Global Network has been outspoken in the fight to abolish ICE. We started the #Free21Savage coalition to bring awareness to the struggles of the black immigrant community," read one press release, in an attempt, apparently, to try to explain away this sprawling focus.[20]

While Black Lives Matter was distracted, Trump continued to sound off on crime, using it as a hot-button issue with his base by calling for more aggressive policing. He made headlines when he told a convention of police officers: "When you see these thugs being thrown into the back of a paddy wagon . . . I said, 'Please don't be too nice.'" Trump again played on racial fears by calling out the Salvadoran street gang MS-13 as "animals" who "transformed peaceful parks and beautiful quiet neighborhoods into blood-stained killing fields."[21]

The only one with the stature to match Trump was former president Obama. Traditionally, former presidents have refrained from criticizing their successors. But Obama broke his silence just before the 2018 midterm election by saying that the rise in hate "did not start with Donald Trump, he is a symptom, not the cause. He is just capitalizing on resentment that politicians have been fanning for years." In a grave tone, he accused Trump of opening a Pandora's Box of hate, scapegoating, and racial grievance. "This is not normal," the former president told a group of students at the University of Illinois. "These are extraordinary times, and they are dangerous times."[22]

Despite the rebuff, Trump pushed ahead with his divisive tactics. He lashed out by feeding the lie that minority voter fraud threatened his rightful power over Congress and the nation. He specifically expressed opposition to early and mail-in voting, and voter registration efforts, especially in minority communities.

Since election night in 2016, Trump had falsely claimed that he had won the popular vote. He said without evidence that he had been robbed because as many as five million votes had been illegally cast for Clinton. He pointed to the large minority turnout in big cities as evidence of supposed fraud. His favorite targets were Black-majority cities. At one point while attacking a Black congressman from Baltimore, Elijah Cummings, Trump denigrated the city as a "disgusting, rat-and-rodent-infested mess."[23] Within four months of taking office, he'd created an Advisory Commission on Election Integrity to try to substantiate his charges that Baltimore and other large, mostly minority cities were engaging in election fraud.

Multiple civil rights groups immediately filed lawsuits against the commission. The NAACP Legal Defense Fund said that the commission's real work was to amplify "the false premise that Black and Latino voters are more likely to perpetrate voter fraud."[24] Within a year's time, the commission failed to find any evidence of voter fraud and was dissolved. Senate Minority Leader Chuck Schumer dismissed the panel as simply a "front to suppress the vote."[25]

Meanwhile, Attorney General Jeff Sessions went further. He used the power of the Justice Department to limit federal scrutiny in how states conducted their local elections. For nearly fifty years, any changes in voting procedures in these mostly Southern states had to be reviewed under the 1965 Voting Rights Act. But that had changed in 2013 with the Supreme Court's decision in *Shelby County v. Holder*. The conservative majority on the court held that the Voting Rights Act was outdated and unfairly punished the South.

This ruling had an immediate impact on American politics. In the days after the Supreme Court decision, Texas made its voter ID laws more restrictive. Other states established laws to purge voter rolls more regularly or shift boundaries of legislative districts to prevent consolidation of minority political power. While traditional civil rights groups condemned these efforts, as did the Obama administration, Donald Trump and his Justice Department took the other side and defended states that sought to implement restrictive rules under the cover of concern about voter fraud.

Despite their proven ability to spark mass opposition, Black Lives Matter activists were notably absent in this major fight over voting rights. Instead, on the progressive side, the spotlight shifted to Stacey Abrams, the Democratic candidate running for governor of Georgia in 2018. She began organizing to get more voters registered, with an emphasis on minorities and women to turn out at the polls.

Abrams, a Yale Law School graduate, had been elected to the Georgia House of Representatives in 2006 and made history when she became minority leader in 2011, a first for a Black woman. Her family story added to her political power. Her parents had been on the front lines in the First Civil Rights Movement, registering Black voters in Mississippi. This was the time of

"Mississippi Burning," of massive white resistance to school integration and Black voting. During this period the NAACP leader Medgar Evers was assassinated. Mississippi became the primary battleground in the 1964 "Freedom Summer" which brought hundreds of mostly white civil rights volunteers to the state to register Black voters.

Three of the most famous individuals in the Freedom Summer voter registration campaign were Michael Schwerner, James Chaney, and Andrew Goodman, who were brutally murdered by the local police and Ku Klux Klan near the town of Philadelphia, Mississippi. That same summer, Stacey Abrams's father, fifteen-year-old Robert Abrams, was arrested in Hattiesburg, Mississippi, for trying to do the same thing.

A generation later, his daughter won enough votes to become the leader of the Democrats in the Georgia legislature and the party's nominee for governor. Trying to make history as the nation's first Black woman governor, she registered a record number of Black and female voters in a state that leaned white and Republican. Her New Georgia Project registered 200,000 new, mostly minority supporters for her 2018 campaign. Abrams wasn't alone in her effort to knock down barriers to Black voters. Another Georgia group, Black Voters Matter, founded before the 2016 election by LaTosha Brown and Cliff Albright, worked to dismantle voter suppression and increase the number of Black voters across the state.

This distinctive effort led by Black women in the South gained national attention as the counter to Trump's work at suppressing minority voter turnout.

But Abrams and her allies ran into an ongoing purge of voter rolls by her white opponent, Secretary of State Brian Kemp. After the Supreme Court weakened the Voting Rights Act, Kemp was quick to act. In the years leading up to the 2018 election, his office imposed draconian new rules on voter registration.

Georgia became "ground zero" for limiting minority votes. The U.S. Commission on Civil Rights identified Georgia as "the only state formerly under federal oversight to adopt all five of the most common voter suppression tactics: strict voter ID laws, proof of citizenship requirements, purges, cuts in early voting, and polling place closures."[26] The Brennan Center for

Justice reported that between the 2012 and 2016 elections, about 1.5 million Georgia voters were purged from the rolls.

Kemp did not act alone. Across the nation, "between 2014 and 2016, [some] states removed almost 16 million voters from the rolls—a 33 percent increase over the period between 2006 and 2008. The increase was highest in states with a history of voting discrimination," according to the Brennan Center.[27]

Oprah Winfrey, former president Obama, and former vice president Joe Biden campaigned for Abrams, and pre-election polls showed the race for governor in Georgia was a dead heat. However, on election day, with voters standing in lines, some poll workers were told to turn away voters who'd come to the wrong precinct or to have them file provisional ballots, which might not be counted. When other election officials found discrepancies in signatures for registration, they simply threw out votes.

Abrams raised the alarm, claiming that thousands of Black voters were being denied their constitutional right. This immediately struck a chord of memory going back to her father's time in the First Civil Rights Movement.

When Abrams lost the race by just over 54,000 votes, her defeat was national news. So was her refusal to concede on the grounds that voter suppression had decided the election, making her a target for constant fury from the right wing. She was called a sore loser and a threat to the nation's trust in "fair" elections. Still, her fight for voting rights made her a national political figure. Two months after her defeat, the Democrats chose her to deliver the party's response, on national television, to President Trump's 2019 State of the Union address.

On the night of the State of the Union, many of the record number of 117 congresswomen defiantly dressed in white. It was both a statement of anger against Trump and a tribute to the suffragettes and the approaching centennial of the passage of the Nineteenth Amendment, which gave American women the right to vote.

In Abrams's televised rebuttal, she squarely laid the blame for her loss on Republican suppression tactics and warned of what was to come in future elections: "While I acknowledge the results of the 2018 election here in Georgia, I did not, and we cannot, accept efforts to undermine our right to vote," Abrams said. "This is the next battle for our democracy, one where all eligible citizens can have their say about the vision we want for our country. . . .

"We fought Jim Crow with the Civil Rights Act and the Voting Rights Act. Yet we continue to confront racism from our past and in our present, which is why we must hold everyone, from the highest offices to our own families, accountable for racist words and deeds and call racism what it is, wrong."[28]

Watching Abrams's response, Dan Pfeiffer, a senior adviser to Obama, immediately tweeted: "Stacey Abrams should run for President."[29] He later told *The New York Times*: "She can inspire people to activism and that is key to a Democrat winning back the White House."[30]

After her loss in Georgia, Abrams turned her attention to a national push for voter registration before the upcoming 2020 presidential election. Her group, Fair Fight, began enrolling voters in battleground states, including North Carolina, Wisconsin, Michigan, and Pennsylvania. A celebrated figure, she was in demand as a speaker, giving new life to calls not seen since the First Civil Rights Movement for the protection of minority voting rights. She raised millions of dollars to register voters.

Fair Fight's online organizing and fundraising mirrored the earlier social media success of Black Lives Matter and became a new pillar of the Second Civil Rights Movement. But where Black Lives Matter had looked for utopian outcomes like abolishing ICE and reparations for Black Americans, Abrams was in line with the thinking that characterized her father's work in the First Civil Rights Movement.

But she was squarely a Second Movement guiding light. A figure cast in the Obama mold, she called for strategic, steady gains to achieve a specific goal—to win elections and thereby gain political power for Black communities. Although she lost her own 2018 gubernatorial race, she came within inches of making history. She would have been the first Black woman governor in the country, and she almost did it in a Southern, formerly Confederate state. Abrams wrote in her autobiography that she believed that the act of voting was now part of a "long game—that battles add up over time and create space for others to feel emboldened to act."[31]

Beyond the political arena occupied by the Squad and Stacey Abrams, there was a cultural battle under way. A new front opened for the Second Civil Rights Movement within establishment America, especially its largest corporations.

The New York Times, the nation's preeminent newspaper and one of the largest media companies, broke ground on how that entrenched American establishment was becoming increasingly willing to talk about race. To commemorate the four hundredth anniversary of the first British slave ship landing in America at Jamestown, Virginia, the *Times* published a special report called "The 1619 Project."[32]

The 1619 Project put slavery at the center of the founding of the country, beginning with the economic structure before the Revolutionary War and the Constitution, which protected slavery while denying equal rights to Blacks. The journalist Nikole Hannah-Jones led The 1619 Project with a provocative article headlined: "Our Democracy's Founding Ideals Were False When They Were Written. Black Americans Have Fought to Make Them True."

"In August 1619, just 12 years after the English settled Jamestown, Va. . . . colonists bought 20 to 30 enslaved Africans from English pirates," Hannah-Jones wrote. "Our Declaration of Independence, approved on July 4, 1776, proclaims that 'all men are created equal' and 'endowed by their Creator with certain unalienable rights.' But the white men who drafted those words did not believe them to be true for the hundreds of thousands of black people in their midst." She argued that there would never have been an American Revolution "if [the colonists] had not believed that independence was required in order to ensure that slavery would continue. It is not incidental that 10 of this nation's first 12 presidents were enslavers, and some might argue that this nation was founded not as a democracy but as a slavocracy."

She made the story of Black people "foundational" to the story of the birth of the United States, arguing that through "centuries of black resistance and protest, we have helped the country live up to its founding ideals."

She added that the Black struggle was "not only for ourselves—black rights struggles paved the way for every other rights struggle, including women's and gay rights, immigrant and disability rights."[33]

The editor of the project, Jake Silverstein, defended the concept of the newspaper's special section by asking readers to question if the lessons "taught in our schools and unanimously celebrated every Fourth of July" were wrong and "the country's true birth date, the moment that its defining contradictions first came into the world, was in late August of 1619?"[34]

The publication of The 1619 Project by the *Times*, a pillar of the establishment, came as a measure of public opinion moving away from Trump's message of racial grievance. Across American life, it was evident that the mainstream was looking for new ways to repair the fraying racial fabric. The country urgently needed to build on the progress and accommodations that were the hallmarks of the First Civil Rights Movement.

Clearly the election of mayors, governors, and even a Black president had not been enough. Black Lives Matter's protests against police violence signaled the need for a new generation to take on race relations, instead of being content with what had been achieved fifty years prior.

The 1619 Project was an immediate sensation, becoming "one of the most talked-about journalistic achievements of the year," in the words of even critics like Professor Leslie M. Harris of Northwestern University.[35] This new framing could have faded into academic debates, but with race relations in turmoil, it came to be seen as a public backlash to "Make America Great Again." This sentiment was evident when Hannah-Jones won the Pulitzer Prize, giving the project more establishment credibility. The 1619 Project was also being used to change school curricula, with support from major corporations. Oprah Winfrey's Harpo Productions soon developed it as a TV series.

The 1619 Project was not without its detractors. Some historians, including some on the left, took aim at Hannah-Jones's charge that slavery was central to the American Revolution. Five preeminent American academics, in a letter to *The New York Times*, wrote: "On the American Revolution, pivotal to any account of our history, the project asserts that the founders declared the colonies' independence of Britain 'in order to ensure slavery would continue.' This is not true," said the historians, who included prize winners from Princeton, Brown, the City University of New York, and Texas State University. "If supportable, the allegation would be astounding—yet every statement offered by the project to validate it is false. . . . Instead, the project is offered as an authoritative account that bears the imprimatur and credibility of The New York Times."[36]

Even inside the *Times*, the project stirred division. The conservative columnist Bret Stephens wrote: "The 1619 Project is a thesis in search of evidence, not the other way around. . . . What makes America most itself isn't four centuries of racist subjugation. It's 244 years of effort by Americans—sometimes halting, but often heroic—to live up to our greatest ideal. That's a struggle that has been waged by people of every race and creed. And it's an ideal that continues to inspire millions of people at home and abroad."[37]

Despite the debate, the publication of The 1619 Project reflected an increased awareness by major U.S. companies, such as the *Times*, of changing attitudes among a new generation of American consumers. It also reflected shifting demographics in the workplace, as in the increased diversity of people editing and writing in *The New York Times*. The leaders of other major corporations, including the biggest blue-chip firms on Wall Street, could see the risks of the economy being dragged down by Trump's racial provocations, which denigrated the largest-growing segments of their markets.

This negative financial impact of racial polarization, including anti-immigrant fervor in a globalized economy, led many American companies to increase their emphasis on diversity, equity, and inclusion (DEI) training. *Time* magazine reported that as early as 2003 companies were spending "an estimated $8 billion a year on diversity efforts." Following the election of Donald Trump, that corporate effort ramped up to an unprecedented level. *Time* wrote that because of "the emergence of movements like #MeToo and Black Lives Matter, the [DEI] industry has exploded." They cited a 2019 survey of more than two hundred companies that found "63% of the diversity professionals had been appointed or promoted to their roles" since Trump's election.[38]

Another novel expression of racial awareness within corporate America came in the heart of Trump country. In Alabama, Bryan Stevenson, a Black lawyer known for successfully defending Black people facing the death penalty, built a museum highlighting the painful history of lynching in America. Major corporations, including Google, joined with mainstream philanthropists such as the Ford Foundation and the Colorado billionaire siblings Pat and Jon Stryker to contribute millions of dollars to construct a site commemorating the victims of white racial violence. According to *The Washington Post*, the National Memorial for Peace and Justice was "one of the most powerful and effective new memorials created in a generation."[39]

The corporate backlash to Trump also reached into the white, male-dominated world of sports ownership. Colin Kaepernick, who spent years condemned to the NFL sidelines for protesting police violence, became celebrated for calling out racism. In 2018, Kaepernick's face appeared on Nike billboards with the slogan: "Believe in something. Even if it means sacrificing everything." He fit into the mold of the heavyweight champion Muhammad Ali, an activist during the First Civil Rights Movement who was stripped of his titles after refusing to be drafted into the Vietnam War. Eventually even the NFL changed its attitude. They issued a statement on their website, NFL .com, which said flatly that Kaepernick's social justice campaign "deserve(s) our attention and action."[40] They also agreed to a financial and legal settlement with the former player.

Trump responded angrily to the celebration of Kaepernick as well as to the changes signaled by The 1619 Project, and corporate DEI efforts. "Look, they want to take your history from you," Trump said specifically in reference to The 1619 Project. "They want to tell you that you're bad. They want to tell you that all of your heroes are not heroes anymore."[41]

He hastily announced the creation of the 1776 Commission, to promote "patriotic education" and a "pro-American curriculum." The president called out the 1619 Project–inspired curriculum as a "twisted web of lies" and said it was "a form of child abuse."

"Critical race theory, the 1619 Project, and the crusade against American history is toxic propaganda, ideological poison that, if not removed, will dissolve the civic bonds that tie us together. It will destroy our country," Trump said.[42]

Concepts elevated to a new level by Black Lives Matter, such as "systemic racism" and "mass incarceration," became increasingly present in the national conversation. Even a previously arcane academic thesis calling attention to racial bias across society, "Critical Race Theory," was becoming a topic of wide discussion. There was also newfound attention from universities and think tanks to the racial wealth gap and racial disparities in education.

Academics writing in the *Proceedings of the National Academy of Sciences* noted that Black Lives Matter was succeeding in changing the terms of debate on race in America: "BLM has successfully leveraged protest events to engender lasting changes in the ways that Americans discuss racial inequality." They went on to note that the new framework introduced "antiracism discourse [that] is distinctive in that it does not view racism as an individual pathology or disfunction," but rather a wider social issue.[43]

Trump doubled down on his criticism in a speech in front of Mount Rushmore, with its granite profiles of iconic American presidents. He decried "cancel culture" coming from left-wing activists against conservatives, saying that it was "driving people from their jobs, shaming dissenters, and demanding total submission from anyone who disagrees. This is the very definition of totalitarianism. In our schools, our newsrooms, even our corporate boardrooms, there is a new far-left fascism that demands absolute allegiance. If you do not speak its language, perform its rituals, recite its mantras, and follow its commandments, then you will be censored, banished, blacklisted, persecuted, and punished."[44]

Trump acted on his denunciations by issuing an executive order to halt all DEI training in the federal workforce, claiming it perpetuated "racial stereotypes and division and can use subtle coercive pressure to ensure conformity of viewpoint." His order appeared to blame the people behind Black Lives Matter and The 1619 Project for undermining a common American identity: "This destructive ideology is grounded in misrepresentations of our country's history and its role in the world." Trump's order added that "this malign ideology is now migrating from the fringes of American society and threatens to infect core institutions of our country."[45]

Trump's criticism was reflected by other conservative public figures, who highlighted fears that American children were being indoctrinated with radical left-leaning ideas that diminished the contributions of the white Founding Fathers. States with conservative legislatures, like Florida and Texas, passed laws banning the teaching of material from The 1619 Project.

Not all corporations were on board with the new discussions of what was becoming known as "woke" culture, after a Black slang term referring to being aware of injustices that may not be immediately apparent. Some corporations were profiting from divisiveness, notably Facebook. Founded in 2004, the social media site boasted more than a billion users worldwide within its first ten years. It was the most common online destination for families and friends to share photos and keep up with one another's birthdays and graduations. It first became a major political force in 2008 when the Obama campaign used it to reach young voters. Its international power became evident during the Arab Spring of 2011, when activists used Facebook to plan protests against authoritarian governments in North Africa and the Middle East.

It was ironic that the social media titan, once celebrated among activists as a springboard for a new civil rights movement, became a major platform of far-right attacks against progressives. White supremacists began using Facebook to bully Black Lives Matter supporters as early as the Ferguson protests, even going so far as publishing their personal information online in a practice known as "doxing." Alicia Garza appealed to Rashad Robinson, the head of Color of Change, for help when her life was threatened by white supremacists on Facebook. She wanted Color of Change to pressure the social media company's executives to stop the abuse of racial activists and limit the online threats.[46]

Facebook failed to go beyond cosmetic changes. The platform continued to be a fountain of threats against liberal activists, including Black Lives Matter, while lies, misinformation, and conspiracies spread on the site like wildfire. Color of Change raised the pressure on Facebook by demanding a "civil rights audit" to address concerns they had about "hate speech, [advertising] discrimination, voter suppression and Facebook's failure to protect the safety and security of Black users and users of color."[47]

The response from the social media giant was angry. Facebook hired a right-wing public relations firm, Definers, to search out negative information about Robinson's organization in a clandestine effort to undermine it. The Definers strategy was to portray Color of Change as a tool of a favorite villain of the right wing. "We started seeing the threats coming in at us, in emails that were physical threats mentioning George Soros in them," Robinson later told the website *Salon*. "For us it was a very weird thing, as a Black racial justice group."[48] *The New York Times* then reported that the Definers campaign was just one part of a larger effort by Facebook to cripple the civil rights group.[49]

Unmasked by the *Times* report, the social media company finally agreed to make changes. It launched an audit of its content, including efforts that blocked some Black opinion on the grounds that it had been too extreme, even as there had been no similar leash on white extremism. That began to change when Facebook finally removed some of the most extreme far-right disinformation on its platform, including permanently banning the infamous Alex Jones, and his *InfoWars* page, which had over 1.7 million followers in 2018.

At the same time, President Trump was also trafficking in disinformation, telling lies and sending off incendiary tweets, some coming in the middle of the night. Now Twitter, as well as Facebook, had to decide what was permissible as political speech, especially if it was coming from the president of the United States.

Trump's online antics made daily headlines; he was spinning out of control with one fight after another. He made furious statements about economic collapse and immigration while instigating the longest government shutdown in American history. His anger was continuing to infect people on the fringes of American society. The anti-immigrant tensions he'd been stoking boiled over in August 2019, when a twenty-one-year-old white Trump supporter took a gun into a Walmart in El Paso, Texas, and killed twenty-three people, mostly Hispanics. It was soon discovered that the gunman had posted a manifesto online that condemned "cultural and ethnic replacement" and what he called a "Hispanic invasion." Trump set off more alarms by downplaying the racism behind the shooting. Just as he did in Charlottesville, the president said he was opposed to hate of any kind, be it "white supremacy, whether it's any other kind of supremacy, whether it's antifa."[50] That deflection and false equivalency led to a tweet storm, with #WhiteSupremicistInChief rising to become the most trending topic.

Just weeks earlier, FBI director Christopher Wray (who had been appointed by Trump) had warned Congress that the greatest source of domestic terrorism in the United States was "white supremacist violence."[51] Yet once again Trump refused to acknowledge the racist anger he was stirring in the country. Instead, he tried to distract from it. After Wray's testimony, the president tweeted that he was considering declaring left-wing protests "a major Organization of Terror (along with MS-13 & others). Would make it easier for police to do their job!"[52]

But for all the online outrage, there was little in the way of street protests, a stark contrast to the earlier Black Lives Matter demonstrations or the Women's March. In fact, Black Lives Matter had not been on the front lines for years, since the police killings of Philando Castile and Alton Sterling back in 2016. But things were about to change. In February 2020, Ahmaud Arbery, a twenty-five-year-old Black man living in Georgia, was intercepted and gruesomely executed by two white men while jogging in his neighborhood. Gregory McMichael, a retired police officer, and his son Travis had been following Arbery in a truck, wrongly suspecting him of being a thief. Initially the local prosecutors took no action in response to the shooting. One prosecutor recused herself from handling the case because McMichael had worked as an investigator in her office. A second prosecutor said there was no evidence to suggest that McMichael had acted illegally in the context of Georgia's self-defense laws. While McMichael was ultimately prosecuted and convicted, there were no immediate national protests despite the initial refusal to bring charges.

Less than three weeks later, on March 13, police in Louisville, Kentucky, broke into the apartment of a twenty-six-year-old Black woman named Breonna Taylor. They were looking for a drug dealer's stash and had acted on the basis of false testimony to get a "no knock" warrant. Taylor, an emergency room technician, was in bed sleeping alongside her boyfriend. She was hit by eight shots out of a barrage of twenty-five bullets fired by the police and died at the scene.

Like the Arbery killing, the Taylor case drew little immediate media attention. Initially there was no video to go viral on social media. The urgency and anger that had attended earlier police shootings of Black people generated only small local protests. There was nothing like what had happened in Ferguson. But under the surface, the racial fever was simmering hot, stoked by anxiety, frustration, and grievance.

But there was an even larger problem brewing in America, one that went far beyond changing demographics, politics, and police violence. This looming crisis would affect the entire planet, as all eyes turned their focus to one single issue—the fear of a pandemic with the potential to kill millions.

Covid-19 would also transform the Second Civil Rights Movement.

8

"I'M DEAD"

The big issue in Black America in the first months of 2020 was the big issue for all of America—fear of catching a killer virus. The very first case in the United States of what would soon be named Covid-19 was confirmed in Washington State on January 20. Two days later, President Trump told the media: "We have it totally under control. It's one person coming in from China. It's going to be just fine."[1]

Nothing could have been further from the truth. Two months later, most Americans were locked down in their homes. Many could not go to work, to school, or to the mall. They were limited to their televisions, phones, and social media, looking for the latest update on the contagion.

Then a cell phone video of a white police officer kneeling on a Black man's neck transfixed the nation.

It was Monday, May 25—Memorial Day. George Floyd, a six-foot, seven-inch-tall man, made a run to pick up cigarettes from Cup Foods, a corner convenience store in Powderhorn, a mostly Black and Hispanic neighborhood of Minneapolis. A few minutes after he left the store, the clerk realized that Floyd had handed him a counterfeit $20 bill.

To the clerk's surprise, when he looked outside, Floyd was still in the vicinity, sitting in a car at the corner with two friends. The clerk approached him to ask for the cigarettes back, but Floyd didn't respond. The young

man then went back inside the store and called the police, telling them that
Floyd was "awfully drunk and he's not in control of himself. He's not acting
right."[2]

When police officers arrived minutes later, Floyd was passed out. One policeman tapped on the window with a flashlight to get his attention. A groggy
Floyd slowly responded by asking, "Please, officer, what's all this for?"[3]

Floyd had trouble keeping his hands visible, according to the two friends
in the car. This led the policeman to draw his weapon. Floyd, with a gun suddenly in his face while he was still high, freaked out. He started to weep while
begging, "Please don't shoot me, man."

He got out of the car, and the two policemen quickly handcuffed him. But
even with Floyd in handcuffs, the officers, one of whom was just five days out
of training, struggled to subdue him. Floyd, forty-six years old, was a former
football player and had been working as a security guard before losing his
job in the pandemic. As the police officers tried to get him into the car, Floyd
resisted, complaining that he'd recently had Covid and feared he was going to
die in the closed, cramped backseat of the squad car.

Two backup officers then arrived on the scene. One, a white officer, a
nineteen-year veteran of the force named Derek Chauvin, grabbed the handcuffed Floyd and forced him onto the ground, placing his knee on Floyd's
back to keep him under control. Chauvin then shifted the weight of his knee
directly onto Floyd's neck.

"I can't breathe," Floyd said, before gasping out calls for his mother. One
officer responded, "You are talking fine." Another officer asked if they should
turn Floyd on his side to let him breathe more easily. But Chauvin refused,
keeping his knee on Floyd's neck.

The whole scene played out at a busy intersection. Chaos ensued as people streamed in and out of the store for late-night food while others stopped to
watch the vicious treatment being applied to George Floyd. Several bystand-
ers began screaming at Chauvin, pointing and saying that Floyd was begging
for his life. One bystander, Darnella Frazier, a seventeen-year-old high school
student, pulled out her cell phone and started recording video.

As Chauvin remained on top of Floyd, Frazier could be heard on the video telling someone near her: "Look how they doing people here. He's Black. They don't care."

Another passerby can be heard directly calling out to Chauvin: "You're enjoying it. Look at you, your body language explains it, you fucking bum."

Floyd continued to squirm, insisting that he was having trouble breathing.

His last words were:

"Please."

"Mama, I love you."

"Tell my kids I love them."

"I can't breathe for nothing man."

"This is cold blooded."

"I'm dead."

After eight minutes and forty-six seconds, Floyd stopped moving. A police officer checked for a pulse. There was none. No one tried to revive him.[4]

The crowd outside Cup Foods continued to grow as word spread that George Floyd was dead. A shaken Darnella Frazier returned to her home, traumatized by what she had just seen. As the flashing lights of the police cars and their wailing sirens turned her neighborhood into a crime scene, she livestreamed herself describing the whole event. Then she uploaded her video of Chauvin kneeling on Floyd's neck with the post: "They killed him right in front of cup foods over south on 38th and Chicago!! No type of sympathy ♥ ♥ #POLICEBRUTALITY."[5]

The Minneapolis Police Department offered a different story. Within hours of the killing, the department posted a press release on social media titled: "Man Dies After Medical Incident During Police Interaction." Floyd's death was deemed a result of "medical distress." The police claimed that he hadn't died on the scene, but later in the hospital. "At no time were weapons of any type used by anyone involved in this incident," the press release said, in a clear attempt to dampen outrage.

Seeing the police statement, Frazier immediately went back online at 3 a.m. to respond: "Medical incident??? Watch outtt they killed him and the proof is clearlyyyy there!!"[6]

By dawn, the horrific video was quickly spreading, and the country woke up to the footage showing a police officer killing a man in a prolonged, cruel act of violence. It immediately set off alarms among people of all races already feeling anxious, threatened, and frustrated from the rising number of Covid deaths. Those alarms rang loudest among young Black activists keeping track of the recent killings of Ahmaud Arbery and Breonna Taylor. Their panic and distress went worldwide with the familiar hashtag #BlackLivesMatter. It created a rush of sharing the video and a flood of commentary about how George Floyd died.

Alicia Garza, Black Lives Matter's cofounder, was quick join the conversation on her Twitter feed: "#GeorgeFloyd should still be alive, along with countless other Black lives taken too soon and too often. Change the laws and the people who make them. Or fail to enforce them equally—from President to prosecutor to Sheriff. #BlackLivesMatter"[7]

Former president Obama posted an online statement: "This shouldn't be 'normal' in 2020 America. It can't be 'normal.' If we want our children to grow up in a nation that lives up to its highest ideals, we can and must be better."[8]

These statements and millions of others added pressure on Minneapolis's mayor and police chief. Even more pressure came when news reports confirmed that the earlier press release from police amounted to lies. Normally in such cases, the policemen involved would be placed on administrative leave while an investigation played out. However, given the harsh and swift public condemnation, the police chief, Medaria Arradondo, took the unusual step of firing the four police officers, while also calling for the FBI to investigate George Floyd's death in the hope of assuring the public that there would be no cover-up.

None of this was enough to stem the anger. #BlackLivesMatter was now being used worldwide more than a million times a day to express outrage and sorrow at Floyd's death. Three days after the killing, the hashtag peaked at over eight million tweets, which according to Pew amounted to "the highest number of uses for this hashtag in a single day."[9] Over the coming weeks, the #BlackLivesMatter hashtag "generated approximately 3.4 million original posts with 69 billion engagements—or roughly 13% of all posts and 15.5% of all engagements on Twitter," a Brookings study later found. Blacks and

Latinos under the age of thirty had the most engagement online about the controversy.[10]

Whether it was a visionary act by BLM's founders, or a matter of chance, the incredible volume of usage indicated beyond any doubt that the hashtag had struck a lasting chord. Local organizers not affiliated with BLM began using #BlackLivesMatter to call together ordinary people from around a mostly white state to join in the marches. *The New York Times* reported that the night following Floyd's murder, "hundreds of protesters flooded into the Minneapolis streets. Some demonstrators vandalized police vehicles with graffiti and targeted the precinct house where the four officers had been assigned." Rioting also started, with businesses set on fire. Police responded to the chaos with rubber bullets and tear gas.[11]

The trouble in Minneapolis quickly spread to other big American cities. On the West Coast, there was a major march around the Los Angeles Civic Center that blocked Highway 101. In St. Louis, near the site of Michael Brown's killing six years earlier, fires and looting broke out, with one man killed. Chicago saw six shootings and one death during demonstrations.

Floyd was an unlikely man to cause a major American social protest. His life in Minnesota was a long way from the dreams he held growing up in Houston. As a teenager, he had won an athletic scholarship to South Florida Community College before transferring to Texas A&M–Kingsville. But the young man with pro-sports aspirations could not maintain his grades and returned to Houston, where he fell into the grip of easy money hustles and began to sell and use drugs. He was jailed several times, including serving five years for aggravated robbery. In 2013, at the age of forty, Floyd was paroled. He was looking for a fresh start but could not get out of the dead-end life of small-time crime, and he struggled to remain sober and out of jail.

He then heard from a friend in Minnesota, who advised him to leave the troubled, poorer precincts of Houston and come to the affluent, white, northern city in 2017. He immediately found a job as a security guard at Minneapolis's largest homeless shelter. Within a year, he took up work as a truck driver and as a part-time bouncer at a nightclub. But Floyd still could not escape his dark past. One of his roommates died of a drug overdose, and he often failed to make the monthly child support payments for his five children back in Houston.[12]

George Floyd's situation worsened when Covid hit Minneapolis. He didn't get the virus right away, but he lost his job at the nightclub as the disease shut down the city. "COVID-19 is hitting the northside community from all angles," Louis King, the head of a Minneapolis vocational school, wrote in an open letter describing how the crisis was hitting Black Minnesotans. King compared what was going on to the high unemployment and turmoil during the Great Depression.[13]

Meanwhile, President Trump was doing nothing but criticizing local leaders for their handling of the Covid crisis. He especially attacked Democratic governors in the Midwest, including Minnesota governor Tim Walz, for taking precautions to protect the people in their states. Walz had issued a stay-at-home order to limit the spread of the virus. In response Trump tweeted: "LIBERATE MINNESOTA!" calling for an end to the lockdown.[14]

In spite of Trump's tweet, the Minnesota State Fair announced that it would cancel that year's event, the first cancellation since 1946, when polio swept through the state. The number of infections in Minnesota grew to more than ten thousand cases in less than two months, a number that included the unemployed George Floyd.

By the time of Floyd's death, Covid had been ravaging the United States for more than four months. Nationwide there had been 1.6 million people infected, and more than 98,000 deaths. Among Black Americans, the pandemic was most devastating.[15] By early June, they would account for more than half of America's cases, and were twice as likely to die from the infection.[16] Minorities' higher rates of being uninsured and unemployed also meant that a Covid case could easily lead to falling behind on rent or a mortgage payment.

That is when the unemployed and recently back-on-drugs George Floyd was accused of passing a counterfeit $20 bill at a corner store.

In an earlier era, Floyd could have been easily dismissed as a statistic—an unemployed former convict killed by police. First Movement leaders stayed away from people like him, fearing that aligning themselves with an imperfect character was a potential liability, a risk that could pull them away from achieving their political goals. But in this generation, after the killings of Trayvon Martin and Michael Brown, there was a sense that a victim's humanity should not be diminished simply because they were not perfect role models.

In other words, Floyd was no Rosa Parks. In 1955 Parks famously refused to give up her seat on a segregated bus in Alabama after being trained to participate in nonviolent protests. This First Civil Rights Movement activist was a model citizen—a steadily employed member of the Black middle class. When the NAACP was filing lawsuits to break down segregation in the 1940s and 1950s, their lead attorney Thurgood Marshall looked for ideal plaintiffs like Parks. They were people with solid reputations in their communities: churchgoers, teachers, and folks with good families who could not easily be trashed by racist segregationists. In public, they all dressed in their Sunday best.

The Second Civil Rights Movement was operating in a universe of different social and cultural realities. This fight was not about integration. The focus now was on continued inequities, such as the number of Black people arrested for drugs and the high percentage of minorities in prison. This group, as well as victims of police violence, were generally not model citizens. For Black Lives Matter, this shift in emphasis was at the heart of their argument.

Black Lives Matter proudly embraced people who were negatively stereotyped and ignored by most of the country. In fact, much of the fervor came from Black America identifying with Floyd. It was not unusual for Black Americans to have a family member in jail, or dealing with drug addiction, joblessness, or trouble in school.

In so many ways George Floyd represented the poor and working-class Black males who were most often victims of police violence. He became a touchstone for Black America's fear that any one of them could be victimized by knee-on-your-neck-style government oppression.

George Floyd was now held up as a martyr. At his funeral, he was celebrated like earlier Black activists who had died for a cause, such as Martin Luther King or Medgar Evers. But the Reverend Al Sharpton made the point that Floyd was just an ordinary man. "If George Floyd had been an Ivy

League school graduate . . . if he'd been a multimillionaire, they would have
said that we were reacting to his wealth," Sharpton said. "If he had been a famous athlete . . . [they'd have said] we were reacting to his fame. But God took
an ordinary brother from the Third Ward, from the housing projects, that
nobody thought much about but those that knew him and loved him. . . . God
took the rejected stone and made him the cornerstone of a movement that's
going to change the whole wide world. . . . And as we lay you to rest today, the
movement won't rest until we get justice."

Attending Floyd's funeral was a somber lineup of relatives of Black people who had been killed by police in the last few years: the parents of Trayvon
Martin, Eric Garner, Michael Brown, and Ahmaud Arbery. Sharpton's mas-
terful eulogy tied together so many events of the Second Civil Rights Movement. "We are not fighting some disconnected incidents," Sharpton preached
to the people in the church and an audience watching on national television.
"We are fighting an institutional, systemic problem that has been allowed to
permeate since we were brought to these shores, and we are fighting wicked-
ness in high places."[17]

By the first week of June, thousands of protests had taken place from
coast to coast, in the largest cities, in suburbs, and even in small, rural, red-
state towns. It was estimated that as many as 26 million people took part in
more than seven thousand demonstrations. In terms of the proportion of the
total U.S. population, this made it the largest protest in American history.[18]

The people involved went beyond Black activists. Families of all races
participated, across generations. Many in the lead were college-educated and
young professionals. As a group, they were wealthier, more politically diverse,
and more racially diverse than previously seen in civil rights protests.

As the majority racial group in the United States, whites also comprised
the largest group of participants in these protests, at 46 percent. Hispanics
surprisingly accounted for the second-largest percentage of Americans taking to the streets, making up 22 percent, which far exceeded their 15 percent
share of the U.S. population. Black Americans accounted for 17 percent of
protesters, compared with their 13 percent share of the population. Asians
were also overrepresented relative to their population, making up 8 percent

of the protests. Overall, Pew found that the participants in the protests were "more likely to be nonwhite and younger than Americans overall . . . also more likely to live in an urban area and to identify with or lean toward the Democratic Party."[19]

This was a dramatically different demographic palette than was present at most of the protests during the First Civil Rights Movement. Professor Deva Woodly of the New School told *The New York Times* that the Floyd protests dwarfed the demonstrations during the 1960s: "If we added up all those protests during that period, we're talking about hundreds of thousands of people, but not millions."[20] Even the most famous demonstration of the First Civil Rights Movement, the 1963 March on Washington featuring Martin Luther King Jr.'s "I Have a Dream" speech, attracted fewer than 250,000 protesters. Though racially diverse, that march was majority-Black. Other minorities were just a small percentage of the American population at that time.

As a hashtag, #BlackLivesMatter extended across the racially diverse makeup of twenty-first-century America. But as a group, Black Lives Matter was not the driving force in setting up the majority of protests. Some chapters did lend material support, provided guidance, and participated, but on the national level, Garza, Tometi, and Cullors were never guiding hands. They continued to resist that role because of their belief in a decentralized leadership model. And even if they hadn't, controlling protests of this size, now taking place around the globe, was in fact much bigger than any of them.

Still, the ideas that had emerged from Black Lives Matter's work and actions had continuing impact. Responding to calls from people protesting under the BLM banner, the Minneapolis City Council began serious discussions about dismantling the city's police department, and elsewhere in the country, a number of Confederate statues were finally removed after many years of protests. The Mississippi legislature voted to replace the state flag with a new banner that did not include the Confederate battle emblem. Even the NFL and NASCAR, not natural allies for Black Lives Matter or civil rights protests of any generation, gave surprising support for people taking to the streets.

At the White House, though, President Trump was fuming. On Twitter he described Americans protesting in the street as "THUGS" and said they were "dishonoring the memory of George Floyd, and I won't let that happen. . . . Any difficulty and we will assume control but, when the looting starts, the shooting starts. Thank you!"[21]

When the protests showed no signs of slowing down, Trump threatened to deploy the military, charging that he needed to protect public safety and restore public order. In fact, what had become apparent was the protests also had strong overtones of opposition to Trump's presidency. The majority of the marches were led by people critical of his policies, including his bungled handling of Covid. Opal Tometi said she thought the protest became so large because people living in a pandemic were "just fed up and thoroughly beside themselves with grief and concern" over Covid as well as George Floyd. What made it worse, she argued, was that the Trump administration did not seem to care or "have a plan of action."[22]

To fight back against growing popular support for the marches, Trump fed the lie that most of the protests were violent. In fact, they weren't. And Twitter took the unprecedented step of flagging the president's tweet about the looting and shooting as a violation of its rules "about glorifying violence." In the end, the post remained on the site. Twitter explained that it was in the public's interest "for the Tweet to remain accessible."[23]

In addition to glorifying violence, Trump's use of the phrase "when the looting starts, the shooting starts" had troubling racist roots extending back to the First Civil Rights Movement. It set off alarms about Trump engaging federal forces against American citizens exercising their right to protest. Professor Clarence Lusane of Howard University noted that the term originated with notorious segregationist Sheriff "Bull" Connor who was known for confronting civil rights protesters with guns, powerful blasts from water hoses, and large German shepherds.

But Trump succeeded in selling his distorted view to his base. He repeatedly lied about big cities being caught in the grip of violent mobs. A Morning Consult poll done a week after Floyd's death found that nearly 60 percent of Republicans agreed that "most of the current protesters are trying to incite violence."[24] That perception, created by Trump's rhetoric and amplified on conservative media, directly contradicted studies that later found that more than 90 percent of protests were peaceful. The Armed Conflict Location & Event Data Project noted that this "disparity [in perception] stems from political orientation and biased media framing . . . such as disproportionate coverage of violent demonstrations."[25]

The president's exaggeration of the violence led the *New York Times*'s Washington correspondent Peter Baker to note that Trump was also falsely attributing the violence "to the Antifa anti-fascist movement, one of his favorite targets."[26] The fact-checking didn't stop Trump. He went further, pushing the idea that the protests were intended as the start of a coup attempt to end his presidency.

With the presidential election just months away, polls available to Trump indicated a third of Republicans backed the marches as a show of support against injustice. Trump claimed that he was the last line of defense against spreading violence in a desperate appeal to win over those straying Republicans.

Protests outside the White House escalated four days after George Floyd's death. On Friday night, some small barriers were knocked over, and inside the Oval Office loud chants could be heard from across Pennsylvania Avenue. Fearing for his safety, Trump briefly retreated to a bunker underneath the White House.

In a Rose Garden speech the following Monday, June 1, Trump spoke in defiant opposition to the marches: "These are not acts of peaceful protest. These are acts of domestic terror. . . . If a city or a state refuses to take the actions that are necessary to defend the life and property of their residents, then I will deploy the United States military and quickly solve the problem for them."[27]

After his remarks, Trump decided to make a show of shutting down the demonstrators at his doorstep. He ordered federal law enforcement into Lafayette Square, in front of the White House, where thousands of Black Lives Matter protesters were chanting and holding signs. Multiple federal agencies used tear gas and rubber bullets to clear the park. "What ensued," *The New York Times* wrote the next day, "was a burst of violence unlike any seen in the shadow of the White House in generations."[28]

Trump, walking alongside the uniformed chairman of the Joint Chiefs of Staff as well as the attorney general, then crossed through the still smoldering park to hold a photo op. When he reached the other side of the park, he proceeded to St. John's Episcopal Church. Outside the church he held a Bible upside down as he posed for photos.

The pointless scene increased criticism of Trump. Even some Republicans felt it was wrong to use force against a peaceful American protest. The whole episode crystallized for the demonstrating millions that they were protesting Trump as much as they were protesting the murder of George Floyd.

Throughout his years in office, from the Women's March, through Charlottesville, and now with his mishandling of Covid, Trump consistently sparked anger. His actions reeked of misogyny, racism, and ineptitude. According to a Kaiser Family Foundation survey, almost one in five Americans even before the summer 2020 had participated in some type of anti-Trump protest since he took office, including a large number of first-time protesters.[29]

Instead of working to bring the country together during the pandemic, Trump remained undeterred in fostering political divisions to generate support for his reelection. Since his 2016 election, there had been a rise in violence against Blacks, Latinos, and Jews. In March and April 2020, during the early months of the pandemic, he lashed out against a new target—Asian Americans. Trump regularly referred to Covid as the "Chinese virus" or the "Wuhan virus."[30] At a campaign rally in Arizona, he got laughs from his supporters by calling it the "Kung Flu."[31]

The impact of the president targeting Asians was immediate and real. One right-winger fatally attacked an Asian family shopping in a Texas supermarket, later saying that he believed they were "carriers" of the coronavirus. In another incident, an attacker yelled, "I lost my job [be]cause [of] Asians." A new advocacy group was created, Stop AAPI Hate (the abbreviation referring to Asian American Pacific Islander), as the United Nations received 1,800 reports of racist incidents against Asian Americans in just eight weeks between March and May 2020.[32]

Online, people were just as vicious. One social media post read: "There is a special place in hell reserved for the fucking Chinese and their archaic culture. . . . [President Trump's] description of COVID-19 as the Chinese virus is the most accurate thing he has ever said."[33]

The George Floyd protests revealed that the damage Trump was doing to divide a racially diverse country was becoming explosive. A majority of Americans told Pew Research that in his three years in office, Trump "had made race relations worse." Almost two thirds of Americans—across racial lines—agreed that "it has become more common for people to express racist or racially insensitive views since Trump was elected president."[34]

Trump's approval rating, which never went above 50 percent, reached a high of 49 percent in the weeks before Floyd's death, according to Gallup. After his response to the protests across the country, the president's rating dropped to 38 percent.[35]

Meanwhile, former vice president Joe Biden had taken a commanding lead in the Democratic presidential primaries. There had been an intense competition among the Democrats, with more than a dozen candidates seeking the nomination. Senator Bernie Sanders of Vermont was the early favorite. But the candidates were as diverse as the country itself, including a Latino from Texas, Representative Julián Castro; the Asian American businessman Andrew Yang; two Black U.S. senators, Cory Booker and Kamala Harris; as well as several white women, notably Senators Elizabeth Warren and Amy Klobuchar. The former mayor of New York, Michael Bloomberg, a billionaire, was also a surprising and self-funded presence in the race.

Early on, Biden struggled. Among young people, he was considered too old and too moderate for a party that had been pushed into an angry stance by years of Trump's extremism. Biden lost the first contest, the Iowa caucus, to a little-known and much younger Pete Buttigieg, a military veteran and gay man who was the former mayor of South Bend, Indiana. Biden lost the second and third contests, in New Hampshire and Nevada, to the tough-talking Bernie Sanders.

Biden's candidacy was on the ropes. His only hope rested with the Black voters in the coming primaries, a major constituency that was largely absent in the early states. The key to a Biden comeback would run through South

Carolina, where a significant number of Blacks would be voting for the first time in this primary season. His secret weapon was support from the state's leading Democrat, Black congressman James Clyburn.

Clyburn's encounter with one Black church woman before the South Carolina primary made front-page news. She asked him who he was backing. Clyburn, who had refused to endorse until then, replied: "We know Joe. But more importantly, Joe knows us."[36]

Blacks made up 56 percent of South Carolina's Democratic primary electorate. After Clyburn's endorsement, they came out in force, with 61 percent voting for Biden. According to Edison Research exit polls, 60 percent cited the endorsement as the key factor in deciding their vote.[37]

Biden's big victory in the Palmetto State dramatically shifted momentum because there were also large Black populations in the upcoming Super Tuesday contests, which were mostly in the South. Out of the fourteen states that voted on Super Tuesday, Biden won ten, with his most reliable support coming from Black women, who were now being hailed as the cornerstone of the Democratic Party. This led to a positive, and perhaps much needed, change in Black Lives Matter's strategy. An organization that had demonstrated real power in raising money to fight racism now put serious effort into mobilizing voters ahead of the fall election. This became more pronounced after the George Floyd protests, when Black Lives Matter's approval rating stood at an astounding 67 percent. *Time* magazine listed the three founders among their 100 Most Influential People of 2020.[38]

The Black Lives Matter webpage received 24 million visitors throughout the protests, a quarter of whom came from outside the United States. The organization's social media followers also expanded—more than four million people on Instagram, more than a million on Twitter, and nearly three quarters of a million on Facebook.[39] This online presence became a powerful fundraising vehicle. In 2020, Black Lives Matter reported receiving $90 million in donations, dwarfing anything received during its earlier years. The organization struggled to control the flood of money coming in, establishing BLM Grassroots as a vehicle for donations to be sent to local chapters.

Patrisse Cullors, the lone member of the founding trio remaining full-time at Black Lives Matter, now took on the role of executive director of a new non-profit, Black Lives Matter Global Network Foundation. Her priority was to mobilize the organization's network and get people to the polls. With a dark view of Trump's tenure, she now appreciated the potentially "transformative change" that came from winning elections. According to the website: "Elections can help eliminate oppressive structures. Elections can help create just economies and governments. Elections can ensure that we remove white supremacists from having legislative power."[40] Black Lives Matter's new appreciation for politics led the organization to set up a political action committee, which put millions of dollars into political ads aimed at Black voters.

Alicia Garza also turned her energy to voter registration drives. Her new group, Black Futures Lab, directed her followers to her Electoral Action Center. "Register to vote; stay up to date on election news & key dates; find out who represents you at the fed., state, & local level; see who is running where you live; and more!" she tweeted.[41]

In particular, she targeted Black women: "I'm all for ambitious Black women," she tweeted. "The Biden campaign should be too—given that Black people, women, and BLACK WOMEN are key to Biden winning the White House. #AmbitiousWoman."[42]

The Black establishment—churches, members of Congress, and locally elected officials—had long backed Biden, as did the top Black leader in the country, former president Obama. But there remained a worry about a lack of enthusiasm among younger Black voters. They had not turned out for Hillary Clinton in 2016 and remained skeptical of establishment Democrats, who they felt were reluctant to confront racial injustice, especially when it came to the police.

When Biden announced his selection of Senator Kamala Harris of California as his running mate, it added to the case for Black Lives Matter and younger Black people to support the ticket. Harris, a woman with Black and Indian parents, had attended Howard University and now was making history as the first woman of color on a major party ticket.

With the announcement, Garza took to Twitter to say, "I'm voting Biden/ Harris. I'm voting down the ticket. I'm registering and moving others to vote.

And I'm going to keep pushing them. It is important to see BLM after all this time. 7 YEARS. Symbols are nice. Policy and practice is essential. Let's go—we got work to do. #DNC2020."[43]

Her "7 YEARS" reference was tied to the anniversary of Black Lives Matter's founding after George Zimmerman's acquittal in Trayvon Martin's death. What started as outrage and frustration in a hashtag had gone from online to the streets and now to political maturity.

Garza said the choice of Harris was a signal to Black women, whom she called the "heart of the Democratic party base" in a piece she wrote that summer for *Glamour* magazine. She noted that voter turnout among Black women had dropped by 10 percent in 2016. In retrospect, Garza was making an implicit criticism of Black Lives Matter's lack of voter mobilization to oppose Trump in that election. Now she saw the political situation differently. She predicted that Harris would "energize" the Democratic Party's most important voting bloc: "It is a signal to Black voters that we matter."[44] By late August, when the Democrats held their national convention in Milwaukee, the George Floyd protests had died down. But the issue of racial violence was central at the convention. Biden saluted Black women at the start of his acceptance speech by honoring Ella Baker, a heroine of the First Civil Rights Movement. Baker had been instrumental in creating the Student Nonviolent Coordinating Committee in the 1960s, a forerunner of take-it-to-the-streets, Black Lives Matter–style activism practiced by young people in the twenty-first century.

Biden quoted Baker: "Give people light and they will find the way." He spoke to racial violence, saying he was passionate to help "communities who have known the injustice of a knee on the neck," a clear reference to Floyd's murder. He then acknowledged the third anniversary of the neo-Nazi march in Charlottesville, calling it reminiscent of the "anti-Semitic bile heard across Europe in the '30s" and lauding the heroism of those who stood up to it. He reminded the national audience of Trump's statement that there were "very fine people on both sides."

"It was a wake-up call for us as a country. And for me, a call to action. At that moment I knew I had to run," Biden told his audience. His message was a salute to the people who had marched, not only the activists but also the moderates and even conservatives who had made a first-time show of activism. He said that the people who had taken to the streets were some of the "most powerful voices we hear in the country today." He was speaking directly to the Second Civil Rights Movement.

In his most emotional appeal of the night, Biden spoke about meeting George Floyd's six-year-old daughter, Gianna. Calling her "an incredibly brave little girl," Biden noted that Gianna's father had once told her that he wanted to "change the world." In life, he had never been able to, but global attention to his murder did just that. Biden told a spellbound audience that the message he got from Gianna was: "Daddy changed the world." He said it was "one of the most important conversations I've had this entire campaign."[45]

Biden maintained a 10-percentage-point lead after the convention. But within three days there was more racial violence. It again happened in the Midwest and threatened to upend his momentum.

The flashpoint took place on August 23, the day before the Republican National Convention, when police responded to a 911 domestic violence call in Kenosha, Wisconsin. When they arrived, they found a twenty-nine-year-old Black man, Jacob Blake, who allegedly had a knife and was resisting arrest. The police tasered Blake and then shot him seven times, though he was not killed.

In response to this latest police shooting, Black Lives Matter issued a statement reiterating its opposition to violent police tactics and calling for more social service and mental health programs: "We need to move away from a culture of punishment and terror and move towards a culture of care and dignity.... Any person who will shoot someone seven times in the back is not shooting to slow someone down. They are shooting to kill."[46]

The next day, as the Republican convention began in North Carolina, protests and rioting broke out in Kenosha; several stores were burned. Kyle Rittenhouse, a seventeen-year-old from neighboring Illinois who had recently attended a Trump rally, drove across the state line to reach Kenosha. He'd seen posts online from store owners who feared their property would be destroyed.

Rittenhouse's own social media accounts included messages that were pro-Trump and included "Blue Lives Matter," a slogan in support of police that was being used to counter Black Lives Matter. The next night, Rittenhouse took to the street as an armed vigilante patrolling the Kenosha business strip. He shot three white Black Lives Matter protesters, two of whom died.[47]

At the convention Trump responded to the shooting in Kenosha by blaming Democrats. In his acceptance speech he said: "Make no mistake, if you give power to Joe Biden, the radical left will defund police departments all across America.... No one will be safe in Biden's America. My administration will always stand with the men and women of law enforcement."[48]

Trump sought to provoke fear among white suburbanites, key to his re-election effort, by running ads about crime, antifa, and anarchy in the streets. Less than a week later, Trump went to Kenosha for his first major post-convention stop. The governor had asked him not to come, for fear that it would prompt more violence. But Trump ignored those warnings.

Touring damaged properties, Trump pointed to the burned buildings as evidence of chaos in Democratic-controlled cities. Trump supporters wearing red MAGA hats faced off against Black Lives Matter supporters. The Rev. Jesse Jackson also showed up in Kenosha that day, and he urged Black Lives Matter supporters to stay away from Trump and his followers. "If they demonstrate, it would be a big mistake. Trump would use it as a commercial," Jackson told reporters. Democrats limited counter protests to setting up voter registration booths.[49]

Biden, who had been making campaign appearances only in his home state of Delaware and neighboring Pennsylvania due to fears about Covid, now broke with that caution to travel to Kenosha. Maintaining distance and wearing a mask, Biden said that Trump was feeding racial division instead of addressing the root of the recent violence. "We're finally now getting to the point of the original sin: slavery. And all the vestiges of it," Biden told a small group of Black leaders, including the local Black Lives Matter spokeswoman, who met with him in a church.[50] The presence of the Black Lives Matter representative marked a big change from the 2016 campaign, during which many Democratic candidates had their events disrupted by Black Lives

Matter activists. But in 2020, Biden's staff invited the organization to be part of a select group with the candidate at a critical stage of a campaign.

As the fall campaign kicked off, neither candidate was able to hold normal rallies due to Covid. The pandemic also prompted several states to expand their use of early voting and mail-in ballots. Black voters in particular took advantage of early voting, even before the presidential debates began.

The first debate took place in the battleground state of Ohio, and race was a central topic. After an extensive discussion about the president's troubled response to the Covid epidemic, the moderator, Chris Wallace of Fox News, asked the candidates who the American people should trust to deal with frayed race relations.

Biden began by calling out Trump's over-the-top response to protests in front of the White House. "He came out of his bunker, had the military use tear gas on them so he could walk across to a church and hold up a Bible. . . . This is a president who has used everything as a dog whistle, to try to generate racist hatred, racist division."

The Democratic nominee acknowledged that there was "systemic injustice in this country, in education and work and in law enforcement and the way in which it's enforced," indicating Black Lives Matter's new presence in the mainstream political conversation. After praising most police as "good, decent, honorable men and women," Biden said that they had to be held accountable. "And that's what I'm going to do as president of the United States."

Trump charged that Biden's support for the Black Lives Matter protests meant that the activists were controlling Biden: "And they've got you wrapped around their finger, Joe, to a point where you don't want to say anything about law and order."

Constantly interrupting Biden's responses, Trump attempted to dominate the conversation. Wallace failed to control a disastrous debate, always verging on collapse. But the defining moment of the night came when Wallace asked Trump to condemn white supremacists.

Trump responded by asking who he should condemn. Biden shot back: "Proud Boys."

Instead of disavowing the violent hate group, the president said: "Proud Boys, stand back and stand by . . . somebody's got to do something about Antifa and the left because this is not a right-wing problem. This is a left-wing problem."[51]

It was incredible that the president appeared to be calling upon an armed militia known for its violent racism to be ready to act. Twitter and Facebook had banned them in 2018 for their extremism, forcing them to turn to other social media sites. "Within minutes [of Trump's debate], members of the group were posting in private social media channels, calling the president's comments 'historic,'" *The New York Times* reported. "In one channel dedicated to the Proud Boys on Telegram, a private messaging app, group members called the president's comment a tacit endorsement of their violent tactics. In another message, a member commented that the group was already seeing a spike in 'new recruits.'"[52]

Biden's running mate, Kamala Harris, said after the debate: "What we saw was a dog whistle through a bullhorn. Donald Trump is not pretending to be anything other than what he is: Someone who will not condemn white supremacists."[53]

A few days later, as the controversy about the Proud Boys continued to dominate the news, the election was thrown into more turmoil. Trump tweeted at 1 a.m. on October 1 to tell the world that he had contracted Covid.[54] The bombshell came after Trump had been on the road for several days of public events. According to his chief of staff, Trump knew that he had tested positive but failed to take precautions to protect those around him. Despite the rising death toll, he acted with bravado, telling the American people that Covid was nothing to be afraid of, even as he was helicoptered to a military hospital, where he remained for several days, getting new treatments not yet publicly available. Upon his return to the White House, Trump acted as though nothing was wrong. He made a public show of ripping off his mask on the White House balcony as he stood in front of TV cameras. Though he acted as if all was normal, campaign events were canceled, as was the second presidential debate.

It was not until almost a month after their first debate that the two candidates met again, on October 22. Once again, racial division was the cutting edge of their confrontation.

Trump bragged that no president had done more for Black people than him "with the exception of Abraham Lincoln . . . nobody has done what I've done."

The moderator for this debate, Kristen Welker of NBC News, reminded the president that he had called Black Lives Matter a "symbol of hate" and had "shared a video of a man chanting, 'white power.'" She asked if he did not recognize that he was creating racial tension. Trump responded that he had seen Black Lives Matter supporters on TV call police "pigs"—"pigs in a blanket, fry 'em like bacon."

"That's a horrible thing," Trump said before asserting, "I am the least racist person in this room."

Biden referred to Trump's boast that he'd done more than any president for Black people with a sarcastic remark that quickly turned serious: "Abraham Lincoln here is one of the most racist presidents we've had in modern history. He pours fuel on every single racist fire, every single one. He started off his campaign coming down the escalator saying he's gonna get rid of those Mexican rapists. He's banned Muslims because they're Muslims. He has moved around and made everything worse across the board. He says to them about the 'Poor Boys,' last time we were on stage here. He said, 'I told him to stand down and stand ready.' Come on. This guy has a dog whistle about as big as a foghorn."[55]

Days before the election, an Idaho white supremacist was arrested on weapons charges and was found to have a list of potential targets, including Alicia Garza. When the FBI notified her, she tweeted, "This is why this President is so dangerous. He is stoking fires he has no intention of controlling. I'm ok y'all, but this shit is not ok. Vote this muthafucka out. For real."[56]

Along with Covid, the racial acrimony surrounding the election captured the public's full attention. Despite the pandemic, two thirds of the American people found a way to vote, the highest percentage of eligible voters casting a ballot than at any time since 1900.[57]

•   •   •

Joe Biden won the election, and the final results showed that his victories in many swing states that Clinton had lost in 2016 were due in large part to a resurgent Black turnout. In Georgia, Stacey Abrams's registration drives generated enough new voters to flip a state that Trump had won in 2016. Across the country and across the races, the record number of people voting suggested that Trump had created a referendum on his provocative, racially charged, and chaotic style of governance.

Black voters' historic turnout for Biden was second only to their support for Barack Obama in the elections of 2008 and 2012. Black social media celebrated with a viral remix of a Black woman twerking at police while handcuffed, rapping, "You about to lose your job." The message, in a raucous hip-hop remix, was aimed at Trump. A later video mash-up that accompanied it had people on the street dancing but also featured prominent politicians, including Obama, grooving in delight at the prospect of Trump's ouster.[58]

According to a Pew voter study, Biden maintained strong support among Black Americans, winning 92 percent of the Black vote. He also improved his support from Black men. Trump won 14 percent in 2016, but only 12 percent in 2020. Biden won among Latinos but made the biggest jump with Asians, with a 10-percentage-point improvement compared to 2016. Trump's anti-Asian attacks had motivated scores of new voters to the polls, and Biden took 59 percent of their support.[59]

But it was Biden's margin of victory among Black women that was larger than any other group. These stalwart Democrats gave him an astonishing 95 percent of their vote.

When the election was called for Biden, Alicia Garza tweeted: "Just woke up and I'm gonna pop some bottles. Woke up to my neighbor screaming HALLELUJAH! #Election2020results."[60]

Patrisse Cullors put out statements celebrating the power of the Black voter to oust Trump: "Once again, Black people—especially Black women—have saved the United States. Whether in Milwaukee, Detroit, Philadelphia, or Atlanta, Black voters showed up in huge numbers to turn this country around and remove the racist in the White House. . . . We worked long and hard to ensure we did all we could to vote Donald Trump out of the White

House—we succeeded. And in doing so, we even elected a Black woman—the first Black woman—to the vice presidency."[61]

In his victory speech, Biden, with Harris by his side, reached back to when his primary campaign was on the rocks and Black voters carried him to the finish line. "Especially at those moments when this campaign was at its lowest ebb," Biden said, "the African American community stood up again for me. You've always had my back, and I'll have yours."[62]

But Trump did not accept the defeat and continued to press Republican state officials to search for votes that could overturn the results. In some cases, he pressured Republican state officials to ignore voters and falsely inform Congress that he had won their states. He claimed without any evidence that there had been voter fraud in big cities with large minority populations.

"Big protest in D.C. on January 6th," Trump wrote in a tweet on December 19. "Be there, will be wild!"[63]

9

A NEW CONFEDERATE
MOVEMENT

Once Donald Trump lost the 2020 presidential election, he decided the best way for him to remain in power was to falsely claim that the election had been stolen. Trump had won the majority of white votes. The base of the Republican Party was nearly all-white, and Trump had come to personify this white party in a country that was increasingly racially diverse. Having won the white vote, his strategy extended to exhorting the most racist elements of his base to threaten violence if he wasn't allowed to stay in the White House. He specifically alleged fraud in areas with large minority populations, where, unsurprisingly, he lost by wide margins.

The country was already full of racial anxiety. Gallup polls showed dissatisfaction with the state of race relations at 71 percent, a twenty-year high. After four years of Trump, this level of dissatisfaction was the same for people of every race.[1]

Even before the election, Trump's own Department of Homeland Security had declared the threat of white supremacist violence to be the biggest terrorist threat to the United States. The Trump administration tried to bury the fact that during Trump's time in office, white supremacists, according to DHS, had "conducted more lethal attacks in the United States than any other DVE [Domestic Violent Extremist] movement." Trump preferred that the agency downplay these threats and instead call attention to potential attacks from foreigners, Black Lives Matter, or antifa. In reality, though, it was the "white supremacist extremists . . . [who] have demonstrated longstanding intent to target racial and religious minorities," DHS officials admitted.[2]

On January 6, 2021, Kevin Seefried, a drywall construction worker from Delaware, came to Washington after swallowing a stew of Trump's rhetoric, including social media posts claiming that the election had been fraudulent and calling on Congress to reject the certification of Biden's victory. Seefried took a Confederate flag to the Ellipse, behind the White House, and waved it as Trump began his "Stop the Steal" speech that morning. Trump egged on the crowd, telling them that they were to go to Capitol Hill and send a message to Congress. "We are going to try and give them the kind of pride and boldness that they need to take back our country," Trump told an increasingly angry sea of mostly white men.[3] The crowd started chanting "USA! USA!" as Seefried and many others left for the Capitol.

Seefried was not a known leader of any white supremacist group. Despite carrying the Confederate flag, he claimed to be a lone actor. Later he described his provocative flag as simply a "symbol of protest," denying it was a banner representing the defenders of slavery.[4] Whether part of an organized group or not, Seefried found himself and his flag leading the charge into the Capitol, alongside organized extremist groups like the Proud Boys and Oath Keepers, whose members included many military veterans, former intelligence officials, and police officers. They were all motivated by Trump's demagogy, with its fiery anger and latent charges of minority voter fraud.

Trump was still speaking when Seefried climbed through a smashed window, leading a surge of people into the Capitol itself. They were at the front of the swarm of ten thousand Trump supporters violently intent on stopping Congress from declaring that Trump had lost the presidential election. Seefried used the flagpole to jab at a Capitol Police officer named Eugene Goodman, who is Black. "Fuck you, I'm not leaving, where are the members at, where are they counting the votes? You can shoot me, man, but we're coming in," he told Goodman.[5]

As Seefried was breaking into the Capitol, Trump ended his speech by telling his supporters that he was joining them to "walk down Pennsylvania Avenue." After he left the stage, Trump told his Secret Service driver that he also wanted to go to the Capitol, but the agent refused, insisting that the president return to the White House because extremists were already over-running the barriers protecting Congress. By now, Proud Boys were smashing windows as other members of their group scaled the scaffolding built for the upcoming inaugural. Members of the Oath Keepers employed military-style formations, complete with walkie-talkie communications, to storm into the Capitol.

Those radicals were joined by lone actors like Seefried, as well as rioters belonging to the right-wing conspiracy-theory community QAnon. One of them, a female Air Force veteran named Ashli Babbitt, was shot by Capitol Police when she tried to climb through a window near the office of Speaker Nancy Pelosi. Babbitt was a follower of the QAnon conspiracy theory that held that Hillary Clinton, Barack Obama, and Joe Biden were part of a Satan-worshipping group of child abusers. She saw Trump as her savior, fighting to protect the country from the evil establishment in Washington.

The rioters, some wearing Trump flags as capes and many with MAGA hats, followed Seefried into the Capitol. They outnumbered law enforcement by nearly 60 to 1. Overrun, the police ordered an evacuation of the Capitol Complex, and the mayor of Washington declared a state of emergency. As the chaos grew, explosive devices were found at the nearby Republican and Democratic Party headquarters.[6]

Meanwhile, Vice President Mike Pence, who was in the Capitol to pre-side at the joint session of Congress, had to be rushed to a secure location as chants of "Hang Mike Pence" echoed in the halls of the Capitol. Even with his vice president under attack, Trump continued to tweet, falsely, that Pence could stop Biden's certification. In fact, Pence had no constitutional or legal authority to do so. "Mike Pence didn't have the courage to do what should have been done," Trump tweeted. The defeated president also worked the phones, reaching out to congressional allies and urging them not to endorse any result that would remove him from power.[7]

The violence engulfing Congress amounted to the biggest threat to democracy since the Civil War. At the White House, an indifferent Trump stubbornly refused demands from staff and family to order the people he'd incited to insurrection to stop. With Trump failing to act, President-elect Joe Biden held a press conference demanding that Trump "step up." He condemned the riot, saying it was "not protest, it's insurrection."[8]

Biden then tweeted: "I call on President Trump to go on national television now to fulfill his oath and defend the Constitution by demanding an end to this siege."[9] Former president Obama also issued a statement on Twitter, squarely blaming Trump for having "incited" the unrest by telling a "lie about the outcome of the lawful election."[10]

Three and a half hours into the bloody riot, even right-wing media personalities like Laura Ingraham and Sean Hannity began pressuring Trump's chief of staff to halt the insurrection. Trump reluctantly agreed to record a video in the Rose Garden, but he refused to acknowledge his part in stirring the violence. Instead, he continued to repeat the lies that provoked the anger of his supporters in the first place. "We had an election that was stolen from us. It was a landslide election, and everyone knows it, especially the other side," Trump said in a video that he released on Twitter. "But you have to go home now. We have to have peace. We have to have law and order. . . . So go home. We love you, you're very special. . . . I know how you feel. But go home and go home in peace."[11]

By nightfall, with reinforcements from the National Guard arriving, the Capitol Police worked to push out the remaining rioters. But it was not until nearly 10 p.m., more than nine hours after Seefried had led the charge, that the building was fully secure. Vice President Pence, who at one point had been hiding in a parking garage, was able to return to the House chamber and restart the certification process: "Today was a dark day in the history of the United States Capitol," he intoned. It wasn't until 3:40 the next morning that Congress certified Biden's election.[12]

The January 6 attacks resulted in assaults on more than 150 members of the U.S. Capitol Police and Metropolitan Police Department, including the killing of Capitol Police officer Brian D. Sicknick. Meanwhile, in addition to Babbitt, three other Trump supporters died in the aftermath of their savage assault that day.[13]

More than a thousand people were eventually charged for their roles in the insurrection; 18 percent of them were veterans, according to information from the University of Maryland and the Justice Department.[14] Some were even active-duty law enforcement officers who had come to Washington. The presence of so many protesters with that background on January 6 was alarming given that only 7 percent of the general American population had ties to military service. In fact, a later study by the RAND Corporation showed that one third of U.S. veterans believed in the "great replacement" conspiracy theory that held that people of color were being brought into the United States to replace the white majority.[15]

Imagine if the protesters storming the Capitol had been people of color. What happened on January 6 stood in stark contrast to the massive law enforcement response to the George Floyd protests the previous summer, despite those protests being mostly peaceful. The juxtaposition was even more pronounced given that U.S. government intelligence agencies had been warned in advance that an attack was being planned by white supremacist Trump supporters. Even as the insurrection started, one Republican senator, Josh Hawley of Missouri, raised his fist in solidarity with the crowd. Incredibly, some U.S. Capitol police were seen taking selfies with insurgents just before the violence began.

The day after the riot, even a white moderate like Joe Biden had to acknowledge the shocking racial double standard in police response. "No one can tell me that if it had been a group of Black Lives Matter protesters yesterday that they wouldn't have been treated very differently than the mob that stormed the Capitol. We all know that's true—and it's unacceptable," Biden said.[16]

The leaders of Black Lives Matter were even more blunt. Patrisse Cullors tweeted: "What is happening today comes from a long history of white supremacist violence against Black people. White supremacist terrorists are willing to hurt, harm and kill to protect themselves and their whiteness."[17]

Makia Green, a Black Lives Matter activist from Washington, D.C., said: "It felt like abuse to see not just white privilege but white supremacy in action. To see the bias from the government, from the police."[18]

Had the races been switched, "there would have been a massacre," wrote Shaun Harper, the executive director of the Race and Equity Center at the University of Southern California. He pointedly said that if outraged Black people had tried to stop the certification of a national election, they would have been "swiftly killed."

"Snipers would have gunned down every Black protester scaling the Capitol. One Jan. 6 insurrectionist was shot and killed; surely, there would have been hundreds, perhaps thousands more had they been Black," Harper wrote.[19]

The glaring double standard even drew attention from Major General William Walker, the head of the D.C. National Guard and a Black man. "I think it would have been more bloodshed if the [racial] composition would have been different," he said.[20]

The most visible immediate response to Trump's violent white supporters was political. Within a week of the attack, the Democratic-controlled House of Representatives voted to impeach Trump for his role inciting the insurrection. It would be Trump's second impeachment trial, unprecedented in American history.

"There's no question—none—that President Trump is practically and morally responsible for provoking the events of the day," said the top Republican in the Senate, Minority Leader Mitch McConnell. "The people who stormed this building believed they were acting on the wishes and instructions of their president."[21] But shortly after Joe Biden took office, McConnell, like most Republicans, refused to convict Trump, using as an excuse the fact that he was no longer in office by the time they voted. Only seven Republicans voted in favor of conviction, not enough to reach the two thirds necessary to win a guilty verdict.

At Biden's inauguration on January 20, on the steps of the Capitol that had recently been under siege, the new president spoke in emotional terms about the racial trauma the nation had been through. "A cry for racial justice some four hundred years in the making moves us," Biden told the crowd, calling attention to race as the central factor in both the insurrection and the George Floyd protests. This was the heart of the Second Civil Rights Movement on display before the entire nation. "The dream of justice for all will be deferred no longer. . . . And now, a rise in political extremism, white supremacy, domestic terrorism that we must confront, and we will defeat."

Referring to the promise of Dr. King's 1963 "I Have a Dream" speech, delivered from the other end of the Mall, Biden told the crowd: "Today, we mark the swearing-in of the first woman in American history elected to national office—Vice President Kamala Harris. Don't tell me things can't change."[22]

Also marking the historic significance of the moment, Biden thanked former president Obama, who was seated behind him. Here was a moment in history where the first Black president not only watched his vice president take office, but also saw the first woman—and the first person of color—assume the vice presidency. Their presence on the dais signaled the extent of the racial change taking place in America, despite the white supremacist riots violently trying to stop it.

There was further political celebration for Democrats. In addition to gaining control of the White House, they had gained control of both the House and Senate for the first time since 2009 and 2010, the first two years of Obama's term.

This was possible because of the late outcome of two U.S. Senate races in Georgia. Both were special run-off elections held in early January, and both saw the Democrats take seats previously held by Republicans. Jon Ossoff, a Jewish candidate, and Raphael Warnock, a Black candidate, defeated two white incumbents. Republican voters failed to turn out, as Trump continued to broadcast lies about voter fraud and to promote the idea that elections should not be trusted. The victories in Georgia meant that the Democrats in Washington now had a 50-50 split in the Senate. With Vice President Harris as the deciding vote, they took control of the legislative agenda in both houses of Congress.

Georgia's new senators owed their victories in part to the work done by Stacey Abrams to register and energize Democratic voters, especially Blacks.

There had been concern about Black voter turnout for the special election at an unusual time of year, but Black voters came out in record numbers, with 94 percent of them, according to AP VoteCast, backing Ossoff and Warnock.[23]

"The work that we've done to build infrastructure absolutely was the game changer," said Abrams, describing the 2020 election. "You compare it to 2018. There is a measurable and meaningful difference in the size of the [Black] electorate participation rates and support rates. That's meaningful."[24]

Black Lives Matter should have been poised to take off at the start of 2021. There was a new energy with diverse leaders in so many positions of power in Washington. A Black politician, James Clyburn, was the number-three ranking member in the House and had unparalleled influence with Biden. Nancy Pelosi, a San Francisco liberal who had expressed support for Black Lives Matter, was speaker of the House. And the Squad was putting left-wing pressure on Biden to enact a progressive agenda that Black Lives Matter favored.

Patrisse Cullors, the organization's remaining leader, asked to meet with Biden and Harris after the election, but Biden never responded. Instead, the president-elect met with Black leaders from every other civil rights group, including the Congressional Black Caucus, the NAACP, and the National Action Network (Al Sharpton's organization). "To set up a meeting with civil rights leaders, without BLM, is unacceptable," Black Lives Matter angrily tweeted.[25] Cullors made the case that her organization had been involved in getting out the vote, enabling Biden and Harris to win the White House. "It's demeaning to the countless times we took our protest to the streets to call for justice for our Black brothers and sisters taken from us at the hands of police," she wrote in an email to her supporters.[26]

Cullors had a point. Black Lives Matter remained popular in the aftermath of the George Floyd protests. In fact, it was far more popular than Martin Luther King Jr. had ever been during his lifetime. The organization's approval rating had declined in the months after the marches had ended, going from 67 percent to 55 percent support, but that was still a high number for any activist civil rights organization.[27]

Even so, the Biden team continued to keep Black Lives Matter at arm's length. Biden stressed his concern that conservatives wanted to paint all Democrats as radicals who sought to eliminate police departments. "That's how they beat the living hell out of us across the country, saying that we're talking about defunding the police. We're not. We're talking about holding them accountable," Biden told civil rights leaders. "We're talking about giving [the police] money to do the right things. We're talking about putting more psychologists and psychiatrists on the telephones when the 911 calls [come] through. We're talking about spending money to enable them to do their jobs better, not with more force, with less force and more understanding."[28]

Biden had support from Black congressional leaders, some of whom were veterans of the First Civil Rights Movement. Like BLM, they were operating in an evolving social and political environment. Unlike BLM, however, these older elected officials were more cautious and open to compromise than the insistent, demanding younger generation. They'd learned tough lessons from errors made during the earlier movement.

"I think the Black Lives Matter today is where SNCC was in the 1960s," said Representative Clyburn. The veteran South Carolina congressman recalled that before Georgia representative and civil rights icon John Lewis died in 2020, the two men sat in the back of the House chamber and discussed the new civil rights activists. Lewis warned him, "'Defund the Police' was going to do to Black Lives Matter what 'Burn, Baby, Burn' did to SNCC." That slogan hurt the First Civil Rights Movement with Middle America when it was used by SNCC leaders during the riots of the 1960s. This hard-earned wisdom was one reason experienced Black leaders were more trusted by Biden; they counseled the president about the need to respond to BLM, but not necessarily meet every demand.[29]

The distance between the White House and Black Lives Matter leadership was about more than just the slogan "Defund the Police." Black Lives Matter had also issued a seven-point "demand" agenda that was unrealistic in a country where Republicans held nearly half the seats in Congress. The organization wanted to expel many Republicans from Congress for trying to overturn the election and inciting "a white supremacist attack." They also wanted to ban Donald Trump from all social media. The recent dip among Americans in their support of Black Lives Matter had been most noticeable among moderate whites, the politically potent group whose support Biden needed to pass his legislative agenda.[30]

While Black Lives Matter was on the defensive in Washington, it was also battling internal conflicts. In late 2020, a group of ten chapters, calling themselves the #BLM10, publicly criticized Cullors for her lack of transparency and her failure to get input from the chapters' grassroots leaders. "Our chapters have consistently raised concerns about financial transparency, decision making, and accountability," the statement read. "Despite years of effort, no acceptable internal process of accountability has ever been produced . . . and [recent] events have undermined the efforts of chapters seeking to democratize [Black Lives Matter's] processes and resources."[31]

The infighting was ironic. Ever since the founding of Black Lives Matter, Cullors had made a point of eschewing the hierarchical, "great man model" of the First Civil Rights Movement. Yet when it came to handling the huge new donations after the George Floyd protests, Cullors sought to consolidate power under her unchecked control.

Black Lives Matter had never been transparent about its donations, having delegated the management of its financial accounting to a larger foundation. The organization's leadership resisted questions about money as unnecessary and obtrusive attacks by critics. But after the tremendous surge in donations in 2020, it filed tax forms under a new name: Black Lives Matter Global Network Foundation.

After reviewing the organization's tax forms, the Associated Press reported that Black Lives Matter had taken in $90 million in donations after the Floyd protests, $60 million of which still sat in the bank the following year. The AP observed that "this marks the first time in the movement's nearly eight-year history that BLM leaders have revealed a detailed look at their finances." In what appeared to be an incredible conflict of interest, members of Cullors's family and close personal friends were employed by the organization or received funding from them. Cullors paid nearly a million dollars to the father of her child for helping stage events. She also paid nearly another million to her brother for security work. And her deputy executive director's consulting firm was paid $2 million by Black Lives Matter.[32]

These disclosures sparked a string of right-wing media attacks. Most of the previous criticisms had to do with Black Lives Matter's leftist ideology and lack of a clear agenda, but now an all-star lineup of conservative media, led by the *New York Post*, Fox News, the *Daily Mail*, and *National Review*, ran a raft of harsh stories portraying Black Lives Matter not merely as an entitled, arrogant group of radical leftists, but corrupt as well.

Conservative attention focused on four houses purchased between 2016 and 2020 under Cullors's name. The houses, in California and Georgia, were valued collectively at $3.2 million. But the biggest story was about the group's purchase of a $6 million "luxury property" in Los Angeles. The six-bedroom house also had a swimming pool and soundstage. Black Lives Matter claimed it was to be used as a retreat for Black artists and to hold events.[33]

The right-wing press went into a frenzy of attacks. It had long wanted to defeat Black Lives Matter because the organization pushed a powerful counterpoint to Trump's narrative about the threat of Black criminals and dangerous big cities. With these revelations of financial mismanagement, criticism became blistering, moving beyond right-wing outlets and into mainstream coverage.

The condemnation came closer to the heart of their cause when two mothers of young Black people killed by police released a public letter critical of Black Lives Matter. The mother of Tamir Rice, a twelve-year-old who had been killed by Cleveland police in 2014, and the mother of Richard Risher, who had been killed by Los Angeles police in 2016, accused the group of raising money off the deaths of their children: "The 'activists' have events in our cities and have not given us anything substantial for using our loved ones' images and names on their flyers. . . . We don't want or need y'all parading in the streets accumulating donations, platforms, movie deals, etc. off the death of our loved ones, while the families and communities are left clueless and broken. Don't say our loved ones' names period! That's our truth!"[34] The torrent of denunciations continued when Tamika Palmer, the mother of Breonna Taylor, also posted emotional, angry comments on Facebook calling out Black Lives Matter as a "fraud."[35]

With news about their confused finances and airing of dirty laundry in the press, Cullors resigned from the Black Lives Matter board. Making no mention of the growing critiques now overshadowing the group and her personally, she said, "I've created the infrastructure and the support, and the necessary bones and foundation, so that I can leave. It feels like the time is right."[36] When news of Cullors's resignation became public, Risher's mother told the *New York Post*, "Now she doesn't have to show her accountability. She can just take the money and run."[37]

Cullors appeared on an MSNBC podcast to admit to "mistakes." She said that she was overwhelmed as someone who had created a group in response to a social injustice. She defended herself as a novice who was given no grace and not allowed to "learn from those mistakes."[38] She later posted a denial of wrongdoing on Instagram, saying that she "never misappropriated funds."[39]

Sean Campbell, a Black writer whose investigations of Black Lives Matter's finances appeared in *New York* magazine, later tweeted that the revelations had been "heartbreaking."[40] He told NPR, "It hurts me that some people might try and twist this in ways that this organization is somehow standing in for the movement as a whole, which is absolutely false. . . . That is not the movement."[41]

These scandals ensured that Black Lives Matter would remain on the outside as the power of the Second Civil Rights Movement shifted from street protests to the halls of power in Washington. The Biden White House may have abandoned Black Lives Matter, but it did not want to abandon the Black voters who had put the president in office. Administration officials began to push two legislative issues to cement President Biden's support with Black voters—police reform and voting rights.

Police reform, the issue that had taken Black Lives Matter to the heights of public awareness and came to define the Second Civil Rights Movement, remained on the front burner for the new administration. Despite the change in the White House, the number of police killings in America continued to rise, according to the *Washington Post* database. In 2021, a record high 1,050 people would die at the hands of police.[42]

At the urging of the liberals in the House, the Democratic majority passed the George Floyd Justice in Policing Act. More than one hundred civil rights groups supported the bill, which banned chokeholds and required that law enforcement keep track of the use of force and officers found guilty of misconduct. The groundbreaking bill required that police use body cameras and prohibited no-knock warrants. It also restricted the transfer of federal military equipment to local police departments. The bill even contained money for training police to stop the use of racial profiling.

When the bill was sent to the Senate, it ran into opposition from Republicans, who objected to a provision that would have ended "qualified immunity," the legal doctrine that protected police officers from personal liability if they committed violent acts while on duty.

Mitch McConnell assigned Senator Tim Scott of South Carolina, the only Black Republican in the Senate, to negotiate a compromise. He reached agreement on no-knock warrants, limiting transfer of military equipment to police, and banning chokeholds. But he could not reach a deal on qualified immunity. The key factor was that Republicans relied on support from police unions, who lobbied vigorously to ensure that qualified immunity remain untouched.

Scott pronounced the bill dead, falsely pointing a finger at Democrats, who he said "could not let go of their push to defund our law enforcement."[43] Senator Cory Booker of New Jersey, who led the Democrats' negotiating team in the Senate, said the deal they were pushing was not about defunding the police, but about raising professional standards.[44] Still, a Republican filibuster prevented any further movement on creating the new law.

In the absence of congressional action, President Biden had no legal power to create new practices for local police departments. The best he could do was to order the Justice Department to resume work with local police by agreeing on consent decrees to limit the use of violent police tactics and to review patterns of abusive, often racist, police behavior. Most of the existing consent decrees under Obama had been undone by the Trump administration.

Biden also ordered the Justice Department to ban federal law enforcement—from the FBI to the Park Police—from using chokeholds and restrict no-knock warrants. The Justice Department also required that federal agents use body cameras when executing search warrants or planning arrests.[45]

The stumbles on police reform were deflating, given the extent of the protests the previous year and the tsunami of public support from people of all colors. As difficult as it was to find a way forward on police reform, there was an even steeper hill to climb when it came to another point of agreement between the Biden administration and the Second Civil Rights Movement—how to combat Republican voter suppression.

Initially the Biden administration put its support behind the John R. Lewis Voting Rights Advancement Act, which sought to maintain laws allowing mail-in voting, extending early voting, and preventing more stringent voter ID requirements in Republican-controlled states. Though the bill passed the House, Republicans once again blocked passage in the Senate.

The administration then pushed for a larger bill—the Freedom to Vote Act—that would have enacted national voting standards and ended a patchwork system that allowed some states to suppress the vote. But Senator McConnell defeated the federal standards bill with a filibuster. He said that the nationwide rules would have "the federal government take over how elections are conducted all over America."[46] Coming on the heels of the failure to pass police reform, Biden came out swinging against his Republican opponents.

"Do you want to be on the side of Dr. King or George Wallace?" Biden asked rhetorically of Republican leadership in Congress. Speaking before an audience from several historically Black colleges and universities (HCBUs) in Atlanta, he said, "Do you want to be on the side of John Lewis or Bull Connor? Do you want to be on the side of Abraham Lincoln or Jefferson Davis?"[47]

Republicans acted as if they were deeply wounded for being compared to defenders of slavery and segregationists. Senator Mitt Romney, who had voted to impeach Trump after the insurrection, said that Biden had unfairly accused "good and principled colleagues in the Senate of having sinister, even racist inclinations. . . .

"He charged that voting against his bill allies us with Bull Connor, George Wallace, and Jefferson Davis. So much for unifying the country and working across the aisle," said Romney.[48] McConnell said that Biden was unfairly invoking the Civil War "to demonize Americans who disagree with him. He compared a bipartisan majority of senators to literal traitors."[49] Still, for all of their indignation over the comparisons to infamous racists, Republicans did nothing to prevent states from suppressing the votes of the young and minorities.

Al Sharpton met with Biden after his address, saying, "I told the president he gave a monumental speech and, though I have been challenging him for months to be forthcoming, it was better late than never."[50] Despite the strength of Biden's remarks and his willingness to be combative with Republicans, he was unable to convince them to act on the bills in the Senate.

The highly charged political environment of Washington allowed for no middle ground. In the First Movement's era, there was a moderate faction in Congress that could be persuaded by passionate, well-reasoned argument; in 2021, due to the polarization created by Trump and the January 6 insurrection, there was no such group of legislators. Republicans dug their heels in and continued to deny the significance of the violence on Capitol Hill. Instead they focused on condemning what they said were violent protests led by antifa and BLM that had destroyed American cities.

Despite this yawning political divide, the Biden administration remained under tremendous pressure to prove that it could deliver concrete results for its political base of white progressives and Black communities. What followed was a series of small victories that could be advertised to the president's supporters.

The first such move was to declare Juneteenth a federal holiday. Juneteenth had long been a celebration in Texas, but never nationwide. The history was compelling. Abraham Lincoln's Emancipation Proclamation had freed the slaves in the Confederate states in January 1863, in the middle of the Civil War, but it took more than two years for news of emancipation to reach the southeastern part of Texas. It wasn't until General Gordon Granger and his Union troops entered the port city of Galveston in June 1865 that the enslaved population finally learned the war had ended two months earlier and that they were free.

Texas made June 19, the anniversary of Granger's proclamation, a statewide holiday in 1980. Now, more than forty years later, after George Floyd's death and Biden's election, this was a neatly packaged symbol for Democrats who wanted to act on behalf of Black America. The bill passed overwhelmingly in Congress, with only minor objections from Republicans.

At the White House signing ceremony, Vice President Harris spoke to the importance of the holiday and its meaning: "We are gathered here in a house built by enslaved people," Harris told the gathering, which included members of the Congressional Black Caucus and civil rights leaders. "We are footsteps away from where President Abraham Lincoln signed the Emancipation Proclamation. We have come far, and we have far to go. But today is a day of celebration. It is not only a day of pride. It's also a day for us to reaffirm and rededicate ourselves to action."[51]

Next, Biden rewarded progressive voters by changing the names of several U.S. military bases. This had been a controversial topic, with strong racial overtones going back to the 1920s, when segregationists in Congress named many military installations in the South to honor Confederate generals. In Biden's first year in office, he established a Pentagon commission to review nine bases that had been named for Confederate leaders.

Historians had long noted that several of these bases were named during a period when Southerners were celebrating the "Lost Cause" of the Confederate army's defeat in the Civil War. The push to remove these Confederate names gained new traction in 2015, after Dylann Roof's massacre of nine Black people at the Emanuel African Methodist Episcopal Church in Charleston, South Carolina, and after Governor Nikki Haley had taken the controversial step of removing the Confederate flag from the grounds of the state capitol. In the aftermath of the Floyd killing, NASCAR had even responded by banning the display of Confederate flags at its races.

Donald Trump, on the other hand, refused to deal with calls to rename the military bases. Dodging the racial implications of bases named for Confederates, he instead turned the debate to the issue of patriotism by tweeting, "My Administration will not even consider the renaming of these Magnificent and Fabled Military Installations. Our history as the Greatest Nation in the World will not be tampered with. Respect our Military!"[52]

Trump's opposition notwithstanding, the mostly white and male military leadership did support changing the names. David Petraeus, the retired general who had been head of U.S. Central Command and later director of the CIA, wrote soon after the Floyd protests began: "The irony of training at bases named for those who took up arms against the United States, and for the right to enslave others, is inescapable to anyone paying attention. Now, belatedly, is the moment for us to pay such attention."[53] Still, nothing changed until Trump left the White House.

President Biden's secretary of defense, Lloyd Austin, a Black man and a retired general himself, quickly agreed to change the names of the nine military installations. Among the notable examples was Fort Lee in Virginia, named after Robert E. Lee, the general who led the Confederate army. The Pentagon renamed this base Fort Gregg-Adams, after two Black soldiers from the World War II era. Fort Hood in Texas (named for John Bell Hood) became Fort Cavazos, named for a Latino leader. Fort Bragg, the country's largest base, located in North Carolina (and named for Braxton Bragg), became Fort Liberty.

The Biden administration knew that in order to have a real impact on the lives of Black Americans, it had to move beyond the symbolism of new names for bases and a new federal holiday. The continued spotlight on police violence against Blacks reignited the nation's memory of its troubled history of lynching. For centuries, Black people were at risk of being grabbed on the street for any reason and hanged from trees or tortured. Lynching was a constant, visible, and vile example of a long line of racial violence used by segregationists to intimidate racial minorities. This practice was especially prevalent in the South, often taking place on hidden back roads and sometimes perpetrated by racist sheriff's departments. Efforts to declare lynching a federal crime had been stuck in Congress, where such bills had failed 250 times in more than 120 years.

Even during the height of the First Civil Rights Movement, Congress would not pass a federal anti-lynching law, despite the efforts of the NAACP, Martin Luther King Jr., and other activists. A little over a year after the 2017 Charlottesville rally, when the Democrats gained majority control of the House of Representatives, an anti-lynching bill was reintroduced, but again the effort went nowhere.

Racial violence—whether by police, hate groups, or lone gunmen—was not a thing of the past. With Trump in office, hate crimes had spiked, with an additional 450 incidents taking place from 2019 to 2020. And yet much of American society remained intent on denying the depths of the brutal problem.

With Biden in office, the effort gained new life. The bill, called the Emmett Till Antilynching Act, finally recognized the damage done by racial terrorism. Many of these murderous episodes remained lost to history. One that did not was the notorious murder of fourteen-year-old Emmett Till, who was lynched in 1955 while visiting Mississippi after allegedly whistling at a white woman. He was beaten, tied to a cotton gin, and thrown into the Tallahatchie River. His mother took his remains home to Chicago for the funeral. With the casket open, showing her son's mutilated body, mourners lined the streets of the city, and news photos of the cadaver were prominently featured in the Black press, especially *Jet* magazine.

The publicity around the Till case was extraordinary. Rarely was there such visible proof of the daily terror inflicted on racial minorities during that time—4,745 confirmed lynchings between 1882 and 1968. These killings occurred after the Civil War and do not include the violent efforts to subjugate slaves. Some of the untold stories were uncovered by the journalist Ida B. Wells, an early crusader in the 1890s, when she published her *Southern Horrors* pamphlets. Her findings suggested the larger magnitude of the fear and violence felt by minority communities, especially among Black people in the South.

The Emmett Till Antilynching Act passed the House with almost unanimous support, 422–3. The three Republicans who voted against the bill argued that it was either unnecessary or, in the words of Representative Chip Roy of Texas, that it was part of an effort by Democrats to "advance a woke agenda under the guise of correcting racial injustice." In the Senate, the bill passed by unanimous consent, which allowed Republicans to have it become law without each individual senator having to cast a vote in support of it.

It was notable that at the signing ceremony, much like the Juneteenth event, President Biden asked Vice President Harris to speak. In her remarks, she noted that the first anti-lynching proposal had reached Congress in 1900, and it failed. "Lynching is not a relic of the past," Harris said. "Racial acts of terror still occur in our nation. And when they do, we must all have the courage to name them and hold the perpetrators to account."[54]

Civil rights groups celebrated the new law. "The most transformative civil rights legislation that we have has been paid for by the blood of Black people," said Damon Hewitt, president of the Lawyers' Committee for Civil Rights Under Law. "When people talk about Black Lives Matter, that's what it means."[55]

But some members of the Second Civil Rights Movement were less effusive. Rashad Robinson noted that while Color of Change celebrated passage of the act, it had little to do with the kind of violence that had ended George Floyd's life. "While we celebrate this historic moment, we cannot pretend that the passage of this bill is an end to the ongoing violence Black people face," he said. "Seeing Congress condemn a tool of political oppression from the last century does not let them off the hook when it comes to addressing the tools of anti-Black political oppression in this century."

A year later, the history-making law had not been used to prosecute anyone, despite continued racial violence. Robinson said that the bill should be just the start of efforts to protect voting rights and urged an end to filibuster rules in the Senate, which had made it impossible to enact police reform and voting rights protection. "We must keep pushing Congress and the White House to deliver real justice for Black people," he said.[56]

It was notable that Black Lives Matter was not involved with the anti-lynching bill and had nothing to say about it once it passed. The organization became insular after the Cullors scandals and her departure, and it continued to be on the defensive, responding to lawsuits and only occasionally raising the cause of police shootings of Black people.

President Biden still faced criticism for lacking a major accomplishment that spoke for Black life in America. The moment arrived when Justice Stephen Breyer announced his retirement from the U.S. Supreme Court in January 2022.

During the South Carolina primary in 2020, Representative Clyburn had pulled Biden aside during a break in a candidates debate to insist that when he went back onstage, he should promise to appoint a Black woman to the Supreme Court. Biden, in dire need of Black support to win the nomination, did just that. "And [in response to] the very last question that was asked that night," Clyburn recalled, "he made the commitment to put a Black woman on the Supreme Court. It got the loudest applause overnight. And that's what it took to solidify support among Black women for that election."[57]

Two years later, following Justice Breyer's retirement, the question was, *Would Biden follow through?* He didn't hesitate. With Breyer by his side at the White House to announce his departure from the court, Biden immediately affirmed his pledge, saying that the nominee "will be someone with extraordinary qualifications, character, experience, and integrity—and that person will be the first Black woman ever nominated to the United States Supreme Court. It's long overdue, in my view."[58]

The court that Biden's nominee would join had a six-to-three majority of conservative justices, including three appointed by Trump. That court had issued rulings that most civil rights groups criticized, including judgments to restrict voting rights. And at the time of Breyer's departure, this conservative court was poised to overturn decades-long legal precedent on cases ranging from abortion rights to affirmative action.

Critics on right-wing cable and radio immediately complained that Biden was unfairly excluding better-qualified candidates. Senator Ted Cruz of Texas did not try to give his argument any veil of decorum, complaining that Biden was simply discriminating against white men: "He's saying, if you're a white guy, tough luck."[59] But Biden didn't budge.

Speculation immediately centered on three judges: Ketanji Brown Jackson, Leondra Kruger, and J. Michelle Childs. In some ways this was a replay of Biden's search for a Black woman to be his vice president. Harris was a U.S. senator and clearly well qualified. But she had to compete with other Black women on a short list of nominees, including two members of Congress, Val Demings and Karen Bass, not to mention the formidable Stacey Abrams.

There was an abundance of qualified candidates in the search for a

Supreme Court nominee, too. But this competition unfolded at an even more
elevated level. It wasn't just about having a strong résumé and political charisma. It also required judicial experience. This would be a lifetime appointment, and Biden needed a nominee who could immediately jump into the fray
against the court's conservative majority.

There were also politics involved. Representative Clyburn, the man
who'd thrown Biden a political lifeline with Black voters in South Carolina,
backed Judge Childs, a federal district court judge from his state. Meanwhile,
Kruger drew support from having served in the Obama Justice Department
and the fact that she'd served in the nation's biggest state as an associate justice on the California Supreme Court.

But Jackson was the front-runner. She already sat on the U.S. Court of
Appeals for the District of Columbia Circuit, which is regarded as the second
most important court in the country. A Harvard graduate and a former Supreme Court clerk, she had served on President Obama's Sentencing Commission and had been Obama's selection for a seat on the U.S. District Court.
In fact, she had been considered for an earlier vacancy on the Supreme Court
in 2016, after the death of Justice Antonin Scalia.

"For too long our government, our courts, haven't looked like America,"
Biden said while nominating Jackson. "I believe it is time that we have a court
that reflects the full talents and greatness of our nation."[60] Even Black Lives
Matter could not dismiss her nomination as symbolic, writing in a statement,
"This is huge—because this takes us on the road to finally ending the 230
years of Black women's exclusion from the Supreme Court."[61]

The hearings were quick and uneventful, with the notable exception of
Jackson being constantly interrupted by Republican white men. There was
one memorable exchange with Senator Ted Cruz. He questioned her role as a
board member of a private school in Washington that allowed books on racial
issues into its curriculum. Holding up a copy of *Antiracist Baby* by Ibram X.
Kendi, he asked Jackson: "Do you agree with this book that is being taught
with kids that babies are racist?"

In front of the cameras and microphones in the Senate hearing room, she
smirked and sighed loudly. "Senator, I do not believe that any child should

be made to feel as though they are racist, or though they are not valued, or though they are less than, that they are victims, that they are oppressors. I do not believe in any of that."[62]

Despite the conservative attempts to portray her as less qualified and pursuing a left-wing agenda, she was confirmed by a vote of 53–47. Only three Republicans supported her.

Unlike anything else Biden had done since the election, putting Ketanji Brown Jackson on the Supreme Court was celebrated across Black America, with her appointment resonating especially among Black women. Their power within the Democratic Party as the most reliable bloc of voters had garnered a major victory.

Jackson's appointment was also widely hailed among civil rights groups and activists of all ages and races. Stacey Abrams captured the historic moment in a euphoric response: "Representation matters. We dismiss it when it feels too obvious. . . . But it matters, it matters to have a black woman on the U.S. Supreme Court."[63]

Jackson cheerfully exalted after her confirmation as well, saying, "It has taken 232 years and 115 prior appointments for a Black woman to be selected to serve on the Supreme Court of the United States, but we've made it! We've made it—all of us."[64]

Getting Justice Jackson on the court was a real victory for the Second Civil Rights Movement, just as getting Thurgood Marshall on the court was a victory for the First Civil Rights Movement. It was also the logical next chapter after the victory that triggered the Second Civil Rights Movement—the election of Barack Obama.

Despite the protestations of Trump's rearguard defenders still in Congress, Biden had succeeded in enacting a number of changes, both symbolic and substantive. But while things were moving ahead on the federal level, a new fight was under way, mostly in Republican-controlled red states and cities. Their "anti-woke" grassroots revolution was the new phase of the battle over shifting racial demographics in a growing culture war.

10

THE BLOWUP

From the outside, Black Lives Matter looked strong in the early 2020s. After its successful, massive protests against the killing of George Floyd, the organization remained supremely well funded, with tens of millions of dollars in the bank and control of the most recognized slogan in the Second Civil Rights Movement. The relative quiet from the group when a Black woman took a seat on the Supreme Court set off no alarms. The organization's lack of attention to Congress passing historic anti-lynching legislation also went largely unremarked upon because the media expected protests, not lobbying, from BLM.

But behind that proud, business-as-usual face, Black Lives Matter was imploding. The organization was preoccupied with lawsuits coming from its own chapters and was spending its energy and time hiding from questions about how the tens of millions donated to the group had been spent.

Other negatives tore away at its heart as well.

Black Lives Matter had never effectively replaced its three founders. It never built a team of people, an institutional structure, to sustain its status as a leading actor in the Second Civil Rights Movement. Its failing in-house operations limited its work on creating allies. It certainly did not build lasting bridges to the Hispanic community, the country's largest minority group. And at a time of a surge in Black immigration, Black Lives Matter never effectively welcomed immigrants from Africa, Asia, the Caribbean, and Latin America into the Second Civil Rights Movement. They missed another opportunity by not forming strategic alliances with established and larger women's organizations, which could have bolstered their profile.

But among all the stumbles, the most troubling were the financial scandals. Critics who opposed Black Lives Matter's racial justice agenda jumped on tax records that revealed an alarming sloppiness, if not corruption. By 2023, the organization had experienced a huge drop in donations. BLM took in nearly $100 million following the George Floyd protests; three years later, they could not even raise $9 million. Two thirds of their previous donations had already been spent on questionable expenses, including payments to friends and relatives of the group's leaders.[1]

Conservative media outlets and websites feasted on the damaging news about Black Lives Matter. The organization settled into a defensive posture, keeping a low profile to avoid the frenzied attention to its troubled financial picture. Opinion polls showed that large percentages of Americans still approved of the Black Lives Matter movement and supported the racial justice appeals behind it. But the group's potential to be a social justice leader was bleeding out, its muscle withering even as the hashtag #BlackLivesMatter remained popular.

Black Lives Matter's public image of rising above politics to speak to injustice was also sinking, as a consequence of rising polarization between Democrats and Republicans. Polls showed more than 80 percent of Democrats approved of the organization and its goals, but more than 80 percent of Republicans opposed it. Across party lines there was one critical point of agreement—only 32 percent thought Black Lives Matter had been effective in improving the lives of Black Americans.[2]

There were even questions about Black Lives Matter's impact in its principal area of focus: police violence against Black people. These concerns grew in 2023, when an unarmed Black man, Tyre Nichols, was brutally beaten to death by five Black police officers in Memphis. This high-profile killing in a majority-Black city demonstrated that the issue had not gone away. Patrisse

Cullors, one of Black Lives Matter's cofounders, called Nichols's killing a "reminder that the people who hold the power have chosen not to wield it on
behalf of Black life. They've chosen to side with violent police forces."

Ten years after the organization first came on the scene, Cullors was full
of regrets. She acknowledged that looking back on the birth of the group
"feels like a painful reminder of what hasn't changed."[3] Beginning with the
acquittal of George Zimmerman in Trayvon Martin's killing and continuing
through George Floyd's violent death, an unprecedented amount of money
had flowed into Black Lives Matter. At the end of a decade of prosperity and
media influence, Cullors now admitted she had been unprepared to handle
the deluge of what she angrily, defensively, and rudely derided as "white guilt
money."[4]

The decline of Black Lives Matter had been evident over the preced-
ing year. During the 2022 midterm election campaign, the organization was
pushed to the fringe of the national debate about politics and even racial issues. Historical trends and polls suggested that the Democrats were likely
to lose majority control of the House and Senate. But Black Lives Matter
showed no interest in rising to the political challenge and coming to the res-
cue by working as part of the Democrats' political coalition. This persistent
lack of political engagement by Black Lives Matter spoke to the organization's
inability to grow and mature.

Black Lives Matter was further marginalized in June 2022, when the Supreme Court overruled *Roe v. Wade* and ended the constitutionally protected
right to abortion access. In *Dobbs v. Jackson Women's Health Organization*,
the nation's highest court said that individual states now had the right to per-
mit or outlaw the procedure as they chose. This upended nearly fifty years of
American constitutional law.

Democrats immediately made protecting abortion rights their top issue
in the coming elections. The outcry over loss of abortion rights overshadowed attention to issues of race and police violence, which had helped turn
out the party's base in 2020.

Intent on distracting women voters from the court's decision to end
abortion rights, the Republican Party launched a series of attacks on gay and

transgender rights. They also started banning books that dealt with LGBTQ issues. These culture wars extended to Republican-led opposition to Covid mandates requiring masks or vaccinations. And the party plunged into conspiracy theories about the 2020 presidential election having been stolen from Donald Trump and Republicans, a claim for which no evidence was ever provided. The party's talking points also included frequent mention of "Defund the Police" and sinister references to Black Lives Matter designed to trigger fear of crime spreading beyond Black neighborhoods to white business districts and suburbs.

Republican candidates also made a big deal of their opposition to affirmative action and diversity, equity, and inclusion workplace training. These programs got hammered on the right for, as their opponents characterized it, making it harder for white students to gain admission to selective public high schools and prestigious colleges, and for making it harder for white workers to be hired and to compete for pay raises and promotion. Polls showed that a majority of Republicans agreed with the "replacement theory" assertion that Democrats, from Soros to Obama to Biden, intended to replace white people as the nation's majority population with an influx of Latino and Asian immigrants as well as Blacks, all of whom have a history of voting for Democrats. Conservatives spoke about racial minorities undoing white American culture and traditions.

In this racially charged atmosphere, Black Lives Matter became a high-visibility scapegoat for the Republicans. Surveys by the Pew Research Center showed that while whites remained the majority in both political parties, in the 2022 election, 85 percent of Republican voters were white, whereas the white majority among Democrats was joined by a base of multiracial voters sympathetic to the ideas and racial conversations prompted by Black Lives Matter to win elections. Pew found that well over 60 percent of Black, Latino, and Asian voters were Democrats.[5]

But for Democrats courting the votes of white moderates, particularly in competitive states, the party's connection to Black Lives Matter became a burden. Every Democratic candidate had to respond to Republicans tying them to the slogan "Defund the Police." Repeating that phrase in white, suburban swing districts was a surefire way to stir anxiety about Democrats doing away with police. That fear was good for Republicans. None of it was good for the Democrats, or for Black Lives Matter, which did not respond to these attacks.

Additional Republican fearmongering centered on the claim that white children were being taught to be ashamed of being white. Republican candidates charged that schoolbooks were promoting the idea that every white child had responsibility for slavery and shared blame for "systemic racial discrimination" in present-day America. With Black Lives Matter protests fading from the streets, Republicans had an open road to change the subject of national media attention from police violence to Critical Race Theory and the idea that this radical ideology was infecting the country's schools, culture, and corporations.

The race-centered culture wars took flight in Florida under its Republican governor, Ron DeSantis. Working with the Republican majority in the Florida state legislature, he passed the Stop WOKE Act in 2022, which explicitly banned workplace and classroom discussions about concepts that were characterized as "inherently racist, sexist, or oppressive, whether consciously or unconsciously." The legislation pushed back against what DeSantis termed "woke indoctrination" and Critical Race Theory.[6]

In reality, Critical Race Theory is a postgraduate-level concept and had never been a feature of American education in elementary or high schools. What began as a theory discussed in law schools about the widespread impact of "systemic racism" was rarely even taught in undergraduate courses, let alone to school-age children.

Meanwhile, the term "stay woke" was Black slang going back to the 1930s. It meant remaining "vigilant against the threat of racist violence."[7] Eighty years later, being "woke" gained new currency during the Ferguson protests and exploded as part of the national lexicon after the George Floyd protests. DeSantis's "anti-woke" efforts reflected a broad conservative push against focusing on racial issues. The Florida governor began a run for the Republican presidential nomination in 2024 by tapping into these culture war emotions to reach a national audience.

His efforts were shaped with the help of a right-wing provocateur named

Christopher Rufo. An obscure documentary filmmaker, Rufo burst onto the scene in 2020 when he wrote an essay for the Manhattan Institute, a conservative think tank, claiming that Black Lives Matter undermined American culture by demonizing white people. He appeared on a Fox News program where he railed against Critical Race Theory, claiming that it "pervaded every aspect of the federal government," as well as corporations, media, and academia.[8]

"This is an existential threat to the United States," Rufo told a prime-time Fox audience. "And the bureaucracy, even under Trump, is being weaponized against core American values." The next morning, Trump's chief of staff, Mark Meadows, called Rufo to ask him to give the White House information about federal agencies that were using diversity programs that vilified white people. Three weeks later, the Trump administration suspended all diversity training across the government.[9]

In truth, *The Wall Street Journal* reported, the information that Rufo provided to the White House did not back up his claim that the federal government was making white people out to be demons.[10]

For years, Trump and DeSantis supporters had been looking for a way to counter the continued popularity of Black Lives Matter. Rufo made the connection, tying Critical Race Theory to Black Lives Matter, saying that the protest movement was a cover for peddling an insidious leftist ideology. "School districts across the country suddenly started adopting 'equity statements,' hiring 'diversity and inclusion' bureaucrats, and injecting heavily political content into the curriculum," he wrote.

Rufo credited Trump's work to stop diversity programs in the federal government as a first step in the movement against Critical Race Theory. It was also the "most successful counterattack against BLM as a political movement. We shifted the terrain and fought on a vector the Left could not successfully mobilize against," he said.[11]

Rufo contrasted Black Lives Matter with the First Civil Rights Movement, which he said had championed freedom and equity. Now, he argued, Black Lives Matter and the Second Civil Rights Movement were advancing a Marxist political and economic agenda. They would destroy, he said, "the remaining structure of the Constitution." He also critiqued Critical Race Theory as a backdoor effort to push the federal government to pay reparations to Blacks for slavery. He even proposed that it might be an effort to undo property rights if they proved harmful to minorities.

He charged that anyone raising concerns about Black Lives Matter's progressive ideology was suddenly "getting mobbed on social media, fired from their jobs, or worse, they remained quiet" for fear of being accused of having unconscious bias or being called a racist. To his thinking, Black Lives Matter activists were using "cancel culture" to silence conservatives.[12]

Despite a lack of evidence that these accusations accurately reflected reality, Rufo's theories were celebrated among conservatives for framing arguments against diversity and inclusion training. Rufo criticized the Walt Disney Company, the largest employer in the state of Florida, for promoting corporate diversity training. DeSantis picked up on Rufo's campaign against Disney as he began his presidential campaign.

Rufo also urged the governor to dismantle diversity offices within state government and at state universities. DeSantis then put Rufo on the board of the state-funded New College, promising to transform it from a decidedly progressive college into an ultraconservative institution. "We are recapturing higher education," Rufo tweeted after his appointment.[13]

Rufo's work with DeSantis in Florida became a model for similar culture-war initiatives in other states with Republican governors or legislatures. At least a dozen states banned Critical Race Theory in public schools.

Rufo, DeSantis, and others in the conservative media aggressively asserted that white people were being demonized in classrooms by Critical Race Theory. They used that fear to justify bans on books that dealt with race, both in the classroom and in public libraries. Banned titles included the *New York Times*'s *1619 Project*, the Nobel laureate Toni Morrison's *The Bluest Eye*, and *The Handmaid's Tale* by Margaret Atwood. The censorship also extended to newer books that dealt with sexual confusion in adolescents, especially those exploring LGBTQ issues, such as *Gender Queer, Flamer*, and *This Book Is Gay*. In addition to the book bans, ten states passed laws that limited treatment for young people questioning their sexual and gender identities, especially transgender youth. They also banned trans girls from competing in girls' sports and prohibited gender-neutral bathrooms.

Rufo's work against Critical Race Theory prompted a group of conservative parents in Florida to take the fight to local school boards. Moms for Liberty, formed in Brevard County, began protesting mandates that children wear masks or receive the Covid vaccine. They saw vaccine mandates as a left-wing edict to control America's children. More than one hundred chapters of Moms for Liberty quickly sprang up around the country. Florida activists Tiffany Justice, Tina Descovich, and Bridget Ziegler described their new movement as "ready to fight those that stand in the way of liberty."[14] Ziegler openly credited Moms for Liberty as a new way to energize women to become Republican voters, and her husband, Christian Ziegler, later became head of the state Republican Party.

After several members of Ziegler's group won school board elections in Sarasota, pictures appeared online showing Zeigler and a large group of parents with members of the Proud Boys flashing white supremacist hand gestures. The Southern Poverty Law Center, which listed Moms for Liberty as an extremist group, noted that its social media posts and programs were in line with conspiracy propaganda, specifically opposition to LGBTQ rights. SPLC reported that some of the group's members had called law enforcement with the claim that children were being sexualized in school and were "pushing into the area of QAnon conspiracies of children being groomed by progressives."[15]

Ziegler's husband was forced to resign as chair of the Florida Republican Party after a woman charged him with rape. Those charges were later dropped, but it was revealed that he and his wife had engaged in a threesome involving another woman. The revelation was humiliating for Ziegler, who had hypocritically pushed "traditional values" and the anti-LGBTQ agenda on the school board and as a member of Moms for Liberty.[16]

Groups similar to Moms for Liberty sprang up in Virginia and helped propel the election of the Republican candidate Glenn Youngkin as governor in 2021. That summer, one person was arrested and another injured as

right-wing activists turned a school board meeting into a brawl in suburban
Loudon County. The activists were protesting accommodations for trans-
gender students, but they principally decried the teaching of Critical Race
Theory, even as the school board assured parents that no schools taught it.

Youngkin used the phrase "Parents Matter," a takeoff on Black Lives
Matter, as a loaded campaign slogan, pledging to "ban teaching critical race
theory in our schools." In a state that was evenly divided between the two parties, he rode a wave of local resentment aimed at school administration and
teachers unions to a victory.[17]

Youngkin's first act as governor was to issue an executive order banning
Critical Race Theory. "Political indoctrination has no place in our classrooms," he said. "Inherently divisive concepts, like Critical Race Theory and
its progeny, instruct students to only view life through the lens of race and
presume that some students are consciously or unconsciously racist, sexist,
or oppressive, and that other students are victims."[18]

Right-wing extremists continued to threaten school board members well
beyond Florida and Virginia. Reuters reported that in 2022 there were more
than 220 threats targeting thirty-three school board members across fifteen
states.[19] The Justice Department decried such intimidation of school board
members, but the aggressive right-wing activism continued to spread. It was
politically potent and led many Republican governors to follow DeSantis by
pushing similar "anti-woke" legislation in Georgia, Alabama, Louisiana, Arkansas, Texas, and Missouri. These developments led to a renewed fight over
voting rights. White conservatives dominated politics in these mostly Southern states, which also had large Black populations. The anti–Critical Race
Theory and anti-LGBTQ fights became part of the white conservative effort
to hold on to political power in the face of a potential wave of Black votes
against them.

In Washington, Biden's signature voting rights bills remained stalled in
Congress, where the threat of Republican filibusters in the Senate prevented
any progress. Ten years after the Supreme Court's 2013 decision in *Shelby
County v. Holder*, when the Court ruled that states with a history of discriminating against Black voters no longer needed federal approval under the

Voting Rights Act to change their voting laws, even if those changes depressed minority voting, the Brennan Center for Justice reported that eleven states had enacted laws making it harder to vote. In contrast, thirteen states, led by Democrats, had expanded voting rights by extending days for voting and increasing the number of polling places.

As this tug-of-war took place among the states over access to the polls, a separate fight broke out after the 2020 U.S. Census as state legislatures drew new maps for congressional districts.

Alabama got the most national attention for its controversial redistricting plan. The state's population was 27 percent Black, but the Republican state legislature drew a map where only one of the state's seven congressional districts had a Black majority. Evan Milligan, the head of a new-generation coalition of civil rights groups called Alabama Forward, led a challenge to the map. The NAACP Legal Defense Fund litigated the case, *Allen v. Milligan*, all the way to the Supreme Court.

But this was not the First Civil Rights Movement pushing for racial integration. This was a new generation of racial strategists whose priority was to concentrate Black voters in congressional districts so they could elect Black officials. Integration was now on a back burner.

In a surprise 5–4 decision—a surprise given the Court's conservative majority—the justices ruled that the remaining protections of the Voting Rights Act required Alabama's legislature to stop splitting up Black populations across the state and to create a second Black-majority district.

The decision brought to light a stark division between the two Black justices. Justice Ketanji Brown Jackson, the celebrated newcomer nominated by Biden, voted with the majority. She said during oral arguments that the Voting Rights Act was intended to make Black Americans "equal to white citizens." But Justice Clarence Thomas wrote a heated dissent. He called the case a "disastrous misadventure" in pursuit of equal rights. Even though race was a protected class under the Voting Rights Act, Thomas argued that the "racial sorting" of voters was wrong. He viewed racial minorities as no different from any other minorities in American society, including those not protected by law, "from environmentalists in Alaska to Republicans in Massachusetts."[20]

After the Court's ruling, however, the Alabama legislature refused to fix its illegal congressional districts. Instead, the legislature created a second district that was just 40 percent Black, which was also ruled to be insufficient by an appeals court—a judgment later affirmed by the U.S. Supreme Court. This set up a standoff between the Alabama legislature and the Supreme Court, which resulted in a second 48 percent Black district. The fight was similar to the "Massive Resistance" of the 1950s, when Southern states (like Alabama) refused to go along with school integration. Back then, white legislators also refused to comply with a Supreme Court ruling. In those cases, Alabama was forced to finally integrate its schools.

The division on the Court over voting rights was a reminder of the unfulfilled goals of the First Civil Rights Movement. And the debate had little to do with the central actors in the Second Civil Rights Movement, President Barack Obama and Black Lives Matter. Things would come to a head in the Supreme Court's decision to revisit its jurisprudence on affirmative action in the 2022–23 term.

The concept of affirmative action was more than sixty years old, having been established in the first days of the Kennedy administration. Soon after taking office, John F. Kennedy signed an executive order calling on the federal government contractors to "take affirmative action to ensure that applicants are employed, and employees are treated [fairly] during employment, without regard to their race, creed, color, or national origin."[21] Kennedy's order did not mandate any requirements or goals for hiring by the federal government or private employers. Over the next decade, affirmative action was expanded under Democratic president Lyndon Johnson and Republican president Richard Nixon.

But affirmative action was unpopular with the public, despite gaining bipartisan support for passage in Congress and from presidents of both parties. Gallup polling in the 1970s showed only 10 percent of Americans agreed with the notion of giving "preferential treatment in getting jobs and places in college."[22] Most said that test scores and past accomplishments should be the basis for admission or hiring, not quotas or purely racial preferences designed to correct past discrimination. Conservatives argued that affirmative action broke with the central tenet of American individual rights, as stated in the Declaration of Independence's claim that all men are created equal.

The clash of ideals led to an early legal test when a white engineer and former Marine, Allan Bakke, applied to the medical school at the University of California, Davis, but was turned down. He argued that he had been rejected because of a university policy to hold sixteen seats at the medical school for Black applicants, and he sued to be admitted.

In 1978, in a 5–4 decision, the Supreme Court found that the university's racial quotas were unconstitutional. The only Black justice on the court, Thurgood Marshall, voted in favor of affirmative action as a necessary corrective for past discrimination. In a memo to the other justices, he wrote: "It must be remembered that during most of the past 200 years, the Constitution as interpreted by this Court did not prohibit the most ingenious and pervasive forms of discrimination against the Negro. Now when the state acts to remedy the effects of that legacy of discrimination, I cannot believe that this same Constitution stands as a barrier."[23]

While Marshall did not carry the day on the idea of legalizing the use of quotas, he was able to convince a majority to agree that the race of applicants could be considered as a compelling interest, such as a university's desire to have a diverse student body. The court endorsed Marshall's view that preparing top students to succeed in an increasingly diverse country required a consideration of race.

The practice of including race as a factor in university admissions held for forty-five years, until two cases came before the Supreme Court for oral argument in the fall of 2022. The cases were brought by conservative activists who argued that affirmative action plans at the University of North Carolina and Harvard University discriminated against Asian and white students. The ruling, issued on June 29, 2023, overturned nearly a half century of decisions allowing affirmative action and signaled a further consolidation of the power of the new conservative majority on the court.

A key precedent used by the justices in outlawing affirmative action was the 2003 case *Grutter v. Bollinger*. In that decision, Justice Sandra Day

O'Connor wrote that "25 years from now, the use of racial preferences will no longer be necessary."[24] O'Connor's decision was certainly reflected in terms of public opinion. Just as polling had found in the 1970s, a majority of Americans remained strongly opposed to affirmative action for university admissions, with 69 percent saying that they did not agree with schools using race as a factor. However, Americans showed much more support for general programs to help minorities, such as internships and apprenticeships, with 49 percent giving their approval.[25]

The two Black justices, who had split on the Alabama voter redistricting case, once again were at odds. In her dissenting opinion, Justice Ketanji Brown Jackson wrote that the majority wanted to look away from "the elephant in the room—the race-linked disparities that continue to impede achievement of our Nation's full potential." As Marshall had argued four decades earlier, Jackson felt that having diverse college campus populations carried "universal benefits" for the country in helping promote racial progress. Both she and Justice Clarence Thomas had been beneficiaries of affirmative action at Ivy League law schools.

But Thomas viewed affirmative action as a burden for its Black beneficiaries, saying that it was a stigma because whites assumed he was less intelligent or capable. Jackson, on the other hand, thought it was a plus in a society burdened with a long history of racial bias. She wrote that Thomas's thinking, shared by the conservative majority, "blinks both history and reality in ways too numerous to count. . . . Our country has never been colorblind." Interestingly, though the lawsuit was about white and Asian students claiming discrimination, Justice Jackson only refers to "Asians" twice in her dissent. In her references to race, she mentioned Black thirty-six times, indicating her focus on combating the historic as well as ongoing discrimination against Black students.[26]

Their argument over America's tortured history of race became personal. For the first time in his thirty-two-year career, Thomas read his decision from the bench. "Treating anyone differently based on skin color is oppression," he told his fellow justices, as well as the rows of the packed onlookers in the chamber.

His opinion called out Justice Jackson directly: "As she sees things, we are all inexorably trapped in a fundamentally racist society, with the original sin of slavery and the historical subjugation of black Americans still determining our lives today." He added: "Justice Jackson uses her broad observations about statistical relationships between race and select measures of health, wealth, and well-being to label all blacks as victims. Her desire to do so is unfathomable to me."

Thomas's disdain continued, as he accused Jackson of putting Black people in a "seemingly perpetual inferior caste."

Without calling out Thomas in the same bitter tone, Jackson wrote in a footnote that he was the one who was lost, trapped in "an obsession with race consciousness that far outstrips my [argument] . . . that race can be a factor that affects applicants' unique life experiences."[27]

The right-wing decision, though unwelcome, did produce a moment of unity across the generations of civil rights leaders. Organizations with their origins in the First Civil Rights Movement were quick to criticize the decision. Derrick Johnson, the president of the NAACP, called it the work of an "extremist minority." He said that "in a society still scarred by the wounds of racial disparities, the Supreme Court has displayed a willful ignorance of our reality."[28]

The Urban League, the NAACP Legal Defense Fund, and the National Action Network also denounced the ruling, and they were joined by newer voices from the Second Civil Rights Movement. Beyond the Black community, UnidosUS, Asian Americans Advancing Justice, and the Mexican American Legal Defense and Educational Fund came together to call the decision a "distressing reminder of the uphill battle we continue to face in dismantling systemic racism."[29]

Notably absent, though, was Black Lives Matter, which had nothing to say on the decision. This had become an unyielding pattern. Beyond police violence, Black Lives Matter never successfully addressed the multiple political and legal issues that confronted minorities in America. Black Lives Matter never rose to the fight as the courts stripped away affirmative action programs, missing in action just as it had been on the issues of redistricting and voter suppression.

Other new organizations in the Second Civil Rights Movement faced similar troubles. The group Color of Change initially had great success in calling attention to right-wing media that promoted negative racial stereotypes through "reality" crime shows like *Cops*. It also had success in calling corporations to account for funding far-right organizations that promoted voter suppression and other racially regressive policies at the state and local level. But it never lived up to its promise to harness the online activism of a new generation seeking to force greater social and political change on major racial issues. Like Black Lives Matter, it suffered from internal dissension ranging from charges of poor financial controls to bullying and even discrimination against women. But unlike Black Lives Matter, this group was more open in acknowledging its problems. "COC's startup culture and systems didn't always meet the demands of the large organization," wrote members of the organization's board in 2023.[30]

There were disappointments among other groups in the Second Civil Rights Movement as well.

For example, the Center for Antiracist Research, a prominent academic institution founded at Boston University by the best-selling author Ibram X. Kendi, had been established with as much as an estimated $50 million in funding in the aftermath of George Floyd's murder. Its stated goal was to "understand, explain and solve seemingly intractable problems of racial inequity and injustice."[31] Yet three years later, the center made front-page headlines for massive staff cuts and for eliminating most of its programs. The *New York Times* columnist Michelle Goldberg observed that there were "considerable questions about what's been accomplished with all that money."[32] There were reports circulated of bickering among academics, many of them Black, who questioned Kendi's leadership. The center's effectiveness was also drowned out by a vagueness in its mission, which never resulted in new academic fields of study on race and only limited research.

Even on the political level, progressive members of Congress, like those in the Squad, could not counter the power and visibility of conservative actors in Washington. They were unable to overcome Senate opposition to pass voting rights legislation or to counter voter suppression efforts. Even after the massive George Floyd protests generated tremendous public support, they were unable to enact police reform, which also hit a roadblock in the Senate. They found time to hold several hearings on establishing a commission to examine whether reparations should be paid to Black Americans to compensate for damage done by slavery, but this effort also led nowhere. Their one legislative victory was the anti-lynching law—a big win after 120 years of effort, but one that felt like leftover work from the First Civil Rights Movement.

Meanwhile, conservatives continued to take pleasure in any missteps made by civil rights groups, loudly countering the argument that the George Floyd protests had brought about a time of racial reckoning. When news broke of the management and financial troubles at the Center for Antiracist Research, Christopher Rufo gleefully tweeted: "It's time for a full investigation into the center's finances. What happened to the $30 million it received?"[33]

On the level of presidential politics, Donald Trump remained the dominant actor among Republicans, and he continued to foment white racial grievance. He was leading the party toward more extreme stances and policies on subjects ranging from race to immigration to gender identity. And his dominance of right-wing media guaranteed support for his lies and appeals to racial division.

This was the landscape as the country moved toward the pivotal 2024 presidential election. Overcoming it was part of the unfinished challenges facing the Second Civil Rights Movement: instituting police reform, confronting voter suppression, and promoting diversity and equity initiatives in an era when affirmative action is no longer constitutional. (Although as Michelle Obama noted at the 2024 DNC, "the affirmative action of generational wealth," which primarily benefits white Americans, remains fully intact.)

Though the Second Civil Rights Movement was far from completing its agenda, it had still achieved remarkable success. In generational terms, it caused a wave of awareness of ongoing racial inequality to flow through the nation's cultural and social life, starting with Barack Obama's election and growing with the rise of Black Lives Matter. The existence of a more diverse America made the historic fight all the more urgent.

The aging white majority of the country struggled with these major cultural changes. White people, especially less educated, older, and more rural white people, were unable or unwilling to adjust to the new reality of an America that included more people with accented voices, some not even speaking English. There was a new prominence for Black voices, previously muted, calling attention to racial disparities in police violence and other racial injustice, and being celebrated for doing so.

In September 2023, on the sixtieth anniversary of the segregationist bombing that killed four Black girls at a church in Birmingham, Alabama, a leading light of the Second Civil Rights Movement was the featured speaker at a memorial service. "Our past is filled with too much violence, too much hatred, too much prejudice, but can we really say that we are not confronting those same evils now?" asked Justice Ketanji Brown Jackson. "We have to own even the darkest parts of our past, understand them, and vow never to repeat them."

At a time when books on Black history were being banned, Justice Jackson made the case for the value of history, no matter how painful, as necessary for the nation's future success.

"Atrocities like the one we are memorializing today are difficult to remember and relive, but I also know that it is dangerous to forget them," the justice said. "We cannot forget because the uncomfortable lessons are often the ones that teach us the most about ourselves. . . . We cannot learn from past mistakes we do not know exist."

Justice Jackson's remarks included a reference to maintaining the ability to "mark forward progress" on civil rights. She was speaking at the site of a racist attack that took place in 1963, almost one hundred years after the end of the Civil War. She was also speaking more than four hundred years after African slaves first came to the American colonies.[34]

Over those centuries, progress on race relations had been a jagged line of ups and downs, from slavery to Reconstruction to Jim Crow to the First Civil Rights Movement, and on to the first Black president and the struggles of today. But through it all, the one constant was action, people standing up for what was right.

As Frederick Douglass said before the Civil War, "Power concedes nothing without a demand. It never did and it never will."[35] The Second Civil Rights Movement made that demand. From Obama's presidency to the Black Lives Matter protests, the Second Civil Rights Movement's legacy is having changed the conversation about race in America and forced more accountability for racist behavior and policy.

It will eventually make way for a Third Civil Rights Movement. That Third Movement will face its own unique cultural, demographic, and political challenges, another phase in history as it demands change to fulfill the promise of life, liberty, and the pursuit of happiness—for all Americans.

CONCLUSION

What Comes Next

In May 2016, during the last year of his presidency, Barack Obama, the man whose rise in national politics marked the start of the Second Civil Rights Movement, gave the commencement address at Howard University. To most observers, it seemed like a victory lap for the first Black president.

But in fact, Obama was addressing an audience that put him face-to-face with people questioning the promise of a post-racial society. These young people were living through the Second Civil Rights Movement, and they wondered why so little had changed in America with the first Black president. They had only just started high school when Obama's election pumped up their hopes of a new morning for Blacks in America. Then they were traumatized by Trayvon Martin's murder and the Ferguson riots. New reasons for hope again filled their hearts and minds with the explosive success of Black Lives Matter. And all along they marched into a new church of activism, faithful people taking part in a conversation on Black Twitter about better days to come. Yet as they sat in their college graduation regalia listening to Obama, they were experiencing a threatening spike in white grievance that was driving the political rise of Donald Trump. Their social media feeds were full of stories about the resurgence of outright white supremacy.

So, despite Obama's election, despite Black Lives Matter, these educated young Black people were fatigued by the daily reality of ongoing racism in American life. They respected Obama but had questions about racial progress.

"Let me say something that may be controversial," Obama told the graduates, "and that is this: America is a better place today than it was when I graduated from college [in 1983]." The president cited lower poverty rates, lower crime rates, more women with jobs, more Black high school graduates, and Black college graduation rates rising from 10 percent in 1983 to more than 20 percent in 2016. It was impossible, Obama said, to deny the amazing work done to improve racial equality by "your mothers and your dads, and grandparents and great-grandparents, who marched and toiled and suffered and overcame to make this day possible."

But Obama did not paint a totally rosy picture. "I am not saying gaps do not persist," he went on. "Obviously, they do. Racism persists. Inequality persists." Still, he told his audience that despite challenges they faced, there was no better time for them to be coming of age. "If you had to choose a time to be, in the words of Lorraine Hansberry, 'young, gifted, and black' in America, you would choose right now," the president said to applause.

Obama warned any impatient listeners to take a step back and look at the bigger picture. He wanted them to recognize that in their short lifetimes the nation had been pushed to higher levels of racial awareness and empathy than ever before. He argued that the students had played a role in successfully making America more woke when it came to racial wrongs, and that they should take pride in their idealism and their progress in creating a "more perfect union." Obama saluted them as part of the Second Civil Rights Movement.

"It's thanks in large part to the activism of young people like many of you, from Black Twitter to Black Lives Matter, that America's eyes have been opened—white, Black, Democrat, Republican—to the real problems, for example, in our criminal justice system," Obama said. But he warned them that "awareness is not enough" and that more was required: mobilization, votes, persistence, and further changes in the law to address deep structural disadvantages for the poor, immigrants, women, Blacks, and other racial minorities. You need "not just hashtags, but votes," he said.[1]

Commenting on the evident tension separating Obama from many young Black people listening to him, Al Sharpton said, "I understood the [young people's] pain, but I think that it was misguided. Because what we ended up getting, we ended up getting Donald Trump. So, the question is, was Barack Obama everything that we wanted? Maybe not. Was he your best alternative . . . ? Absolutely. And I think politics is about being able to advance the ball. And I think they're not going to score a touchdown every time but when you get some yards toward the goal line, you take them."[2]

From a veteran political perspective, Congressman Jim Clyburn agreed with Sharpton. He said that "Obama had the weight of history on his shoulders. And I think that he had to be strategic in doing and saying things. . . . Everybody wants fast food and instant gratification over here."[3]

In spite of Trump's eventual rise to the White House, Obama laid the foundation for Joe Biden's election in 2020, which came with the first Black woman to serve as vice president and the appointment of the first Black woman to the Supreme Court. Obama also achieved the lowest level of Black unemployment in fifty years and spearheaded health care legislation that was the biggest help for the poor since the Great Society.

Obama hit the nail on the head in his Howard speech. His presidency, Black Lives Matter, and even the Trump backlash are all essential parts of the Second Civil Rights Movement. And today's movement is making progress.

The young Howard graduates who listened to Obama, now in their thirties, may be understandably impatient with what they see as slow-moving change. But no matter the speed, it is also true that they are living through an epoch of historic impact.

Just as the First Civil Rights Movement ignited the national consciousness—the defiant Rosa Parks refusing to give up her bus seat to a white man and the brave John Lewis being beaten bloody as he marched for voting rights—Obama's appeal across racial lines caused the Second Civil Rights Movement to catch fire. He spoke to the reality of so many Black men being sent to jail, so many bad public schools, the harsh reality of low pay for most Black workers, and shocking cases of police violence against Black people. Current demands for racial equality are clearly built on the work of earlier generations that began the fight by breaking through even more severe segregation. People working for racial justice today have a legitimate claim as leading figures in the next chapter in the history of civil rights struggles.

"I think the impact of the Trayvon Martin case was very significant. It raised the consciousness level in America," said the noted civil rights attorney Ben Crump, who played an important role in many of the police violence cases that were the hallmark of the Second Civil Rights Movement. Crump saw progress even when Trayvon Martin's family lost its fight to get the man who shot their son convicted of murder. It was a step forward, Crump said, because the fury generated by the teenager's tragic death had a significant impact on public opinion. It launched Black Lives Matter, pushing the Second Civil Rights Movement and racial justice to the forefront of the larger society.

"I think Emmett Till is one of those cases. I think Rodney King was one of those cases. I believe Trayvon Martin was one of those cases," he continued. "And because of Trayvon Martin, we see other landmark cases like George Floyd, Ahmaud Arbery. You know, without Trayvon Martin, and there's no way you get police officers convicted" in the George Floyd case and other police brutality cases.[4]

It can be hard to see the Second Civil Rights Movement's achievements through the blizzard of constant backlash, especially the rising public profile of white supremacists. That understandably leads to frustration among young people looking for quick results. But they are wrong to think of the backlash as evidence of failure or diminishing the value of their entire movement. It is simply another phase in a long-term fight, a struggle across time for equal rights. It stands in line with "Massive Resistance," the historic backlash the First Civil Rights Movement dealt with after the Supreme Court's ruling in *Brown v. Board of Education* in 1954.

Wayne Frederick, the president of Howard University when Obama spoke in 2016, saw the issues of race and American democracy as a pendulum. "It corrects based on what has happened before," he said. "So, the reality is that you don't have an Obama if you did not have a George W. Bush," he said, referring to the economic troubles at the end of Bush's tenure as well as an unpopular, lingering war effort in Afghanistan. "He gives rise to an Obama and Obama gives rise to a Trump. Whether or not we like that or not, it's a reality."[5]

The truth is that civil rights activism is never finished. Trump's 2016 campaign exploited white grievances and delighted in the worst stereotypes of Black people as scary, poorly educated criminals. In Trump's first year in office, white supremacists violently rallied in Charlottesville. Hate crimes spiked across the country, and the FBI noted that the biggest threat to the safety of American citizens was not foreign terrorism but domestic white supremacy. Attacks against synagogues, Hispanics, Asians, and gays all exploded, with Trump as the leading figure in the backlash.

It took the video of the torturous nearly-nine-minute killing of George Floyd to fully awaken and mobilize a broad coalition across class and race around the nation. Americans of all backgrounds filled the streets and provoked responses from corporate leaders and mainstream media. They came from the largest urban centers. They even came from white suburbs and small towns. This contributed to Biden's victory over Trump in 2020. But inevitably, it sowed the seeds of another backlash. Soon a Confederate flag was paraded through the halls of the Capitol, as Trump supporters violently attacked Congress in the hopes of denying certification of Biden's victory in a democratic election.

The Trump supporters who stormed the Capitol are playing the role of villains in the Second Civil Rights Movement, in another parallel to the First Civil Rights Movement. Their insurrection evoked the image of Governor George Wallace of Alabama standing in the schoolhouse door to prevent integration. Wallace's actions also sparked riots and deadly violence.

Trump's "Make America Great Again" theme succeeded as an emotional trigger, stirring rage in people who felt uncomfortable with the rapid demographic changes that had led to increased attention to racial differences. They saw themselves being eclipsed. They feared that the rising number of minorities undermined their political and economic status. More off-putting, Trump's followers saw any celebration of multiculturalism by the Second Civil Rights Movement as a threat to their own place in society. In their minds, they were being displaced as the heroes of American history. People trying to hold on to past visions of a white-dominated nation, saw themselves as victims of politically correct thinking, as more minority voices complained about white colonialists, slaveholders, and segregationists. Extremist politicians fed them fear of their identity being washed away by changes beyond their control, provoking them to violently lash out.

Just as former Confederates waylaid the post–Civil War Reconstruction efforts in the nineteenth century, Trump's insurrectionists hoped to delay the inevitable changes coming in the twenty-first century. But despite their efforts, it is impossible to stop the reality of demographic and cultural shifts.

Thanks to Obama, Black Lives Matter, and activists of all colors, there is more positive thinking about racial diversity and it is impossible to ignore. It is evident in the culture, which celebrated arts and music from well beyond Black and white categories. Bad Bunny, rapping in Spanish over reggaetón beats, became a best-selling American artist. Hip-hop, now beyond its fiftieth anniversary, has become the nation's top musical genre. *Everything Everywhere All at Once*, a movie with a predominantly Asian cast, won the Academy Award for best picture, and Shohei Ohtani is widely considered the best baseball player of his generation—with a $700 million contract to show for it.

The Census Bureau estimates that by the year 2045 the United States will cease to be a white-majority country.[6] This tectonic shift on the horizon remains the driving factor behind the new era of racial consciousness. Hispanics will make up a quarter of that future population. Asians will remain its fastest growing racial group. Blacks have already lost their status as the nation's biggest minority group, and many in the Black community already fear the loss of recognition for their past as slaves and any presumption that they deserve a leading role in future movements for equal rights. Now there is fear that the Black experience and Black leadership will lose their primacy and will no longer set the tone for debates over equity and racial justice.

Leading the fight for racial justice has been an almost sacred space for Black people in America. Iconic leaders like Frederick Douglass fought slavery. Dr. King inspired with his dream of Black and white coming together. Jesse Jackson raised Black pride when he proclaimed, "I Am Somebody."

These are hallmarks of American history. The Black role in American society has been to take the lead in reminding the nation of the great American promise that all men and women are created equal.

A 2023 poll by *USA Today*/Ipsos found that "two in five (40%) say they consider 'woke' to be an insult, but about a third (32%) consider it a compliment." Again, this reflected a political divide in the country, with Democrats being far more likely to embrace the term and Republicans being more likely to reject it.[8]

The concept of being "woke" itself came directly out of the heart of the Second Civil Rights Movement, signaling another success by Black Lives Matter at changing the terms of the debate in the United States around issues of race. The question for this growing, diverse population will be whether it can successfully build coalitions across racial and economic lines. Can poor minorities and poor whites come together to unite around their mutual interests? Can people awaken across economic lines? Can people awaken to find common ground, regardless of their ethnicity, gender, or religion?

That means the coming movement for racial justice will be a search for common ground among people with different experiences of America, people of different races and ethnicities. Wade Henderson, the former head of the largest coalition of civil rights groups in the country, said the key to the next generation's success will be coalition building. He points to the enduring presence of some groups, such as the National Urban League and the NAACP, as a testament to their success in attracting allies.[7]

Stacey Abrams has argued that this variety of voices has the potential to move from a cacophony to a harmony of previously unseen solutions: "We're looking forward. You have to educate; you have to engage. Demographic changes are real. And that's one of the reasons we're seeing the speed of the [counter] attack." In her mind, "Demography is not destiny. It is opportunity." And that opportunity is to join with new allies to gain leverage for more powerful change.

For example, the leaders of America's biggest businesses kept their distance from civil rights activism for most of the country's history. But now America's businesses see a need to appeal to a new generation of workers and consumers, no matter their religion, race, or country of origin. This is especially important as the white population is aging. "If I can convince you that the cost of your racism is more expensive than the purity of it, then that's how we make progress," Abrams said.[9]

The positive potential coming from demographic diversity is also increasingly reflected in America's elected leaders. The 118th Congress, which took office in January 2023, was the most diverse ever elected—more than one hundred members were non-white—and included a twenty-five-year-old from Generation Z as its youngest member. The two houses of Congress had 153 women (28 percent), and this diversity in gender representation is representative of profound shifts elsewhere in American society.[10] Almost half the U.S. workforce is female, and 60 percent of U.S. college students are women.[11] These facts indicate that future political leaders, corporate bosses, and workers will also be more heavily female, and potentially another engine driving social justice.

There are also new multiracial categories. As marriages across ethnic lines continue, we will see more multiracial couples and multiracial children, whose experiences and expectations about race will be vastly different than those of the people who made up the First and Second Civil Rights Movements. In the decades since the Supreme Court made interracial marriage legal in 1967, with the case *Loving v. Virginia*, there has been an explosion of interracial couples. In the 1960s, only 3 percent of marriages were interracial; that number has grown to more than 20 percent today. According to Gallup, 94 percent of Americans, across all racial lines, approve of interracial marriages.[12] Support for gay marriage also stands above 70 percent approval.[13] These changes reflect wide social and demographic realities that will only increase through the twenty-first century.

Immigration will bring more change to the U.S. and beyond. According to the International Organization for Migration 2022 World Migration Report, migration trends show that more than 280 million people around the world are on the move, with Europe and Asia seeing even more immigration than the United States. An estimated 61 percent of global migrants, more than 170 million people, are moving to those regions. Meanwhile, North America

(Canada, the United States, and Mexico) receives about 21 percent of the world's migrants—more than 59 million people.[14]

As Stacey Abrams noted, most of the legislative change will come not at the federal level, but from the states: "When I think about this next wave of [the civil rights] movement, 56 percent of Black people live in the South. The Latino population is largely concentrated in the South and Southwest. AAPI communities are growing fast in the South and Southwest. And so, if we want to see antiracism, if we want to see expansion of civil rights, we have to focus on what's happening in the South and Southwest."[15]

Because of the success of the First and Second Civil Rights Movements, America stands out in the international community. It is a model for adjusting to heightened racial and gender diversity. The question now is exactly what the definition of social justice will be for the next or Third Civil Rights Movement as the country approaches 2045 and a majority-minority country.

Whatever the definition, it will have to be accepted by people who see themselves as American but are also multiracial, multiethnic, and multinational. It will have to work for people who speak different languages, practice different religions, and have ties to different countries. A consensus on racial justice will have to attract everyone, from racial minorities with a long history in the United States and women of all colors to immigrants who want economic opportunity, political stability, and a better education for their children. Some of those people won't know about the First Civil Rights Movement or even have sympathies for the Second Civil Rights Movement. But they will share a common desire that grew out of these movements—to be treated equally, to have protection under the law, and to participate in a democratic system. They will not want to be scapegoated or threatened with deportation by white supremacist demagogues.

Marc Morial, the president of the National Urban League, called this transition a period of extreme uncertainty: "We can't predict what the millennials, and the Gen Zs are going to bring when they achieve power. I think they're going to be much more focused on multiracial equity and that those issues become more mainstream."[16]

The coming Third Civil Rights Movement, featuring so many immigrants, will inevitably face a backlash. Newcomers will be demeaned as interlopers and not fully American. They will be accused of taking advantage of public schools or a health care system that they didn't establish. The backlash against them won't simply be the result of white supremacy.

Though the MAGA crowd remains the heart of that resistance to newcomers, it may also include older Blacks, Asians, or Hispanics who have lived for generations in the United States. The cases engineered by far-right activists to dismantle affirmative action, for example, often included Asians as plaintiffs. Even though some Asians had suffered discrimination in college admissions, MAGA's cynical focus was not to overcome historic discrimination; their goal was to maintain white racial dominance by assuring that access to elite schools remained based purely on test scores, an area where Blacks and Hispanics have generally underperformed relative to whites and Asians.

The Third Movement will also need to learn from the mistakes of the Second Movement. Black Lives Matter made some big mistakes, ranging from a lack of clear leadership and strong organizational structure, to not doing enough to build a lasting multiracial movement. Many of the people supporting Black Lives Matter are still locked in an amorphous struggle against "systemic racism" that often seems to lack attainable goals. And as Jim Clyburn, a key player on Capitol Hill in the Second Movement, asserts, one of those big mistakes by BLM was the knee-jerk embrace by some after the George Floyd protests of the provocative slogan "Defund the Police." The phrase ultimately proved to be an instrument that divided Black Lives Matter from some of its allies. The phrase also proved to be a weapon for opponents. It was held up by conservatives to damage the movement and prompted some moderates across racial lines to dismiss it entirely.

MAGA's exploitation of "Defund the Police" extended to efforts limiting access to the voting booth. Continued voter suppression efforts will generate a Third Movement counteroffensive which must move beyond traditional racial lines to bring people of different races into coalitions. "We're going to start to see the need for marginalized and disadvantaged communities for voting rights to take on a very different complexion, no pun intended," said Stacey Abrams. "And that complexion is going to include bringing together strange bedfellows. . . . We've got to build coalitions that don't rest on us having the same belief systems, but rest on us wanting the same behaviors."[17]

Patrick Gaspard, a former U.S. ambassador to South Africa who now serves as the president of the Center for American Progress, argues that it is important to remain optimistic and for people not to lose faith in the power of coalitions: "So I want to see this nascent new civil rights movement have in its core, a set of organizers who have a theory of power, and who understand that power comes from being able to create governing majorities."[18] This is the very point that Barack Obama made to the students at Howard University.

Even with these lessons, it is important to admit that we are still coping with problems of the past. The Second Civil Rights Movement's complaints over police violence have not been solved. There is more awareness of the problem and greater accountability for police, but the issue remains.

And there are additional problems with gun violence, high rates of incarceration, and economic disparities that are particularly felt in minority communities. Troubled public schools in poor neighborhoods also belong on this list of ongoing challenges.

The most far-reaching goal for coalitions under a Third Civil Rights Movement will be to create new strategies that break down the fundamental antidemocratic structures that are rooted in America's founding. At the time the Constitution was written, the elites were all white landowners, and many were slaveholders. They had no interest in the popular vote of people who would rebel against their authority and economic interests.

Such reforms will require rethinking the lack of proportional representation in the Senate and devising creative solutions that recognize the fact that the Senate's composition cannot be changed, even by constitutional amendment, unless the states vote to do it. While each state has two senators, those senators do not equally represent the people of the United States. California, which is home to 12 percent of the American population, has the same number of senators as Wyoming, which has only 0.17 percent of the U.S population. This disparity also has a strong immigrant and racial aspect. California is already a majority-minority state, while Wyoming remains 92 percent white.[19] The Senate's use of the filibuster compounds this tyranny of the minority, because sixty votes are required to pass certain legislation or to confirm most nominees.

Similarly, the Third Civil Rights Movement will be challenged to reform the Electoral College. It remains radically unfair in its failure to give every American a meaningful vote in electing their nation's leader. The popular vote for the presidential candidates really does not matter under the Electoral College. Instead, ballots cast by voters are tallied by each state to select a slate of electors pledged to vote for the popular vote winner within that state. But it is possible for individual electors not to support that winner, or—as proposed (without success) during Donald Trump's failed effort to overturn the 2020 election—to reject the popular vote completely. The Electoral College, even when it works as designed, sometimes rewards the candidate who received fewer popular votes nationally. In fact, Republicans have won the popular vote only once in the last eight presidential races, yet they have held the White House for twelve of those years.

Judges in courts around the country remain overwhelmingly white and disproportionately male. Today's Supreme Court, despite being more diverse than ever, is ruled by a conservative majority which reveres a doctrine of "originalism." That thinking is locked into eighteenth-century views of the law, which do not fit with today's very modern nation. Originalism comes from a time when American society was far less racially diverse and when the voting population did not include minorities or even women. It's worth noting that until 1967, none of the justices were anything other than white men.

A more fully representative Congress and Supreme Court will have a better chance to create reforms that address issues ranging from voting suppression to police violence and hate crimes. But given the continued antidemocratic composition of the court and Congress, these institutions are unlikely to see changes in the near future.

Correcting this lack of democratic representation will be the greatest challenge for a multiracial, diverse Third Civil Rights Movement. And a backlash to these reforms is almost a certainty.

If it has success in changing these major institutions of American life, the

Third Civil Rights Movement has the potential to redefine social justice. It will achieve the goal of a truly democratic American system.

The First Civil Rights Movement was about integration, breaking down segregation in schools, housing, voting. Its victories went from the courts in the 1950s to the streets in the 1960s. Then it went into politics in the 1970s, electing more diverse people to local government and Congress. It produced civil rights legislation, voting rights, and affirmative action laws.

The Second Civil Rights Movement was about justice, police reform, and continued voting protections. But instead of starting with judges who ruled racial segregation to be unconstitutional, the Second Movement started with increased diversity in political leaders that culminated in the election of Barack Obama. Where the First Civil Rights Movement relied on small, orderly, nonviolent marches to change public opinion, the Second Civil Rights Movement created marches of historic number nationwide in response to police violence. Where the First Civil Rights Movement started in the courts, the Second Civil Rights Movement wants to see its work finished in the courts, with rulings that certify that justice is to be found in affirmative action and protecting voting rights.

The Second Civil Rights Movement is the door to a burgeoning Third Civil Rights Movement, and to innovative steps to redefine civil rights, racial justice, and democracy itself. It will be about giving people, whether they are Black, white, Hispanic, Asian, gay, or transgender, a chance to succeed and a chance to decide our country's future together: to make America excellent— great for the first time.

Acknowledgments

This book had a near-death experience.

The casket was closing when Jon Karp, the CEO of Simon & Schuster, raised his hand to say this book had to live.

He introduced me to Paul Golob, a skilled editor and good man, who brilliantly guided me home on the first draft. Ian Straus, a top editor at Simon & Schuster, took it higher, challenging me to polish stories to create the book before you.

Gentlemen, thank you for working with me to produce a compelling book for today's readers—with lasting value for future generations. That was the standard set in 1987 by its best-selling predecessor—*Eyes on the Prize: America's Civil Rights Years, 1954–1965.*

Day-to-day, creation of this book, from research to writing, would not have been possible without Christopher Teal.

Currently U.S. consul general in Mexico, Chris sat with me, laughed with me, and lunched with me, to make this book happened. As a graduate student, Chris was the extraordinary researcher for my biography of former Supreme Court justice Thurgood Marshall. Chris then joined the Foreign Service. He also wrote a book of his own—*Hero of Hispanola: America's First Black Diplomat, Ebenezer D. Bassett.*

His intellect and friendship go beyond any simple thank-you. So, I dedicate this book to him.

Robert Barnett, my lawyer and friend, kept me and the book afloat even at low tide moments. He joined with Jon Karp in seeing the importance of telling this generation's civil rights story.

Men with terrific minds, political wisdom, and real-life experience advised me along the way—Nate Fredman, Jim Hudson, Jim Kessler, Bill Lightfoot, Ghebre Mehreteab, Arnon Mishkin, Barrett Nnoka, and Armstrong Williams.

Thank you to my mentors in the writing life—Herbert Denton at *The Washington Post*; Henry Hampton at Blackside; and Sam Boyle at the *Philadelphia Evening Bulletin*.

Thanks to Oakwood Friends School and Haverford College.

Every word you read here was touched by caring professionals at Simon & Schuster, beginning with Priscilla Painton, editorial director; Lisa Healy, senior production editor; Fred Chase, copyeditor; Jackie Seow, executive art director; Ruth Lee-Mui, associate design director; and Anna Hauser, editorial assistant.

Post-production thanks to Julia Prosser, associate publisher; Stephen Bedford, vice president of marketing; Larry Hughes, deputy director of publicity; and Tyanni Niles, marketing manager.

Here is to my speaking agency—American Program Bureau. Hats off to my colleagues at The Hill.com—Bob Cusack, Daniel Allot, David Freddoso, and Niall Stanage.

Thanks to my Fox colleagues—Bret Baier; Bryan Boughton; Dianne Brandi; Shannon and Sheldon Bream; Porter Berry; Dana Blanton; Megan Clarke; Kevin Corke; Jason Chaffetz; Rick DiBella; Andrea DiVito; Mary Pat Dennert; Mike Emmanuel; Jennifer Griffin; Brit Hume; Jessica Loker; Martha MacCallum; Mary Katharine Ham; John Roberts; Katy Ricalde; Patricia Pert; Jama Podell Vitale; Christina Svolopoulos Robbins; Doug Rohrbeck; Suzanne Scott; Gillian Turner; Jay Wallace, Ted Williams, and Caroline Whiteman.

Thank you to my family for their love.

My wife, Delise, has been a true partner and guardian at every turn. My daughter, Regan, once brought over her husband, Patrick, and my grandchildren Elias, Pepper, and Wesley to show support. Yes, they carried balloons. Raffi and Antonio, my sons, consistently pumped out confidence in the book's success. Grandchildren Margo and August were heaven-sent, a gift, born as I worked on this book.

Special thanks to Morgan and Erika, my daughters-in-law, and their families John and Donna Chalfant and Gordon and Jan Nuber, for riding the roller coaster of a distracted book writer's life.

Deep affection to my brother, Roger, and my sister, Elena. Thank you to Roger's wife, Ginger, and their children, Ashley and Christoper. Their sweet grandchildren are Chloe, Haley, Abby, and Eleanor. Love to Elena's children—Alexandra and Jonathan—and grandchildren—Chiara, Paul, and Rafael.

That spirit of gratitude also goes to my brother-in-law, Dr. Arthur West, and his wife, Leathia, their children, Marisa and Chip, and grandchildren, Maya and Miles.

Thanks to my cousins—Ligia, Carlito, Haroldo (and his wife, Lupita), Donna, Ruby Linda, Rilda, and Rudy. That appreciation extends to my family in Panama: Javier, Ricardo, Rogelio, and Armonia.

The Trinity Episcopal Church family is a living blessing, beginning with longtime rector, Rev. John Harmon, now bishop of Arkansas, and current priest in charge, Rev. Shayna J. Watson.

My friends are always bumping with ideas and opinions—Arthur Aidala; Susan Alexander; Bishop Nathan Baxter; LaSharah Bunting; Dana Canedy; Jim Clifton; Frank Craig; Chris and Lynne Cowan; Eric and Tina Easter; John Eshun; Jimmy Finkelstein; Michael and Ulrika Francis; David Garrow; Cheryl Gibert; Ken Gormley; Donald Graham; Warren Graves; Gina Wishnick; Cherie Grzech; Scot Hagerthey, Karen Vossler, and their son, Gavin; Bill Herald; Jerry Higgins; Anne Ashmore Hudson; Dante James; Jordan Jean; Colby King; Michael Medved; Cynthiana Lightfoot; Mara Liasson; James Loadholt; Cam MacQueen; Thurgood Marshall Jr.; Michael Meyers; Sarah Mullins; Jerralynn Ness; Judy Nnoka; Ali Noorani and Toya

Gavin; Franco Nuschese; Cathleen O'Brien; Jeremy Peters; Jennifer Pond; Joe Quinlan; Diane Rehm; Jason Riley; Eugene Robinson; Steve Selden; Dr. Sian Spurney; Noah Shachtman; Ben Smith; Jessica Tarlov; Paul and Mindy Thaler; Diane Thomson; Leland Vittert; George Will; Chris Wilson; Jason Wrenn, and David Zinn.

In memory and Roger and Alma Williams; Annie Elias Cox; Arthur and Minna West.

As I say too often, "Check it out!" To all above—this book is for you.

Notes

INTRODUCTION

1. Juliet Eilperin and Greg Jaffe, "Obama After Ferguson: Youth Leaders Urge President to Be 'More Out in Front' on Race," *Washington Post*, December 2, 2014, www.washingtonpost.com/politics/obama-after-ferguson-youth-leaders-urge-president-to-be-more-out-in-front-on-race/2014/12/01/eca65690-7980-11e4-84d4-7c896b90abdc_story.html.

2. Dudley L. Poston Jr. and Rogelio Sáenz, "Majority to Minority: The Declining U.S. White Population," N-IUSSP, September 11, 2017, https://www.niussp.org/migration-and-foreigners/majority-minority-declining-u-s-white-population/.

3. Mohamad Moslimani et al., "Facts About the U.S. Black Population," Pew Research Center, January 18, 2024, https://www.pewresearch.org/social-trends/fact-sheet/facts-about-the-us-black-population/.

4. Christine Tamir, "The Growing Diversity of Black America," Pew Research Center, March 25, 2021, https://www.pewresearch.org/social-trends/2021/03/25/the-growing-diversity-of-black-america/.

5. Andre M. Perry and Carl Romer, "The Black Middle Class Needs Political Attention, Too," Brookings, February 27, 2020, https://www.brookings.edu/articles/the-black-middle-class-needs-political-attention-too/.

6. Liz Mineo, "Making American Schools Less Segregated," *Harvard Gazette*, July 14, 2020, https://news.harvard.edu/gazette/story/2020/07/how-to-make-american-schools-less-segregated/.

7. Criminal Justice Fact Sheet, NAACP, https://naacp.org/resources/criminal-justice-fact-sheet.

8. "New National UMASS Amherst Poll on Issue Finds One-Third of Americans Believe 'Great Replacement' Theory," University of Massachusetts-Amherst, October 25, 2022, www.umass.edu/news/article/new-national-umass-amherst-poll-issues-finds-one-third-americans-believe-great.

9. Steve Phillips, "Democrats Need to Have an Honest Talk About White People," *The Atlantic*, September 14, 2023, https://www.thenation.com/article/politics /democrats-white-voter-turnout/.

1: A POST-RACIAL AMERICA?

1. William Bunch, "Who the Heck Is This Guy?," *Philadelphia Daily News*, July 27, 2004, p. 3.
2. "Obama to Give Keynote Address," *Chicago Tribune*, July 15, 2004, www.chicago tribune.com/2004/07/15/obama-to-give-keynote-address/.
3. David Plouffe, *The Audacity to Win: The Inside Story and Lessons of Barack Obama's Historic Victory* (New York: Viking, 2009).
4. "Obama to Give Keynote Address," *Chicago Tribune*.
5. Ibid.
6. David Mills, "Sister Souljah's Call to Arms," *Washington Post*, May 12, 1992, https://www.washingtonpost.com/archive/lifestyle/1992/05/13/sister-souljahs -call-to-arms/643d5634-e622-43ad-ba7d-811f8f5bfe5d/.
7. Jennifer Liberto, "Origin of Obama's Run Is on the South Side," *Tampa Bay Times*, October 2, 2008, www.tampabay.com/archive/2008/10/26/origin-of-obama-s-run -is-on-south-side/.
8. Jeff Zeleny, "When It Comes to Race, Obama Makes His Point—with Subtlety," *Chicago Tribune*, June 26, 2005, https://www.chicagotribune.com/2005/06/26 /when-it-comes-to-race-obama-makes-his-point-with-subtlety/.
9. Martin Luther King Jr., "I Have a Dream," August 28, 1963, https://www.digitalhis tory.uh.edu/disp_textbook.cfm?smtid=3&psid=4063.
10. "Obama to Give Keynote Address," *Chicago Tribune*.
11. "Transcript: Illinois Senate Candidate Barack Obama Keynote Address at the Democratic National Convention, July 27, 2004," https://www.washingtonpost .com/wp-dyn/articles/A19751-2004Jul27.html.
12. Ibid.
13. "Ex-Wife of GOP Senate Candidate Alleged Sex Club Forays," CNN, June 22, 2004, https://www.cnn.com/2004/ALLPOLITICS/06/22/ryan.divorce/.
14. Mark Porter, "Keyes Ready to 'Fight' for Illinois Senate Seat," NBC News, August 9, 2004, https://www.nbcnews.com/id/wbna5652009.
15. Barack Obama, "Katrina and Gulf Recovery," September 6, 2005, http://obama speeches.com/029-Statement-on-Hurricane-Katrina-Relief-Efforts-Obama -Speech.htm.
16. Barack Obama, "Presidential Announcement," February 10, 2007, http://obama speeches.com/099-Announcement-For-President-Springfield-Illinois-Obama -Speech.htm.
17. "Senator Obama Interview with Steve Inskeep," NPR, February 28, 2007, www .npr.org/2007/02/28/7630250/obama-to-attend-selma-march-anniversary.
18. Author's interview with Rev. Al Sharpton, May 9, 2022.
19. John Whitesides, "Black Voters Still Unsure About Obama," Reuters, August 9, 2007, https://www.reuters.com/article/idUSN08292517/.
20. Katherine Seelye, "A Former President, Back in the Thick of Politics," *New York Times*, January 7, 2008, https://www.nytimes.com/2008/01/27/us/politics/27bill.html.

21. "Bill Clinton Says He Was 'Race Card' Victim," *Los Angeles Times*, April 23, 2008, https://www.latimes.com/archives/la-xpm-2008-apr-23-na-clintonrace23-story.html.
22. Geoff Bennett, "Andrew Young: Obama's Time Will Come," NPR, December 7, 2007, www.npr.org/sections/newsandviews/2007/12/andrew_young_obamas_time_will.html.
23. Author's interview with Andrew Young, May 8, 2022.
24. Roddie Burris, "Jackson Slams Obama for 'Acting White,'" *Politico*, September 19, 2007, www.politico.com/story/2007/09/jackson-slams-obama-for-acting-white-005902.
25. Carrie Brown, "First Black President? Obama Doesn't Say It," *Politico*, December 9, 2007, www.politico.com/story/2007/12/first-black-president-obama-doesnt-say-it-007274.
26. Christi Parsons, "Rev. Jackson Critical of Obama," *Chicago Tribune*, September 19, 2007, www.chicagotribune.com/2007/09/19/rev-jackson-critical-of-obama/.
27. "Statement by Senator Obama on Repeal of Jena 6 Conviction," September 14, 2007, www.presidency.ucsb.edu/documents/statement-senator-obama-repeal-jena-6-conviction.
28. Jeff Zeleny, "Black Leader Changes Endorsement to Obama," *New York Times*, February 28, 2008, www.nytimes.com/2008/02/28/us/politics/28lewis.html.
29. Jesse Jackson Jr. interview with NPR, "Jesse Jackson, Jr. Helps Obama Win Black Vote," October 24, 2007, https://www.npr.org/templates/story/story.php?storyId=15603662.
30. "Jackson Apologizes for Obama Remarks," *Chicago Tribune*, July 10, 2008, https://www.chicagotribune.com/2008/07/10/jackson-apologizes-for-obama-remarks-2/.
31. Barack Obama, "Remarks at the Selma Voting Rights March Commemoration in Selma, Alabama," March 4, 2007, https://www.presidency.ucsb.edu/documents/remarks-the-selma-voting-rights-march-commemoration-selma-alabama.
32. "Wright's Controversial Comments," *Politico*, March 17, 2008, https://www.politico.com/story/2008/03/wrights-controversial-comments-009089.
33. "Transcript: Barack Obama's Speech on Race," NPR, March 18, 2008, www.npr.org/templates/story/story.php?storyId=88478467.
34. "Obama and Wright Controversy Dominate News Cycle," Pew Research Center, March 27, 2008, www.pewresearch.org/politics/2008/03/27/obama-and-wright-controversy-dominate-news-cycle/.
35. "Transcript: Barack Obama's Acceptance Speech," NPR, August 28, 2008, www.npr.org/templates/story/story.php?storyId=94087570.
36. "Transcript of Barack Obama's Victory Speech," NPR, November 5, 2008, www.npr.org/2008/11/05/96624326/transcript-of-barack-obamas-victory-speech.
37. Barack Obama, "President Barack Obama's Inaugural Address," The White House, https://obamawhitehouse.archives.gov/blog/2009/01/21/president-Barack-obamas-inaugural-address.

2: BURSTING THE BUBBLE

1. Matt Taibbi, "The Truth About the Tea Party," *Rolling Stone*, September 28, 2010, www.rollingstone.com/politics/politics-news/the-truth-about-the-tea-party-188228/.

2. Michael Eric Dyson, "President Obama's Racial Renaissance," *New York Times*, August 1, 2015, www.nytimes.com/2015/08/02/opinion/sunday/president-obamas -racial-renaissance.html.

3. Lucy Madison, "Gingrich Singles Out Blacks in Food Stamp Remark," CBS News, January 6, 2012, www.cbsnews.com/news/gingrich-singles-out-blacks-in-food -stamp-remark/.

4. "Glenn Beck: Obama Is a Racist," CBS News, July 29, 2009, www.cbsnews.com /news/glenn-beck-obama-is-a-racist/.

5. Tad Barker, "Barack the Magic Negro?," *The Hill*, December 30, 2008, thehill.com /blogs/pundits-blog/the-administration/27827-barack-the-magic-negro/.

6. Brian Montopol, "Obama: Cops Acted 'Stupidly' in Professor's Arrest," CBS News, July 22, 2009, www.cbsnews.com/news/obama-cops-acted-stupidly-in-professors -arrest/.

7. "Obama's Ratings Slide Across the Board," Pew Research Center, July 30, 2009, www.pewresearch.org/politics/2009/07/30/obamas-ratings-slide-across-the-board/.

8. "How One Scholar's Arrest Tainted the President's Image as a Racial Healer," *Washington Post*, April 22, 2016, www.washingtonpost.com/graphics/national /obama-legacy/henry-louis-gates-jr-arrest-controversy.html.

9. Jamelle Bouie, "The Professor, the Cop, and the President," *Slate*, September 21, 2016, slate.com/news-and-politics/2016/09/the-henry-louis-gates-beer-summit -and-racial-division-in-america.html.

10. "A Black Agenda: Mr. President, Would You Just Answer the Phone," *Chicago Defender*, March 16, 2012, chicagodefender.com/a-black-agenda-mr-president -would-you-just-answer-the-phone/.

11. Sean Sullivan, "CBC Chairman Suggests Obama May Get a Pass from Black Community," *Washington Post*, September 18, 2012, www.washingtonpost.com/news /post-politics/wp/2012/09/18/cbc-chairman-suggests-obama-may-get-a-pass -from-black-community/.

12. Barack Obama, "Remarks by the President at Congressional Black Caucus Foundation Annual Phoenix Awards Dinner," September 24, 2011, https://obama whitehouse.archives.gov/realitycheck/the-press-office/2011/09/24/remarks -president-congressional-black-caucus-foundation-annual-phoenix-a.

13. Interview with Dr. Cornel West, "Obama," Kunhardt Film Foundation, November 15, 2018, https://www.lifestories.org/attachment/en/65946ce4179a0efae903 8462/TextOneColumnWithFile/61f034f6e660a85b5e55aec1.

14. Kim Severson, "Digital Age Drives Rally to Keep a Georgia Inmate from Execution," *New York Times*, September 16, 2011, www.nytimes.com/2011/09/17/us /supporters-rally-to-save-troy-davis-from-execution-in-georgia.html.

15. "Troy Davis Amidst 11th Hour Plea to High Court," CBS News, September 21, 2011, www.cbsnews.com/news/troy-davis-amidst-11th-hour-plea-to-high-court/.

16. Kim Severson, "Davis Is Executed in Georgia," *New York Times*, September 21, 2011, www.nytimes.com/2011/09/22/us/final-pleas-and-vigils-in-troy-davis-exe cution.html.

17. "DPIC Releases Report Placing Death Penalty in Historical Context as a 'Descendant of Slavery, Lynching, and Segregation,'" Death Penalty Information

Center, September 15, 2020, deathpenaltyinfo.org/facts-and-research/dpic-reports /in-depth/enduring-injustice-the-persistence-of-racial-discrimination-in-the-u-s -death-penalty.

18. Concurrence of Justice Thurgood Marshall, *Furman v. Georgia*, 408 U.S. 238 (1972), https://supreme.justia.com/cases/federal/us/408/238/.

19. Elizabeth Flock, "U.S. Supreme Court Rejects Appeal; Troy Davis Executed," *Washington Post*, September 22, 2011, www.washingtonpost.com/blogs/blogpost/post /troy-davis-executed-after-us-supreme-courtrefuses-to-block-sentence/2011 /09/22/gIQAWQdhnK_blog.html.

20. Jake Tapper, "White House Declines Comment on Troy Davis Case," ABC News, September 21, 2011, abcnews.go.com/blogs/politics/2011/09/white-house-de clines-comment-on-troy-davis-case.

21. Joy Freeman-Coulbary, "Obama Silent on Troy Davis," *Washington Post*, September 21, 2011, www.washingtonpost.com/blogs/therootdc/post/obama-silent-on -troy-davis/2011/09/21/gIQAH9tIlK_blog.html.

22. Author's interview with Rev. Al Sharpton, May 9, 2022.

23. "High Court Denies Stay of Execution for Troy Davis," CBS News, September 21, 2011, www.cbsnews.com/news/high-court-denies-stay-of-execution-for-troy-davis/.

24. Author's interview with Benjamin Jealous, May, 26, 2022.

25. Erick Schonfeld, "The Top Spiking Tweets of 2011," Techcrunch, December 6, 2011, https://techcrunch.com/2011/12/06/top-spiking-tweets-2011/.

26. Supreme Court of the United States, Order in Pending Case, September 21, 2011, https://www.supremecourt.gov/orders/courtorders/092111.zr.pdf.

27. Greg Bluestein, "Witness to the Execution: Davis' Last Moments," Associated Press, September 22, 2011, https://www.savannahnow.com/story/news/2011/09 /22/ap-reporter-describes-witnessing-davis-execution/13421433007/.

28. Jen Marlowe and Keeanga-Yamahtta Taylor, "The Execution That Birthed a Movement," *In These Times*, September 17, 2016, inthesetimes.com/article/the-execu tion-that-birthed-a-movement.

29. Derek Dingle, "Oval Office Interview with President Barack Obama," *Black Enterprise*, August 6, 2012, www.blackenterprise.com/president-obama-interview-small -business-unemployment-exclusive/.

3: SKITTLES AND A HOODIE

1. "Trayvon Martin Shooting Fast Facts," CNN, February 14, 2024, https://www.cnn .com/2013/06/05/us/trayvon-martin-shooting-fast-facts/index.html.

2. "Trayvon Martin Investigator Wanted Manslaughter Charge," ABC News, March 27, 2012, abcnews.go.com/US/trayvon-martin-investigator-wanted-charge -george-zimmerman-manslaughter/story?id=16011674.

3. Paul Farhi, "Trayvon Martin Story Found the Media," *Washington Post*, April 12, 2012, www.washingtonpost.com/lifestyle/style/trayvon-martin-story-found-the -media/2012/04/12/gIQA9VGmDT_story.html.

4. Author's interview with Ben Crump, June 21, 2023.

5. Farhi, "Trayvon Martin Story Found the Media."

6. Mark Memmot, "Three Key Moments as Trayvon Martin's Story Went Viral," NPR,

March 29, 2012, www.npr.org/sections/thetwo-way/2012/03/29/149615333/three
-key-moments-as-trayvon-martins-story-went-viral.

7. Tracy Martin and Sybrina Fulton, Petition: "Prosecute the Killer of Our Son,
    17-Year-Old Trayvon Martin," Change.org, March 8, 2012, www.change.org/p
    /prosecute-the-killer-of-our-son-17-year-old-trayvon-martin.

8. Sam Schlinkert and Brian Ries, "Trayvon Martin Killing Inspires 13 Tweets from
    Celebrities," *Daily Beast*, March 21, 2012, www.thedailybeast.com/trayvon-martin
    -killing-inspires-13-tweets-from-celebrities.

9. Author's interview with Wade Henderson, June 27, 2022.

10. Derrick Bryson Taylor, "Hundreds Gather for 'Million Hoodie March' in New
    York," *Essence*, March 22, 2012, www.essence.com/news/hundreds-gather-for
    -million-hoodie-march-in-new-york/.

11. Michael Scherer, "Obama Speaks Out on Trayvon Martin: A Personal Appeal with
    Political Risk," *Time*, March 23, 2012, swampland.time.com/2012/03/23/obama
    -speaks-out-on-trayvon-martin-a-personal-appeal-with-political-risk/.

12. "George Zimmerman Speaks w/ FoxNews Sean Hannity (Full Interview)," July 19,
    2012, www.buzzfeednews.com/article/jose3030/george-zimmerman-full-interview
    -with-sean-hannity.

13. Michael Brendan Dougherty, "NBC: We're Sorry We Edited the Trayvon Tape to
    Make George Zimmerman Sound Racist," *Business Insider*, April 4, 2012, www
    .businessinsider.com/nbc-apologizes-to-george-zimmerman-for-editing-a-911-call
    -to-make-him-sound-really-racist-2012-4.

14. Patrick Jonsson, "Geraldo Rivera (Again) Says Trayvon Martin's 'Thug Wear' Got
    Him Profiled," *Christian Science Monitor*, May 19, 2012, www.csmonitor.com
    /USA/Justice/2012/0519/Geraldo-Rivera-again-says-Trayvon-Martin-s-thug-wear
    -got-him-profiled.

15. Karen Grigsby Bates, "A Look Back at Trayvon Martin's Death, and the Movement
    It Inspired," *Code Switch*, NPR, July 31, 2018, www.npr.org/sections/codeswitch
    /2018/07/31/631897758/a-look-back-at-trayvon-martins-death-and-the-move
    ment-it-inspired.

16. Author's interview with Ben Crump, June 21, 2023.

17. Reis Thebault, "Trayvon Martin's Death Set Off a Movement That Shaped a
    Decade's Defining Moments," *Washington Post*, February 25, 2022, www.wash
    ingtonpost.com/nation/2022/02/25/trayvon-martins-death-set-off-movement-that
    -shaped-decades-defining-moments/.

18. Author's interview with Ben Crump, June 21, 2023.

19. Aniko Bodroghkozy, *Equal Time: Television and the Civil Rights Movement* (Chi-
    cago: University of Illinois Press, 2012), 2.

20. Martin Luther King Jr. to Andrew Young, as cited in David J. Garrow, *Bearing the
    Cross: Martin Luther King, Jr., and the Southern Leadership Conference* (New York:
    Morrow, 1986).

21. Alexis C. Madrigal, "When the Revolution Was Televised," *The Atlantic*, April 11,
    2018, www.theatlantic.com/technology/archive/2018/04/televisions-civil-rights
    -revolution/554639/.

22. Aaron Smith, "African Americans and Technology Use," Pew Research Center,

January 6, 2014, www.pewresearch.org/internet/2014/01/06/african-americans
-and-technology-use/.

23. Chris Wilson, "uknowurblack," *The Root*, September 9, 2009,https://web.archive
.org/web/20130524032758/http://www.theroot.com/views/uknowurblack.

24. Farhad Manjoo, "How Black People Use Twitter," *Slate*, August 10, 2010, slate
.com/technology/2010/08/how-black-people-use-twitter.html.

25. "Big Racial Divide over Zimmerman Verdict," Pew Research Center, July 22, 2013.

26. "On Twitter: Anger Greets the Zimmerman Verdict," Pew Research Center, July 17,
2013, www.pewresearch.org/short-reads/2013/07/17/on-twitter-anger-greets-the
-zimmerman-verdict/.

27. "Remarks by the President on Trayvon Martin," The White House, July 19, 2013,
https://obamawhitehouse.archives.gov/the-press-office/2013/07/19/remarks
-president-trayvon-martin#:~:text=The%20judge%20conducted%20the%20
trial,and%20they%20rendered%20a%20verdict.

28. John Gramlich, "Black Imprisonment Rate in the U.S. Has Fallen by a Third
Since 2006," Pew Research Center, May 6, 2020, www.pewresearch.org
/short-reads/2020/05/06/share-of-black-white-hispanic-americans-in-prison
-2018-vs-2006/.

29. Ibid.

30. Jessica Guynn, "Meet the Woman Who Coined #BlackLivesMatter," *USA Today*,
March 4, 2015, www.usatoday.com/story/tech/2015/03/04/alicia-garza-black-lives
-matter/24341593/.

31. "#BlackLivesMatter: The Birth of a New Civil Rights Movement," *The Guardian*,
July 19, 2015, www.theguardian.com/world/2015/jul/19/blacklivesmatter-birth
-civil-rights-movement.

32. Ibid.

4: #BLACKLIVESMATTER

1. Susanna Capelouto, "Eric Garner: The Haunting Last Words of a Dying Man," CNN,
December 8, 2014, www.cnn.com/2014/12/04/us/garner-last-words/index.html.

2. Jazzy T., "Broadway Performs 'I Can't Breathe' Poem," Power 93, WBLK, wblk
.com/broadway-performs-i-cant-breathe-poem-video/.

3. Alice Speri, "A Chokehold Didn't Kill Eric Garner, Your Disrespect for the NYPD
Did," *Vice News*, August 6, 2014, www.vice.com/en/article/59a4en/a-chokehold
-didnt-kill-eric-garner-your-disrespect-for-the-nypd-did.

4. "Fatal Police Violence by Race and State in the USA, 1980–2019: A Network Meta-
Regression," *The Lancet*, October 2, 2021, www.thelancet.com/journals/lancet/ar
ticle/PIIS0140-6736(21)01609-3/fulltext.

5. "Violence Flares Again in Harlem; Restraint Urged," *New York Times*, July 20,
1964, www.nytimes.com/1964/07/20/archives/violence-flares-again-in-harlem-re
straint-urged-19-hurt-in-new.html.

6. "Police Board Absolves Gilligan in Slaying of Negro Teen-Ager; No Violation of
Rules Found—Shooting Led to Riots in Harlem and Brooklyn," *New York Times*,
November 7, 1964, www.nytimes.com/1964/11/07/archives/police-board-ab
solves-gilligan-in-slayin-g-of-negro-teenager-no.html.

7. Jason Pollock, *Stranger Fruit*, 2017, www.imdb.com/title/tt6642264/.
8. "Department of Justice Report Regarding the Criminal Investigation into the Shooting Death of Michael Brown by Ferguson, Missouri Police Officer Darren Wilson," March 4, 2015, https://www.justice.gov/sites/default/files/opa/press-releases/attachments/2015/03/04/doj_report_on_shooting_of_michael_brown_1.pdf.
9. Jim Dalrymple II, "A Witness to the Police Shooting of Michael Brown Live-Tweeted the Entire Event," *Buzzfeed News*, August 15, 2014, www.buzzfeednews.com/article/jimdalrympleii/a-witness-to-the-police-shooting-of-michael-brown-live-tweet.
10. "Ferguson, Missouri Crowd After Fatal Shooting of Unarmed Teen: 'Kill the Police,'" Associated Press, August 9, 2014, newsone.com/3042999/missouri-crowd-after-shooting-kill-the-police/.
11. Jim Dalrymple II, "This Is Why Darren Wilson Supporters Are Rallying In St. Louis," *Buzzfeed News*, August 25, 2014, www.buzzfeednews.com/article/jimdalrympleii/why-darren-wilson-supporters-are-rallying-in-st-louis.
12. Joyce Jones, "This Ain't Your Granddaddy's Civil Rights Movement," BET, December 5, 2014, www.bet.com/article/debcim/this-ain-t-your-granddaddy-s-civil-rights-movement.
13. #TeamEbony, "And the Young Ones Shall Lead Them," *Ebony*, October 2, 2014, www.ebony.com/and-the-young-ones-shall-lead-them-the-ferguson-rebellion-and-the-crisis-in-blac/.
14. "Remarks by the President After Announcement of the Decision by the Grand Jury in Ferguson, Missouri," The White House, November 24, 2014, https://obamawhitehouse.archives.gov/the-press-office/2014/11/24/remarks-president-after-announcement-decision-grand-jury-ferguson-missou.
15. Juliet Eilperin and Greg Jaffe, "Obama After Ferguson: Youth Leaders Urge President to Be 'More Out in Front' on Race," *Washington Post*, December 2, 2014, www.washingtonpost.com/politics/obama-after-ferguson-youth-leaders-urge-president-to-be-more-out-in-front-on-race/2014/12/01/eca65690-7980-11e4-84d4-7c896b90abdc_story.html.
16. "Breaking: Ferguson Activists Meet with President Obama to Demand an End to Police Brutality Nationwide," Funders for Justice, December 1, 2014, fundersforjustice.org/breaking-ferguson-activists-meet-with-president-obama-to-demand-an-end-to-police-brutality-nationwide/.
17. Bruce Drake, "Divide Between Blacks and Whites on Police Runs Deep," Pew Research Center, April 28, 2015, www.pewresearch.org/short-reads/2015/04/28/blacks-whites-police/.
18. Jake Miller, "Why Did Chris Christie Go After Black Lives Matter?," *Face the Nation*, CBS News, October 28, 2015, www.cbsnews.com/news/why-did-chris-christie-go-after-black-lives-matter-election-2016/.
19. Joe Coscarelli, "Watch Al Sharpton Bring the House Down at Michael Brown's Funeral: 'This Is Not About You! This Is About Justice!,'" *New York*, August 25, 2014, nymag.com/intelligencer/2014/08/al-sharpton-eulogy-michael-brown-funeral.html.
20. Byron York, "At Michael Brown Funeral, Al Sharpton's Double-Edged Eulogy Evokes Anger," *Washington Examiner*, August 25, 2014, www.washingtonexaminer

.com/opinion/1724434/at-michael-brown-funeral-al-sharptons-double-edged-eu logy-evokes-anger/.

21. Jeff Smith, "In Ferguson, Black Town, White Power," *New York Times*, August 17, 2014, www.nytimes.com/2014/08/18/opinion/in-ferguson-black-town-white-pow er.html.

22. "Investigation of the Ferguson Police Department," United States Department of Justice Civil Rights Division, March 4, 2015, www.justice.gov/sites/default/files /opa/press-releases/attachments/2015/03/04/ferguson_police_department_re port_1.pdf.

23. Patrisse Khan-Cullors, "We Didn't Start a Movement. We Started a Network," *Medium*, February 22, 2016, medium.com/@patrissemariecullorsbrignac/we-didn't -start-a-movement-we-started-a-network-90f9b5717668.

24. "Black Lives Matter Co-Founder Opal Tometi on the Fight for Racial Justice in the US," *Seeking Peace* podcast featuring Opal Tometi, Georgetown University's Institute for Women, Peace and Security, January 13, 2021, giwps.georgetown.edu/black -lives-matter-co-founder-opal-tometi-on-the-fight-for-racial-justice-in-the-us/.

25. "Herstory," Black Lives Matter, https://blacklivesmatter.com/herstory/.

26. "Black Lives Matter Movement Wins Sydney Peace Prize," University of Sydney, May 23, 2017, www.sydney.edu.au/news-opinion/news/2017/05/23/black-lives -matter-movement-wins-sydney-peace-prize.html.

27. "Black Lives Matter Co-Founder Opal Tometi on the Fight for Racial Justice in the US," *Seeking Peace* podcast.

28. Monica Anderson, "The Hashtag #BlackLivesMatter Emerges: Social Activism on Twitter," Pew Research Center, August 15, 2016, www.pewresearch.org/inter net/2016/08/15/the-hashtag-blacklivesmatter-emerges-social-activism-on-twitter/.

29. "Black Lives Matter Co-Founder Opal Tometi on the Fight for Racial Justice in the US," *Seeking Peace* podcast.

30. Anderson, "The Hashtag #BlackLivesMatter Emerges: Social Activism on Twitter."

31. Issac Chotiner, "A Black Lives Matter Co-Founder Explains Why This Time Is Different," *The New Yorker*, June 3, 2020, www.newyorker.com/news/q-and-a/a-black -lives-matter-co-founder-explains-why-this-time-is-different.

32. Ibid.

33. "Black Lives Matter," *Time*, April 20, 2015, time.com/magazine/us/3814960/april -20th-2015-vol-185-no-14-u-s/.

34. Alex Altman, "Black Lives Matter," *Time*, December 2015, https://time.com/time -person-of-the-year-2015-runner-up-black-lives-matter/.

5: WHITE BACKLASH

1. Amber Phillips, "'They're Rapists.' President Trump's Campaign Launch Speech Two Years Later, Annotated," *Washington Post*, June 16, 2017, www.washington post.com/news/the-fix/wp/2017/06/16/theyre-rapists-presidents-trump-cam paign-launch-speech-two-years-later-annotated/.

2. Jeremy Stahl, "The Exploitation of 'Beautiful Kate,'" *Slate*, August 10, 2017, slate .com/news-and-politics/2017/08/the-death-of-kate-steinle-and-the-rise-of-donald -trump.html.

3. Christopher Ingraham, "On Twitter, Trump Accuses Blacks of Racism Three

Times as Often as Whites," *Washington Post*, August 14, 2017, www.washington
post.com/news/wonk/wp/2017/08/14/on-twitter-trump-accuses-blacks-of-racism
-three-times-as-often-as-whites/.

4. MJ Lee, "Trump Says He Still Doesn't Know Where Obama Was Born," CNN,
July 9, 2015, www.cnn.com/2015/07/08/politics/donald-trump-illegal-immigrant
-workers/index.html.

5. "Donald Trump Links Shooting Death in San Francisco with Border Control,"
The Guardian, July 4, 2015, www.theguardian.com/us-news/2015/jul/04/donald
-trump-links-shooting-death-in-san-franciso-with-border-control?CMP=gu
_com.

6. Lee, "Trump Says He Still Doesn't Know Where Obama Was Born."

7. Michael Harriot, "Kate Steinle and the Return of the Angry White Lynch Mob,"
The Root, December 5, 2017, www.theroot.com/kate-steinle-and-the-return-of-the
-angry-white-lynch-mo-1820984744.

8. "Bill O'Reilly: The Vilification of Donald Trump over Illegal Immigration," Fox
News, July 7, 2015, www.foxnews.com/transcript/bill-oreilly-the-vilification-of
-donald-trump-over-illegal-immigration.

9. Ibid.

10. Erik Wemple, "Fox News's Bill O'Reilly Embraces Activism with 'Kate's Law,'"
Washington Post, July 14, 2015, washingtonpost.com/blogs/erik-wemple/wp/2015
/07/14/fox-newss-bill-oreilly-embraces-activism-with-kates-law/.

11. David Frum, "The Problem with Downplaying Immigrant Crime," *The Atlantic*,
July 29, 2015, www.theatlantic.com/politics/archive/2015/07/the-problem-with
-downplaying-immigrant-crime/399905/.

12. Doug Criss, "This Is the 30-Year-Old Willie Horton Ad Everybody Is Talking
About Today," CNN, November 1, 2018, www.cnn.com/2018/11/01/politics/wil
lie-horton-ad-1988-explainer-trnd/index.html.

13. David Kaczynski, "David Duke Urges His Supporters to Volunteer and Vote for
Trump," *BuzzFeed News*, February 25, 2016, www.buzzfeednews.com/article/an
drewkaczynski/david-duke-urges-his-supporters-to-volunteer-and-vote-for-tr#
.bsP0pjXpae.

14. "Why White Nationalists Hear a Political Ally in Donald Trump, *PBS NewsHour*,
October 26, 2016, www.pbs.org/newshour/show/white-nationalists-hear-political
-ally-donald-trump.

15. "Interview with Presidential Candidate Donald Trump," *State of the Union*, CNN,
February 28, 2016, www.cnn.com/TRANSCRIPTS/1602/28/sotu.01.html.

16. Philip Bump, "In 1927, Donald Trump's Father Was Arrested After a Klan Riot
in Queens," *Washington Post*, February 29, 2016, www.washingtonpost.com/news
/the-fix/wp/2016/02/28/in-1927-donald-trumps-father-was-arrested-after-a-klan
-riot-in-queens/.

17. "Southwest Border Unaccompanied Alien Children FY 2014," U.S. Customs and
Border Protection, October 13, 2016, https://www.cbp.gov/newsroom/stats/south
west-border-unaccompanied-children/fy-2014.

18. Nolan Malone, Kaari F. Baluja, Joseph M. Costanzo, and Cynthia J. Davis, "Census 2000 Brief: The Foreign-Born Population: 2000," U.S. Census Bureau,

December 1, 2003, www.census.gov/library/publications/2003/dec/c2kbr-34.html
#:~:text=Census%202000%20measured%20a%20population,of%20whom%20
were%20foreign%20born.

19. "1960 Census of the Population: Supplementary Reports: Race of the Population of
the United States, by States: 1960," U.S. Census Bureau, September 7, 1961, www
.census.gov/library/publications/1961/dec/pc-s1-10.html.

20. "The White Population: 2010," U.S. Census Bureau, September 2011, www2.cen
sus.gov/library/publications/cen2010/briefs/c2010br-05.pdf.

21. "The Hispanic Population: 2010," U.S. Census Bureau, May 2011, www.census
.gov/history/pdf/c2010br-04-092020.pdf.

22. "2010 Census Shows America's Diversity," U.S. Census Bureau, March 24, 2011,
www.census.gov/newsroom/releases/archives/2010_census/cb11-cn125.html.

23. Michael Hoefer, Nancy Rytina, and Bryan C. Baker, "Estimates of the Unauthorized
Immigrant Population Residing in the United States: January 2010," Department
of Homeland Security, February 2011, www.dhs.gov/sites/default/files/publications
/Unauthorized%20Immigrant%20Population%20Estimates%20in%20the%20
US%20January%202010_0.pdf.

24. "Remarks by the President on Immigration," The White House, June 15, 2012,
obamawhitehouse.archives.gov/the-press-office/2012/06/15/remarks-president
-immigration.

25. Robert Barnes, "Supreme Court Upholds Key Part of Arizona Law for Now, Strikes
Down Other Provisions," *Washington Post*, June 25, 2012, www.washingtonpost
.com/politics/supreme-court-rules-on-arizona-immigration-law/2012/06/25/gJ
QA0Nrm1V_story.html.

26. Jens Manuel Krogstad, "On Views of Immigrants, Americans Largely Split Along
Party Lines," Pew Research Center, September 30, 2015, www.pewresearch.org
/short-reads/2015/09/30/on-views-of-immigrants-americans-largely-split-along
-party-lines/.

27. John Gramlich, "Trump Voters Want to Build the Wall, but Are More Divided on
Other Immigration Questions," Pew Research Center, November 29, 2016, www
.pewresearch.org/short-reads/2016/11/29/trump-voters-want-to-build-the-wall
-but-are-more-divided-on-other-immigration-questions/.

28. Chuck Sudo, "Indiana Cop Sells 'Breathe Easy Don't Break the Law' T-Shirts,"
Chicagoist, December 16, 2014, chicagoist.com/2014/12/16/breathe_easy_dont
_break_the_law_t-s.php.

29. "Across Racial Lines, More Say Nation Needs to Make Changes to Achieve Racial Equality," Pew Research Center, August 5, 2015, www.pewresearch.org
/politics/2015/08/05/across-racial-lines-more-say-nation-needs-to-make-changes
-to-achieve-racial-equality/.

30. Janet Hook, "U.S. Split Along Racial Lines on Backlash Against Police, Poll Finds,"
The Wall Street Journal, May 4, 2015, www.wsj.com/articles/BL-WB-54943.

31. "William J. Bratton Remarks at NOBLE William R. Bracey CEO Symposium,
March 13, Atlanta, Georgia," trustandjustice.org/resources/article/william-bratton
-remarks-at-noble-friday-march-13-atlanta-ga.

32. James B. Comey, "Hard Truths: Law Enforcement and Race," Georgetown

University, Washington, D.C., February 12, 2015, www.fbi.gov/news/speeches/hard-truths-law-enforcement-and-race.

33. Eva Frazer, MD, et al., "The Violence Epidemic in the African American Community: A Call for Comprehensive Reform," National Medical Association White Paper on Violence 2017, National Minority Health Institute, https://www.mhinst.org/pdf/NMA_WhitePaper.pdf.

34. Kiana Cox and Christine Tamir, "Place and Community," Pew Research Center, April 14, 2022, www.pewresearch.org/race-ethnicity/2022/04/14/black-americans-place-and-community/.

35. German Lopez, "Watch: Hillary Clinton's Tense, Closed-Door Meeting with Black Lives Matter Activists," *Vox*, August 18, 2015, www.vox.com/2015/8/18/9171905/hillary-clinton-black-lives-matter.

36. Sam Sanders, "Bill Clinton Gets into Heated Exchange with Black Lives Matter Protester," NPR, April 7, 2016, www.npr.org/2016/04/07/473428472/bill-clinton-gets-into-heated-exchange-with-black-lives-matter-protester#:~:text=%22I%20don't%20know%20how,were%20good%20citizens%20.

37. "Transcript of Facebook Video in Fatal Police Shooting," Associated Press, July 7, 2016, apnews.com/general-news-3ec9863050bc4ded954cf7a0f3256f70.

38. twitter.com/HillaryClinton/status/751081918712676352.

39. Ben Wolfgang, "Hillary Clinton Meets with Philando Castile's Family in Minnesota," *Washington Times*, July 19, 2016, www.washingtontimes.com/news/2016/jul/19/clinton-meets-philando-castiles-family-minnesota/.

40. Barack Obama, Facebook, July 7, 2016, www.facebook.com/potus44/posts/507884336068078.

41. Ibid.

42. Nicole Gaouette and Steve Visser, "Dallas Police Shooter a Reclusive Army Reservist," CNN, July 11, 2016, www.cnn.com/2016/07/08/us/micah-xavier-johnson-dallas-shooter/index.html.

43. Stephen Sawchuk, "In AFT Talk, Hillary Clinton Doubles Down on Support for Teachers," *Education Week*, July 18, 2016, www.edweek.org/policy-politics/in-aft-talk-hillary-clinton-doubles-down-on-support-for-teachers/2016/07.

44. Chris Summers, "'Too Often, We Judge Other Groups by Their Worst Examples While Judging Ourselves by Our Best Intentions': Moving Quote by George W. Bush at Dallas Police Memorial Inspires America," *Daily Mail*, July 13, 2016, www.dailymail.co.uk/news/article-3687974/Too-judge-groups-worst-examples-judging-best-intentions-Moving-quote-George-W-Bush-Dallas-police-memorial-inspires-America.html.

45. "Remarks by the President at Memorial Service for Fallen Dallas Police Officers," The White House, July 12, 2016, obamawhitehouse.archives.gov/the-press-office/2016/07/12/remarks-president-memorial-service-fallen-dallas-police-officers.

46. David Weigel, "Three Words That Republicans Wrestle with: 'Black Lives Matter,'" *Washington Post*, July 12, 2016, www.washingtonpost.com/politics/three-words-that-republicans-wrestle-with-black-lives-matter/2016/07/12/f5a9dfdc-4878-11e6-90a8-fb84201e0645_story.html.

47. "Fatal Force: 1,150 People Have Been Shot and Killed by Police in the Past 12 Months," www.washingtonpost.com/graphics/investigations/police-shootings-database/.

48. "Kaepernick Voices Support for Racial Justice, Condemns Police Brutality," NBC Bay Area, August 28, 2016, www.nbcbayarea.com/news/sports/kaepernick/130588/.

49. Yamiche Alcindor, "Colin Kaepernick Says Presidential Candidates Were Trying to 'Debate Who's Less Racist,'" *New York Times*, September 28, 2016, www.nytimes.com/2016/09/29/us/colin-kaepernick-says-presidential-candidates-were-trying-to-debate-whos-less-racist.html.

50. Eric Edholm, "Colin Kaepernick: Donald Trump, Hillary Clinton Are 'Proven Liars,'" *Yahoo Sports*, September 27, 2016, https://sports.yahoo.com/news/colin-kaepernick-donald-trump-hillary-clinton-are-proven-liars-215536317.html.

51. Melissa Harris-Perry, "Why #BlackLivesMatter's Alicia Garza Won't Support Hillary Clinton," *Elle*, June 27, 2016, www.elle.com/culture/career-politics/news/a37416/alicia-garza-black-lives-matter-hillary-clinton/.

52. Jesse Holland, "Black Lives Matter Movement Won't Endorse a Presidential Candidate," PBS, September 19, 2015, www.pbs.org/newshour/politics/black-lives-matter-movement-wont-endorse-presidential-candidate.

53. Aislinn Pulley, "Black Struggle Is Not a Sound Bite: Why I Refused to Meet with President Obama," *Truthout*, February 18, 2016, https://truthout.org/articles/black-struggle-is-not-a-sound-bite-why-i-refused-to-meet-with-president-obama/.

54. "Remarks by President Obama in Town Hall with Young Leaders of the UK," The White House, April 23, 2016, https://obamawhitehouse.archives.gov/the-press-office/2016/04/23/remarks-president-obama-town-hall-young-leaders-uk.

55. Jim Norman, "U.S. Worries About Race Relations Reach a New High," Gallup, April 11, 2016, https://news.gallup.com/poll/190574/worries-race-relations-reach-new-high.aspx.

56. Frank Bruni, "Has Barack Obama Hurt Race Relations?," *New York Times*, July 13, 2016, www.nytimes.com/2016/07/13/opinion/has-barack-obama-hurt-race-relations.html.

57. "Khizr Khan's Speech to the 2016 Democratic National Convention," ABC News, August 1, 2016, abcnews.go.com/Politics/full-text-khizr-khans-speech-2016-democratic-national/story?id=41043609.

58. "Donald Trump to Father of Fallen Soldier: 'I've Made a Lot of Sacrifices,'" ABC News, July 30, 2016, abcnews.go.com/Politics/donald-trump-father-fallen-soldier-ive-made-lot/story?id=41015051.

59. "An Examination of the 2016 Electorate, Based on Validated Voters," Pew Research Center, August 9, 2018, www.pewresearch.org/politics/2018/08/09/an-examination-of-the-2016-electorate-based-on-validated-voters/.

60. Remarks of President Donald J. Trump—as prepared for delivery, Inaugural Address, January 20, 2017, https://trumpwhitehouse.archives.gov/briefings-statements/the-inaugural-address/.

6: THE ALT-RIGHT WHITE HOUSE

1. Julia Felsenthal, "These Criminal Justice Activists Are Taking the System Head On," *Vogue*, March 8, 2018, https://www.vogue.com/projects/13541665/criminal-justice-reform.

2. Arwa Mahdawi, "Black Lives Matter's Alicia Garza: 'Leadership Today Doesn't Look Like Martin Luther King,'" *The Guardian*, October 17, 2020, www.the guardian.com/world/2020/oct/17/black-lives-matter-alicia-garza-leadership-today -doesnt-look-like-martin-luther-king.

3. Greg Jaffe, "Obama Counsels Black Lives Matter Activists: 'You Can't Just Keep on Yelling,'" *Washington Post*, April 23, 2016, www.washingtonpost.com/news/post -politics/wp/2016/04/23/obama-counsels-black-lives-matter-activists-you-cant -just-keep-on-yelling/.

4. "Commencement Address at Howard University," May 7, 2016, www.presidency .ucsb.edu/documents/commencement-address-howard-university-1.

5. Alicia Garza, *The Purpose of Power: How We Come Together When We Fall Apart* (New York: Random House, 2020), p. 171.

6. Jens Manuel Krogstad and Mark Huge Lopez, "Black Voter Turnout Fell in 2016, even as a Record Number of Americans Cast Ballots," Pew Research Center, May 12, 2017, www.pewresearch.org/short-reads/2017/05/12/black-voter-turnout-fell-in -2016-even-as-a-record-number-of-americans-cast-ballots/.

7. Garza, *The Purpose of Power*, p. 172.

8. Margaret Talbot, "The Populist Prophet," *The New Yorker*, October 5, 2015, www .newyorker.com/magazine/2015/10/12/the-populist-prophet.

9. Dara Lind, "Black Lives Matter vs. Bernie Sanders, Explained," *Vox*, August 11, 2015, www.vox.com/2015/8/11/9127653/bernie-sanders-black-lives-matter.

10. Patrisse Cullors, "#BlackLivesMatter Will Continue to Disrupt the Political Process," *Washington Post*, August 18, 2015, www.washingtonpost.com/news /powerpost/wp/2015/08/18/opinion-blacklivesmatter-will-continue-to-disrupt -the-political-process/.

11. Reena Flores, "Congressional Black Caucus Backs Hillary Clinton," CBS News, February 11, 2016, www.cbsnews.com/news/congressional-black-caucus-to-back -hillary-clinton/.

12. Vanessa Williams and Scott Clement, "Despite Black Lives Matter, Young Black Americans Aren't Voting in Higher Numbers," *Washington Post*, May 14, 2016, www.washingtonpost.com/politics/despite-black-lives-matter-young-black-amer icans-arent-voting-in-higher-numbers/2016/05/14/e1780b3a-1176-11e6-93ae -50921721165d_story.html.

13. David Neiwert, *Alt-America: The Rise of the Radical Right in the Age of Trump* (New York: Verso, 2017).

14. Don Gonyea, "Majority of White Americans Say They Believe Whites Face Discrimination," NPR, October 24, 2017, www.npr.org/2017/10/24/559604836 /majority-of-white-americans-think-theyre-discriminated-against.

15. "Dylann Roof's Manifesto Is Fluent in White Nationalist Ideology," Southern Poverty Law Center, June 21, 2015, www.splcenter.org/hatewatch/2015/06/20/dylann -roofs-manifesto-fluent-white-nationalist-ideology.

16. Debbie Elliott, "The Charlottesville Rally 5 Years Later: 'It's What You're Still Trying to Forget,'" NPR, August 12, 2022, www.npr.org/2022/08/12/1116942725 /the-charlottesville-rally-5-years-later-its-what-youre-still-trying-to-forget.

17. Joe Heim, "Recounting a Day of Rage, Hate, Violence and Death," *Washington Post*,

August 14, 2017, www.washingtonpost.com/graphics/2017/local/charlottesville
-timeline/.

18. https://twitter.com/VSPPIO/status/896434685206822912.

19. https://www.facebook.com/shaunking/photos/a.799605230078397/1508327
532539493/?type=3.

20. https://twitter.com/realDonaldTrump/status/896420822780444672?lang=en.

21. "Full text: Trump's Comments on White Supremacists, 'Alt-Left' in Charlottesville," *Politico*, August 15, 2017, www.politico.com/story/2017/08/15/full-text
-trump-comments-white-supremacists-alt-left-transcript-241662.

22. Scott Clement and David Nakamura, "Poll Shows Clear Disapproval of How
Trump Responded to Charlottesville Violence," *Washington Post*, August 21,
2017, www.washingtonpost.com/politics/poll-shows-strong-disapproval-of-how
-trump-responded-to-charlottesville-violence/2017/08/21/4e5c585c-868b-11e7-a
94f-3139abce39f5_story.html.

23. "Trump, Again, Casts Blame on Both Sides for Deadly Violence in Virginia," Reuters, August 16, 2017, www.reuters.com/article/idUSL8N1L137F/.

24. "The Hate He Dares Not Speak Of," *New York Times*, August, 13, 2017, www
.nytimes.com/2017/08/13/opinion/trump-charlottesville-hate-stormer.html.

25. Thomas J. Main, *The Rise of the Alt-Right* (Washington, D.C.: Brookings Institution
Press, 2018).

26. Jeff Greenfield, "Trump Is Pat Buchannan with Better Timing," *Politico Magazine*,
September/October 2016, www.politico.com/magazine/story/2016/09/donald
-trump-pat-buchanan-republican-america-first-nativist-214221/.

27. Kevin Drum, "Is Steve Bannon Racist? Let's Find Out!," *Mother Jones*, November 14, 2016, www.motherjones.com/kevin-drum/2016/11/steve-bannon-racist-lets
-find-out/.

28. Sarah Posner, "How Steve Bannon Created an Online Haven for White Nationalists," *Mother Jones*, August 22, 2016, www.motherjones.com/politics/2016/08
/stephen-bannon-donald-trump-alt-right-breitbart-news/.

29. P. R. Lockhart, "How Russia Exploited Racial Tensions in America During the 2016 Elections," *Vox*, December 17, 2018, www.vox.com/identi
ties/2018/12/17/18145075/russia-facebook-twitter-internet-research-agency
-race.

30. Karen Yourish and Larry Buchanan, "Mueller Report Shows Depth of Connections
Between Trump Campaign and Russians," *New York Times*, April 19, 2019, https://
www.nytimes.com/interactive/2019/01/26/us/politics/trump-contacts-russians
-wikileaks.html#:~:text=Campaign and Russians.

31. Jason Wilson, "Leaked Emails Reveal Trump Aide Stephen Miller's White Nationalist Views," *The Guardian*, November 14, 2019, www.theguardian.com/us
-news/2019/nov/14/stephen-miller-leaked-emails-white-nationalism-trump.

32. James Higdon, "Jeff Sessions' Coming War on Legal Marijuana," *Politico Magazine*,
December 2016, www.politico.com/magazine/story/2016/12/jeff-sessions-coming
-war-on-legal-marijuana-214501/.

33. Tim Walker, "Donald Trump Builds Cabinet Team of Far-Right Figures,
Nationalists—and White Men Named Mike," *The Independent*, November 19,

2016, www.independent.co.uk/news/world/americas/donald-trump-president-lat est-cabinet-sessions-flynn-pompeo-racist-mike-a7426046.html.

34. "Trump Targets Sanctuary Cities, Promises Border Wall in Executive Orders," ABC News, January 25, 2017, abcnews.go.com/Politics/trump-signs-executive -orders-border-wall-immigration/story?id=45045056.

35. "Executive Order: Enhancing Public Safety in the Interior of the United States," The White House, January 25, 2017, https://trumpwhitehouse.archives.gov/presi dential-actions/executive-order-enhancing-public-safety-interior-united-states/.

36. https://twitter.com/realDonaldTrump/status/936437372706836480?s=20.

37. "Attorney General Sessions Statement on the Verdict in People of the State of California vs. Jose Ines Garcia Zarate aka Juan Francisco Lopez Sanchez," Department of Justice, November 30, 2017, www.justice.gov/opa/pr/attorney-general-sessions -statement-verdict-people-state-california-vs-jose-ines-garcia.

38. Nicole Goodkind, "Jeff Sessions Blames Gun Deaths Increase on Antifa, Black Lives Matter and ACLU—But Not Guns," *Newsweek*, September 20, 2018, www .newsweek.com/jeff-sessions-antifa-gun-death-blm-1130796.

39. Eliana Plott, "The Fall of Jeff Sessions, and What Came After," *New York Times Magazine*, June 30, 2020, www.nytimes.com/2020/06/30/magazine/jeff-sessions.html.

40. Alicia Garza, "BLM Co-Founder: Obama Should Help the People Who His Presidency Failed," *Time*, January 24, 2017, time.com/4599447/barack-obama-black -lives/.

41. Sharon Cohen and Deepti Hajela, "Obama Racial Legacy: Pride, Promise, Regret and Deep Rift," Associated Press, January 4, 2017, apnews.com/article/jackie -robinson-barack-obama-chicago-politics-il-state-wire-29b24a7985a442d8b 890261da99cad86.

42. Garza, *The Purpose of Power*, p. 176.

43. Garza, "BLM Co-Founder: Obama Should Help the People Who His Presidency Failed."

44. Richard A. Oppel Jr., "States Trim Penalties and Prison Rolls, Even as Sessions Gets Tough," *New York Times*, May 18, 2017, www.nytimes.com/2017/05/18/us /states-prisons-crime-sentences-jeff-sessions.html.

45. Joshiah Ryan, "'This Was a Whitelash': Van Jones' Take on the Election Results," CNN, November 9, 2016, www.cnn.com/2016/11/09/politics/van-jones-results -disappointment-cnntv/index.html.

46. Author's interview with Van Jones, September 28, 2022.

47. *The First Step*, 2021, www.firststepfilm.com/.

48. Author's interview with Van Jones, September 28, 2022.

49. https://twitter.com/VanJones68/status/1062852237779554304.

50. "JustLeadershipUSA joins with National Partner Organizations in Opposing Revised First Step Act Legislation," JustLeadershipUSA, November 20, 2018, jlusa .org/media-release/justleadershipusa-joins-with-national-partner-organizations-in -opposing-revised-first-step-act-legislation/.

51. "Black Lives Matter Global Network Responds to the United States Senate Passage of the First Step Act, A Criminal Reform Package," Black Lives Matter, December 20, 2018, blacklivesmatter.com/black-lives-matter-global-network-responds-to -the-united-states-senate-passage-of-the-first-step-act-a-criminal-reform-package/.

52. "Computational Propaganda, Jewish-Americans and the 2018 Midterms: The Amplification of Anti-Semitic Harassment Online," ADL, October 26, 2018, www.adl.org/resources/report/computational-propaganda-jewish-americans-and -2018-midterms-amplification-anti.

53. "2017 Audit of Anti-Semitic Incidents," ADL, February 25, 2018, www.adl.org /resources/report/2017-audit-anti-semitic-incidents.

54. Heidi Beirich and Susy Buchanan, "2017: The Year in Hate and Extremism," Southern Poverty Law Center, February 11, 2018, www.splcenter.org/fighting-hate /intelligence-report/2018/2017-year-hate-and-extremism.

55. John Wagner, "Trump Says He 'Wouldn't Be Surprised' if Unfounded Conspiracy Theory About George Soros Funding Caravan Is True," *Washington Post*, November 1, 2018, www.washingtonpost.com/politics/trump-wouldnt-be-surprised -if-democratic-megadonor-george-soros-is-funding-the-migrant-caravan/2018 /11/01/9ea196a0-ddcf-11e8-85df-7a6b4d25cfbb_story.html.

56. https://twitter.com/repmattgaetz/status/1052629557826736129.

57. Jarrett Renshaw, "Who Is Robert Bowers, the Pittsburgh Synagogue Shooting Suspect?," Reuters, October 29, 2018, https://www.reuters.com/article/idUSKCN 1N31S4/.

58. "11 Dead, Several Others Shot at Pittsburgh Synagogue," KDKA News, October 27, 2018, https://www.cbsnews.com/pittsburgh/news/heavy-police-presence -near-synagogue-in-squirrel-hill/.

59. Ibid.

7: STACEY AND THE SQUAD

1. Arit John, "A Brief History of Squads," *New York Times*, July 18, 2019, www.ny times.com/2019/07/18/style/squad-aoc-trump.html.

2. https://twitter.com/realDonaldTrump/status/1150381395078000643.

3. Michael Crowley, "At Rally, President Accuses Liberal Critics of Seeking the Nation's 'Destruction,'" *New York Times*, July 17, 2019, www.nytimes.com/2019/07/17/us /politics/trump-send-her-back-ilhan-omar.html.

4. https://twitter.com/realDonaldTrump/status/1153315875476463616.

5. https://twitter.com/AOC/status/1150445185438035968.

6. https://twitter.com/AyannaPressley/status/1150460489199173632.

7. Bobby Allyn, "Congresswomen Denounce Trump Tweets Telling Them to 'Go Back' to Their Home Countries," NPR, July 14, 2019, www.npr.org /2019/07/14/741630889/congresswomen-denounce-trump-tweets-telling-them -to-go-back-to-their-home-countr.

8. Eli Watkins, "Ocasio-Cortez Says 'AOC Sucks' Chant at Trump Rally Shows Trump Needs a Woman to 'Vilify,'" CNN, March 30, 2019, www.cnn.com/2019/03/30 /politics/alexandria-ocasio-cortez-donald-trump/index.html.

9. Aaron Rupar, "New Congress Member Creates Stir by Saying of Trump: 'We're Going to Impeach This Motherfucker!,'" *Vox*, January 4, 2019, www.vox.com/policy-and -politics/2019/1/4/18168157/rashida-tlaib-trump-impeachment-motherfucker.

10. Katharine Seely, "Ayanna Pressley Upsets Capuano in Massachusetts House Race," *New York Times*, September 4, 2018, www.nytimes.com/2018/09/04/us/politics /ayanna-pressley-massachusetts.html.

11. Karl Vick, "Perhaps the Largest Protest in U.S. History Was Brought to You by Trump," *Time*, January 26, 2017, time.com/4649891/protest-donald-trump/.

12. #TeamEbony, "#WAKANDATHEVOTE Allows for Voter Registration at 'Black Panther' Screenings," *Ebony*, February 15, 2018, www.ebony.com/voter-registra tion-black-panther/.

13. Matthew Schneier, "The Stars of September," *New York Times*, August, 9, 2018, www.nytimes.com/2018/08/09/style/diversity-september-issue-magazines.html.

14. "Black Impact: Consumer Categories Where African Americans Move Markets," Nielsen, February 2018, www.nielsen.com/insights/2018/black-impact-consumer -categories-where-african-americans-move-markets/.

15. Doreen St. Félix, "What Kendrick Lamar's Pulitzer Means for Hip-Hop," *The New Yorker*, April 17, 2018, www.newyorker.com/culture/cultural-comment/what-kend rick-lamars-pulitzer-means-for-hip-hop.

16. National Domestic Workers Alliance, "About NDWA | National Domestic Workers Alliance," June 8, 2022, https://www.domesticworkers.org/about-ndwa/.

17. Black Futures Lab, "The Black Census Project Final," n.d., https://blackfutureslab .org/black-census-project-2/.

18. Ayo Tometi, "How Black Lives Matter Cofounder Ayọ Tometi Makes Sure She Can 'Weather the Storm'," August 25, 2021, https://ayotometi.org/how-black-lives-matter -cofounder-opal-tometi-makes-sure-she-can-weather-the-storm/.

19. Washington Post Staff, "Police Shootings Database 2015–2024: Search by Race, Age, Department," *Washington Post*, December 5, 2022, https://www.washington post.com/graphics/investigations/police-shootings-database/.

20. Patrisse Cullors, "21 Savage Released on Bond Following Black Lives Matter Led Consortium Demanding His Release, the Fight Is Not Over," Black Lives Matter, February 2019, blacklivesmatter.com/21-savage-released-on-bond-fol lowing-black-lives-matter-led-consortium-demanding-his-release-the-fight-is -not-over/.

21. Melanie Eversley, "Trump Tells Law Enforcement: 'Don't Be Too Nice' with Sus- pects," *USA Today*, July 28, 2017, www.usatoday.com/story/news/2017/07/29 /trump-tells-law-enforcement-dont-too-nice-suspects/522220001/.

22. "Obama Unleashes on Trump and GOP Ahead of Midterms," CNN, September 7, 2018, us.cnn.com/TRANSCRIPTS/1809/07/wolf.01.html.

23. Wilborn P. Nobles III, "Trump Calls Baltimore 'Disgusting . . . Rodent Infested Mess,' Rips Rep. Elijah Cummings over Border Criticism," *Baltimore Sun*, July 27, 2019, www.baltimoresun.com/2019/07/27/trump-calls-baltimore-disgusting-ro dent-infested-mess-rips-rep-elijah-cummings-over-border-criticism/.

24. Christopher Ingraham, "Trump's Voter Commission Is Now Facing at Least 7 Fed- eral Lawsuits," *Washington Post*, July 18, 2017, www.washingtonpost.com/news /wonk/wp/2017/07/18/trumps-voter-fraud-commission-is-now-facing-at-least -7-federal-lawsuits/.

25. Josh Gerstein and Matthew Nussbaum, "Trump Disbands Voter Fraud Commis- sion," *Politico*, January 3, 2018, www.politico.com/story/2018/01/03/trump-dis bands-voter-fraud-commission-322621.

26. Angela Caputo, Geoff Hing, and Johnny Kauffman, "After the Purge: How a Mas- sive Voter Purge in Georgia Affected the 2018 Election," *APM Reports*, October 29,

2019, www.apmreports.org/story/2019/10/29/georgia-voting-registration-records
-removed.

27. "Voter Purges," Brennan Center for Justice, www.brennancenter.org/issues/ensure
-every-american-can-vote/vote-suppression/voter-purges.

28. "Full Transcript: Stacey Abrams Democratic Rebuttal," *New York Times*, February 6,
2019, www.nytimes.com/2019/02/05/us/politics/stacey-abrams-speech.html.

29. twitter.com/danpfeiffer/status/1092993571391586304.

30. Astead W. Herndon, "Stacey Abrams Isn't Running for President. Should She
Be?," *New York Times*, February 6, 2019, www.nytimes.com/2019/02/06/us/poli
tics/stacey-abrams-president.html.

31. Stacey Abrams, *Minority Leader: How to Lead from the Outside and Make Real
Change* (New York: Henry Holt, 2018).

32. New York Times Magazine, "The 1619 Project," *New York Times Magazine*, May 29,
2024, https://www.nytimes.com/interactive/2019/08/14/magazine/1619-america-slav
ery.html.

33. Nikole Hannah-Jones, "Our Democracy's Founding Ideals Were False When They
Were Written. Black Americans Have Fought to Make Them True," 1619 Project,
New York Times, August 14, 2019, www.nytimes.com/interactive/2019/08/14/mag
azine/black-history-american-democracy.html.

34. Jake Silverstein, "On Recent Criticism of The 1619 Project," *New York Times*, October 16, 2020, www.nytimes.com/2020/10/16/magazine/criticism-1619-project
.html.

35. Leslie Harris, "I Helped Fact-Check the 1619 Project. The Times Ignored Me,"
Politico, March 6, 2020, https://www.politico.com/news/magazine/2020/03/06
/1619-project-new-york-times-mistake-122248.

36. "We Respond to the Historians Who Critiqued The 1619 Project," *New York
Times*, December 20, 2019, www.nytimes.com/2019/12/20/magazine/we-respond
-to-the-historians-who-critiqued-the-1619-project.html.

37. Bret Stephens, "The 1619 Chronicles," *New York Times*, October 9, 2020, www
.nytimes.com/2020/10/09/opinion/nyt-1619-project-criticisms.html.

38. Pamela Newkirk, "Diversity Has Become a Booming Business. So Where Are the
Results?," *Time*, October 10, 2019, time.com/5696943/diversity-business/.

39. Philip Kennicott, "A Powerful Memorial in Montgomery Remembers the Victims of
Lynching," *Washington Post*, April 24, 2018, www.washingtonpost.com/entertain
ment/museums/a-powerful-memorial-in-montgomery-remembers-the-victims-of-ly
nching/2018/04/24/3620e78a-471a-11e8-827e-190efaf1f1ee_story.html.

40. National Football League, "NFL: Issues Raised by Kaepernick Deserve Attention,"
September 4, 2018, https://www.nfl.com/news/nfl-issues-raised-by-kaepernick
-deserve-attention-0ap3000000958222.

41. Arun Venugopal, "'1619 Project' Journalist Says Black People Shouldn't Be an As-
terisk in U.S. History," *Fresh Air*, NPR, November 17, 2021, https://www.npr.org
/transcripts/1056404654.

42. "Remarks by President Trump at the White House Conference on American History," The White House, September 17, 2020, https://trumpwhitehouse.archives
.gov/briefings-statements/remarks-president-trump-white-house-conference-amer
ican-history/.

43. Zackary Okun Dunivin, Harry Yaojun Yan, Jelani Ince, and Fabio Rojas, "Black Lives Matter Protests Shift Public Discourse," *Proceedings of the National Academy of Sciences*, March 3, 2022, https://www.pnas.org/doi/full/10.1073/pnas.2117320119.

44. "Remarks by President Trump at South Dakota's 2020 Mount Rushmore Fireworks Celebration | Keystone, South Dakota," The White House, July 4, 2020, https://trumpwhitehouse.archives.gov/briefings-statements/remarks-president-trump-south-dakotas-2020-mount-rushmore-fireworks-celebration-keystone-south-dakota/.

45. "Executive Order on Combating Race and Sex Stereotyping," The White House, September 22, 2020, https://trumpwhitehouse.archives.gov/presidential-actions/executive-order-combating-race-sex-stereotyping/.

46. Author's interview with Rashad Robinson, April 16, 2022.

47. "Color of Change Secure Agreement from Facebook to Create Civil Rights Accountability Infrastructure," Color of Change, colorofchange.org/press_release/color-of-change-secures-agreement-from-facebook-to-create-civil-rights-accountability-infrastructure/.

48. Nicole Karlis," A Racial Justice Group Got Death Threats After Facebook Launched Secret Smear Campaign," *Salon*, February 19, 2018, www.salon.com/2018/11/19/a-racial-justice-group-started-getting-death-threats-after-facebook-launched-secret-smear-campaign/.

49. Mike Issac and Jack Nicas, "Facebook Cuts Ties with Washington Firm That Sought to Discredit Social Network's Critics," *New York Times*, November 15, 2018, www.nytimes.com/2018/11/15/technology/facebook-definers-soros.html.

50. Philip Bump, "Trump Keeps Framing the El Paso Shooting as His Side Against His Opponents,'" *Washington Post*, August 7, 2019, www.washingtonpost.com/politics/2019/08/07/trump-keeps-framing-el-paso-shooting-his-side-against-his-opponents/.

51. Matt Zapotosky, "Wray Says FBI Has Recorded About 100 Domestic Terrorism Arrests in Fiscal 2019 and Many Investigations Involve White Supremacy," *Washington Post*, July 23, 2019, www.washingtonpost.com/national-security/wray-says-fbi-has-recorded-about-100-domestic-terrorism-arrests-in-fiscal-2019-and-most-investigations-involve-white-supremacy/2019/07/23/600d49a6-aca1-11e9-bc5c-e73b603e7f38_story.html.

52. twitter.com/realDonaldTrump/status/1155205025121132545.

8: "I'M DEAD"

1. "CNBC News Release CNBC transcript: President Donald Trump Sits Down with CNBC's Joe Kernen at the World Economic Forum in Davos, Switzerland," CNBC, January 22, 2020, www.cnbc.com/2020/01/22/cnbc-transcript-president-donald-trump-sits-down-with-cnbcs-joe-kernen-at-the-world-economic-forum-in-davos-switzerland.html.

2. Peter Martinez, "Minneapolis Releases Transcript of George Floyd 911 Call," CBS News, May 29, 2020, www.cbsnews.com/news/george-floyd-death-911-transcript-minneapolis-police/.

3. Erica L. Green and Katie Benner, "Witness Who Was in Floyd's Car Says His Friend Did Not Resist Arrest," *New York Times*, June 4, 2020, www.nytimes.com/2020/06/04/us/politics/george-floyd-witness-morries-lester-hall.html.

4. www.facebook.com/darnellareallprettymarie/posts/1425398217661280/.

5. Ibid.

6. www.facebook.com/darnellareallprettymarie/posts/pfbid02CpBxUYDBh3K8EM
   D9UUvme4vei5wYX55n4B5jkb2cC3BrUt6TBX4qxV1bgCorjAoil.

7. twitter.com/aliciagarza/status/1265481390985900032.

8. www.instagram.com/p/CAxyXWOAPiL.

9. Monica Anderson, Michael Barthel, Andrew Perrin, and Emily A. Vogels, "#Black-
   LivesMatter Surges on Twitter After George Floyd's Death," Pew Research Center, June 10, 2020, www.pewresearch.org/short-reads/2020/06/10/blacklives
   matter-surges-on-twitter-after-george-floyds-death/.

10. Valerie Wirtschafter, "How George Floyd Changed the Online Conversation
    Around BLM," Brookings, June 17, 2021, www.brookings.edu/articles/how
    -george-floyd-changed-the-online-conversation-around-black-lives-matter/.

11. Derrick Bryson Taylor, "George Floyd Protests: A Timeline," *New York Times*, No-
    vember 5, 2021, www.nytimes.com/article/george-floyd-protests-timeline.html.

12. Robert Samuels and Toluse Olorunnipa, *His Name Is George Floyd* (New York: Vi-
    king, 2022).

13. Louis King, "The NCRT 2020: An African American Community Response,"
    March 30, 2020, https://s3.documentcloud.org/documents/6827036/NCRT-Col
    lectiveResponse-March30.pdf.

14. twitter.com/realDonaldTrump/status/1251168994066944003.

15. Ben Westcott et al., "May 25 Coronavirus News," CNN, May 25, 2020, www.cnn
    .com/world/live-news/coronavirus-pandemic-05-25-20-intl/promise.

16. Latoya Hill and Samantha Artiga, "COVID-19 Cases and Deaths by Race/Ethnicity:
    Current Data and Changes over Time," KFF, August 22, 2022, www.kff.org/racial
    -equity-and-health-policy/issue-brief/covid-19-cases-and-deaths-by-race-ethnicity
    -current-data-and-changes-over-time/.

17. "Reverend Al Sharpton George Floyd Funeral Eulogy Transcript," June 9, 2020,
    www.rev.com/blog/transcripts/reverend-al-sharpton-george-floyd-funeral-eulogy
    -transcript-june-9.

18. Larry Buchanan, Quoctrung Bui, and Jugal K. Patel, "Black Lives Matter May Be
    the Largest Movement in U.S. History," *New York Times*, July 3, 2020, www.ny
    times.com/interactive/2020/07/03/us/george-floyd-protests-crowd-size.html.

19. Amanda Barroso and Rachel Minkin, "Recent Protest Attendees Are More Racially
    and Ethnically Diverse, Younger than Americans Overall," Pew Research Center,
    June 24, 2020, www.pewresearch.org/short-reads/2020/06/24/recent-protest-at
    tendees-are-more-racially-and-ethnically-diverse-younger-than-americans-overall/.

20. Buchanan, Bui, and Patel, "Black Lives Matter May Be the Largest Movement in
    U.S. History."

21. twitter.com/realDonaldTrump/status/1266231100780744704.

22. Isaac Chotiner, "A Black Lives Matter Co-Founder Explains Why This Time Is Dif-
    ferent," *The New Yorker*, June 3, 2020, www.newyorker.com/news/q-and-a/a-black
    -lives-matter-co-founder-explains-why-this-time-is-different.

23. twitter.com/realDonaldTrump/status/1266231100780744704.

24. Cameron Easley, "Floyd Protests Are Backed by Most Americans as More Say
    Racism Isn't Taken Seriously Enough," Morning Consult, June 1, 2020, pro

.morningconsult.com/articles/floyd-protests-are-backed-by-most-americans-as
-more-say-racism-isnt-taken-seriously-enough.

25. Roudabeh Kishi and Sam Jones, "Demonstrations and Political Violence in America: New Data for Summer 2020," ACLED, September 3, 2020, https://acleddata.com/2020 /09/03/demonstrations-political-violence-in-america-new-data-for-summer-2020/.

26. Peter Baker, "A Long History of Language That Incites and Demonizes," *New York Times*, August 31, 2020, www.nytimes.com/2020/08/31/us/politics/trump-police -protests.html.

27. "Statement by the President," The White House, June 1, 2020, trumpwhitehouse .archives.gov/briefings-statements/statement-by-the-president-39/.

28. Peter Baker et al., "How Trump's Idea for a Photo Op Led to Havoc in a Park," *New York Times*, June 2, 2020, www.nytimes.com/2020/06/02/us/politics/trump-walk -lafayette-square.html.

29. Mary Jordan and Scott Clement, "Rallying Nation," *Washington Post*, April 6, 2018, www.washingtonpost.com/news/national/wp/2018/04/06/feature/in-reaction-to -trump-millions-of-americans-are-joining-protests-and-getting-political/.

30. Veronica Stracqualursi, "Congress' Asian Pacific American Caucus Chair: It's Dangerous for Trump to Call Coronavirus 'the Chinese Virus,'" CNN, March 21, 2020, www.cnn.com/2020/03/21/politics/judy-chu-coronavirus-trump-china/index.html.

31. "President Trump Calls Coronavirus 'Kung Flu,'" BBC, June 24, 2020, www.bbc .com/news/av/world-us-canada-53173436.

32. "Mandates of the Special Rapporteur on Contemporary Forms of Racism, Racial Discrimination, Xenophobia and Related Intolerance; the Special Rapporteur on the Human Rights of Migrants; and the Working Group on Discrimination Against Women and Girls," United Nations, August 12, 2020, https://spcommreports .ohchr.org/TMResultsBase/DownLoadPublicCommunicationFile?gId=25476.

33. Ibid.

34. Juliana Menasce Horowitz, Anna Brown, and Kiana Cox, "Race in America 2019," Pew Research Center, April 9, 2019, www.pewresearch.org/social -trends/2019/04/09/race-in-america-2019/.

35. "Presidential Approval Ratings—Donald Trump," Gallup, https://news.gallup .com/poll/203198/presidential-approval-ratings-donald-trump.aspx.

36. Donna M. Owens, "Jim Clyburn Changed Everything for Joe Biden's Campaign. He's Been a Political Force for a Long Time," *Washington Post*, April 1, 2020, www.washingtonpost.com/lifestyle/style/jim-clyburn-changed-everything-for-joe -bidens-campaign-hes-been-a-political-force-for-a-long-time/2020/03/30/7d054e9 8-6d33-11ea-aa80-c2470c6b2034_story.html.

37. Chris Kahn, "POLL-Clyburn's Endorsement of Biden 'a Factor' for a Majority of South Carolina Voters," Reuters, February 29, 2020, www.reuters.com/article/usa -election-south-carolina/poll-clyburns-endorsement-of-biden-a-factor-for-a-major ity-of-south-carolina-voters-idUSL1N29Z1KX/.

38. Sybrina Fulton, "Black Lives Matter Founders Alicia Garza, Patrisse Cullors and Opal Tometi," *Time*, September 22, 2020, time.com/collection/100-most-influen tial-people-2020/5888228/black-lives-matter-founders/.

39. "Black Lives Matter 2020 Impact Report," Black Lives Matter, blacklivesmatter .com/wp-content/uploads/2021/02/blm-2020-impact-report.pdf.

40. "Get Ready to Vote," Black Lives Matter, https://blacklivesmatter.com/vote/.
41. twitter.com/aliciagarza/status/1290767518055796736.
42. twitter.com/aliciagarza/status/1289695334747127808.
43. twitter.com/aliciagarza/status/1296667186698653696.
44. Alicia Garza, "With Kamala Harris in the VP Slot, We Just Made History—Let's Do It Again in November," *Glamour*, August 12, 2020, www.glamour.com/story/alicia-garza-kamala-harris-vice-president-history.
45. "Transcript: Joe Biden's DNC Speech," CNN, August 21, 2020, www.cnn.com/2020/08/20/politics/biden-dnc-speech-transcript/index.html.
46. "Statement by Patrisse Cullors, Executive Director, Black Lives Matter Global Network on the Attempted Murder of Jacob Blake," Black Lives Matter, August 25, 2020, blacklivesmatter.com/statement-by-patrisse-cullors-executive-director-black-lives-matter-global-network-on-the-attempted-murder-of-jacob-blake/.
47. Faith Karimi, "Kenosha Shooting Suspect Called a Friend to Say He 'Killed Somebody,' Police Say, and then Shot Two Others," CNN, August 28, 2020, www.cnn.com/2020/08/28/us/kyle-rittenhouse-kenosha-shooting/index.html.
48. "Transcript: Donald Trump's RNC speech," CNN, August 28, 2020, www.cnn.com/2020/08/28/politics/donald-trump-speech-transcript/index.html.
49. "As Trump Visits Kenosha, Hundreds Gather Where Jacob Blake Was Shot," *New York Times*, September 1, 2020, www.nytimes.com/live/2020/09/01/us/trump-vs-biden.
50. Matt Viser and Dan Simmons, "Biden, in Kenosha, Vows That America Will Address Racism and 'Original Sin' of Slavery," *Washington Post*, September 3, 2020, www.washingtonpost.com/politics/biden-kenosha-jacob-blake/2020/09/03/adb60b36-edfd-11ea-b4bc-3a2098fc73d4_story.html.
51. "September 29, 2020 Presidential Debate Transcript," The Commission on Presidential Debates, www.debates.org/voter-education/debate-transcripts/september-29-2020-debate-transcript/.
52. Sheera Frenkel and Annie Karni, "Proud Boys Celebrate Trump's 'Stand by' Remark About Them at the Debate," *New York Times*, September 29, 2020, www.nytimes.com/2020/09/29/us/trump-proud-boys-biden.html.
53. Marina Pitofsky, "Harris Blasts Trump for Refusing to Denounce White Supremacy," *The Hill*, September 30, 2020, thehill.com/homenews/campaign/518896-harris-blasts-trump-for-not-condemning-white-supremacy/.
54. twitter.com/realDonaldTrump/status/1311892190680014849.
55. "Transcript of the Presidential Debate at Belmont University in Nashville, Tennessee," The Commission on Presidential Debates, October 22, 2020, www.debates.org/voter-education/debate-transcripts/october-22-2020-debate-transcript/.
56. twitter.com/aliciagarza/status/1319730484390227969.
57. "Voter turnout, 2018–2022," Pew Research Center, July 12, 2023, www.pewresearch.org/politics/2023/07/12/voter-turnout-2018-2022/.
58. twitter.com/sartorialgirl/status/1324738648970010627.
59. Ruth Igielnik, Scott Keeter, and Hannah Hartig, "Behind Biden's 2020 Victory," Pew Research Center, June 30, 2021, www.pewresearch.org/politics/2021/06/30/behind-bidens-2020-victory/.
60. twitter.com/aliciagarza/status/1325117593485602819.

61. "Black Lives Matter Global Network Statement About Biden-Harris Victory," Black Lives Matter, November 7, 2020, blacklivesmatter.com/black-lives-matter-global-network-statement-about-biden-harris-victory/.

62. "Address in Wilmington, Delaware Accepting Election as the 46th President of the United States," The American Presidency Project, November 7, 2020, www.presidency.ucsb.edu/documents/address-wilmington-delaware-accepting-election-the-46th-president-the-united-states.

63. twitter.com/realDonaldTrump/status/1340185773220515840.

9: A NEW CONFEDERATE MOVEMENT

1. "Race Relations," Gallup, 2021, news.gallup.com/poll/1687/race-relations.aspx.

2. "Homeland Threat Assessment," Department of Homeland Security, October 2020, https://www.dhs.gov/sites/default/files/publications/2020_10_06_homeland-threat-assessment.pdf.

3. *The Lead with Jake Tapper*, CNN, January 12, 2021, www.cnn.com/TRANSCRIPTS/2101/12/cg.01.html.

4. "Rioter Who Menaced Officer with Confederate Flag Gets Prison," Associated Press, February 9, 2023, https://news.yahoo.com/rioter-menaced-officer-confederate-flag-231350174.html.

5. Caleb Newton, "Trump Goon Who Chased Officer Goodman Given 2 Years in Jail," *Bipartisan Report*, October 25, 2022, https://bipartisanreport.com/2022/10/25/trump-goon-who-chased-officer-goodman-given-2-years-in-jail/.

6. Dalton Bennett et al., "17 Requests for Backup in 78 Minutes," *Washington Post*, April 15, 2021, https://www.washingtonpost.com/investigations/interactive/2021/dc-police-records-capitol-riot/.

7. Matthew Brown, "How Pence Came to Finally Blame Trump for Jan. 6 Capitol Attack," March 15, 2023, https://www.washingtonpost.com/national-security/2023/03/15/mike-pence-trump-january-6/.

8. Michael D. Shear and Jim Tankersley, "Biden Denounces Storming of Capitol as a 'Dark Moment' in Nation's History," *New York Times*, January 6, 2021, www.nytimes.com/2021/01/06/us/politics/biden-capitol-congress.html.

9. twitter.com/JoeBiden/status/1346929533774159876.

10. twitter.com/BarackObama/status/1346983894298595330.

11. "Videotaped Remarks During the Insurrection at the United States Capitol," The American Presidency Project, January 6, 2021, www.presidency.ucsb.edu/documents/videotaped-remarks-during-the-insurrection-the-united-states-capitol.

12. "Mike Pence's Statement to the Senate on the Storming of the Capitol," *U.S. News & World Report*, January 6, 2021, www.usnews.com/news/elections/articles/2021-01-06/read-mike-pences-statement-to-the-senate-on-the-storming-of-the-capitol.

13. Chris Cameron, "These Are the People Who Died in Connection with the Capitol Riot," *New York Times*, January 5, 2022, www.nytimes.com/2022/01/05/us/politics/jan-6-capitol-deaths.html.

14. Irene Loewenson, "Mattis Says Vets at Jan. 6 Capitol Riot 'Don't Define the Military,'" *Marine Corps Times*, November 6, 2023, www.marinecorpstimes.com/news/your-marine-corps/2023/11/06/mattis-says-vets-at-jan-6-capitol-riot-dont-define-the-military/.

15. Todd C. Helmus, Ryan Andrew Brown, and Rajeev Ramchand, "Prevalence of Veteran Support for Extremist Groups and Extremist Beliefs," RAND, September 11, 2023, www.rand.org/pubs/research_reports/RRA1071-2-v2.html.

16. Astead W. Herndon, "America in 2021: Racial Progress in the South, a White Mob in the Capitol," *New York Times*, January 8, 2021, www.nytimes.com/2021/01/08/us/politics/trump-georgia-capitol-racism.html.

17. twitter.com/Blklivesmatter/status/1346930035324645377.

18. "Capitol Siege: If Rioters Were Black, 'Hundreds' Would Be Killed," *Al Jazeera*, January 8, 2021, www.aljazeera.com/news/2021/1/8/if-rioters-who-stormed-capitol-hundreds-would-have.

19. Shaun Harper, "The U.S. Capitol Insurrection Was a Case Study in White Privilege. Teach It That Way," *Education Week*, January 5, 2022, www.edweek.org/teaching-learning/opinion-the-u-s-capitol-insurrection-was-a-case-study-in-white-privilege-teach-it-that-way/2022/01.

20. Derek Major, "Former Head of D.C. National Guard Says if Black People Led Capitol Riot, More People Would've Died," *Black Enterprise*, December 29, 2022, www.blackenterprise.com/former-head-of-d-c-national-guard-says-if-jan-6th-rioters-were-black-more-people-would-have-2/.

21. Barbara Sprunt, "After Voting to Acquit, McConnell Torches Trump as Responsible for Riot," NPR, February 13, 2021, www.npr.org/sections/trump-impeachment-trial-live-updates/2021/02/13/967701180/after-vote-mcconnell-torched-trump-as-practically-and-morally-responsible-for-ri.

22. "Inaugural Address by President Joseph R. Biden, Jr.," The White House, January 20, 2021, www.whitehouse.gov/briefing-room/speeches-remarks/2021/01/20/inaugural-address-by-president-joseph-r-biden-jr/.

23. Josh Boak and Hannah Fingerhut, "AP VoteCast: Competing Coalitions Define GA Senate Races," Associated Press, January 6, 2021, apnews.com/ap-votecast-competing-coalitions-define-ga-senate-races-6ff7ce7c61e9e5e812a2665ccc4c66b2.

24. Author's interview with Stacey Abrams, August 1, 2023.

25. twitter.com/Blklivesmatter/status/1336817575976726532.

26. Marisa Schultz, "Black Lives Matter Accuses Biden of Ignoring Them: 'It's Demeaning to Our Hurt and Trauma,'" Fox News, December 11, 2020, www.foxnews.com/politics/black-lives-matter-biden-ignoring-demeaning.

27. Juliana Menasce Horowitz, Kiley Hurst, and Dana Braga, "Support for the Black Lives Matter Movement Has Dropped Considerably from Its Peak in 2020," Pew Research Center, June 14, 2023, www.pewresearch.org/social-trends/2023/06/14/support-for-the-black-lives-matter-movement-has-dropped-considerably-from-its-peak-in-2020/.

28. Ryan Grim, "Inside Biden's Meetings with Civil Rights Leaders," *The Intercept*, December 10, 2020, theintercept.com/2020/12/10/biden-audio-meeting-civil-rights-leaders/.

29. Author's interview with Rep. James Clyburn, August 22, 2023.

30. "BLM's 7 Demands," Black Lives Matter, blacklivesmatter.com/blm-demands/.

31. "It Is Time for Accountability," #BLM10, November 10, 2020, www.blmchapterstatement.com/no1/.

32. Aaron Morrison, "AP Exclusive: Black Lives Matter Opens Up About Its Finances,"

Associated Press, February 23, 2021, apnews.com/article/black-lives-matter
-90-million-finances-8a80cad199f54c0c4b9e74283d27366f.

33. Alex Hammer, "Black Lives Matter Secretly Used $6 Million in Donations to Buy
Luxurious 6,500-Square Foot Mansion with Seven Bedrooms and Parking for 20
Cars in Southern California in 2020 Where Leaders Have Filmed YouTube Vid-
eos," *Daily Mail*, April 4, 2022, www.dailymail.co.uk/news/article-10685303/Black
-Lives-Matter-secretly-used-6-million-donations-buy-luxurious-6-500-square
-foot-mansion.html.

34. Sean Campbell, "The Murky Finances of Black Lives Matter," *New York*, January 21, 2022, nymag.com/intelligencer/2022/01/black-lives-matter-finances.html.

35. Kelly Byrne, "Breonna Taylor's Mom Slams BLM Chapter in Louisville as a
'Fraud,'" *New York Post*, April 17, 2021, nypost.com/2021/04/17/breonna-taylors
-mom-slams-blm-louisville-as-a-fraud/.

36. Aaron Morrison, "BLM's Patrisse Cullors to Step Down from Movement Foundation," Associated Press, May 27, 2021, apnews.com/article/ca-state-wire-george
-floyd-philanthropy-race-and-ethnicity-0a89ec240a702537a3d89d281789adcf.

37. Isabel Vincent, "Mothers Criticize BLM Activists for Profiting off Their Dead
Sons," *New York Post*, May 29, 2021, nypost.com/2021/05/29/mothers-criticize
-blm-activists-for-profiting-off-their-dead-sons/.

38. "A Conversation with Patrisse Cullors," *Into America*, MSNBC, May 16, 2022,
www.msnbc.com/podcast/into-america/transcript-patrisse-cullors-making-mis
takes-n1295454.

39. Trace William Cowen, "Patrisse Cullors, BLM Co-Founder, Addresses Accusa-
tion Organization Used Donations to Buy $6 Million House," *Yahoo Finance*,
April 6, 2022, finance.yahoo.com/news/patrisse-cullors-blm-co-founder-204
251405.html.

40. twitter.com/Sean_Kev/status/1511008589322022912.

41. Ailisa Chang, "Secret $6 Million Home Has Allies and Critics Skeptical of BLM
Foundation's Finances," *All Things Considered*, NPR, April 7, 2022, www.npr
.org/2022/04/07/1091487910/blm-leaders-face-questions-after-allegedly-buying
-a-mansion-with-donation-money.

42. Washington Post Staff, "Police Shootings Database 2015–2024: Search by Race,
Age, Department," *Washington Post*, December 5, 2022, https://www.washington
post.com/graphics/investigations/police-shootings-database/.

43. "Scott Statement on Police Reform Negotiations," Senator Tim Scott (R-SC), September 22, 2021, www.scott.senate.gov/media-center/press-releases/scott-state
ment-on-police-reform-negotiations/.

44. "Booker Statement on Bipartisan Policing Reform Negotiations," Senator Cory
Booker (D-NJ), September 22, 2021, www.booker.senate.gov/news/press/booker
-statement-on-bipartisan-policing-reform-negotiations.

45. "Department of Justice Announces Department-Wide Policy on Chokeholds and
'No-Knock' Entries," U.S. Department of Justice, September 14, 2021, www.jus
tice.gov/opa/pr/department-justice-announces-department-wide-policy-choke
holds-and-no-knock-entries.

46. Juana Summers and Deirdre Walsh, "Democrats' Biggest Push for Voting
Rights Fails with No Republicans on Board," NPR, October 20, 2021, www.npr

.org/2021/10/20/1040238982/senate-democrats-are-pushing-a-voting-rights-bill
-republicans-have-vowed-to-bloc.

47. "Remarks by President Biden on Protecting the Right to Vote," The White House, January 11, 2022, www.whitehouse.gov/briefing-room/speeches-remarks /2022/01/11/remarks-by-president-biden-on-protecting-the-right-to-vote/.

48. "Democrats Conveniently Ignore Their Own Impassioned Defense of the Filibuster," Senator Mitt Romney (R-UT), January 11, 2022, www.romney.senate.gov /romney-democrats-conveniently-ignore-their-own-impassioned-defense-fili buster/.

49. "Profoundly Unpresidential," Senate Mitch McConnell (R-KY), January 12, 2022, www.republicanleader.senate.gov/newsroom/remarks/profoundly-unpresidential.

50. Seung Min Kim, Mike DeBonis, and Amy B Wang, "Biden Calls for Changing the Filibuster in Major Voting Rights Speech," *Washington Post*, January 12, 2022, www.washingtonpost.com/politics/biden-voting-rights-filibuster/2022/01/11 /ada7ce66-72dd-11ec-b202-b9b92330d4fa_story.html.

51. Alana Wise, "Juneteenth Is Now a Federal Holiday," NPR, June 17, 2021, www .npr.org/2021/06/17/1007602290/biden-and-harris-will-speak-at-the-bill-signing -making-juneteenth-a-federal-holi.

52. twitter.com/realDonaldTrump/status/1270787978626052096.

53. David Petraeus, "Take the Confederate Names off Our Army Bases," *The Atlantic*, June 9, 2020, www.theatlantic.com/ideas/archive/2020/06/take-confederate -names-off-our-army-bases/612832/.

54. "Remarks by Vice President Harris at Signing of H.R. 55, 'The Emmett Till Antilynching Act,'" The White House, March 29, 2022, www.whitehouse.gov /briefing-room/speeches-remarks/2022/03/29/remarks-by-vice-president-harris -at-signing-of-h-r-55-the-emmett-till-antilynching-act/.

55. Fabiola Cineas, "What an Anti-Lynching Law Means in 2022," *Vox*, March 29, 2022, www.vox.com/22995013/anti-lynching-act-emmett-till.

56. "Statement from Rashad Robinson, President of Color of Change, on passage of Emmett Till Antilynching Act," Color of Change, March 29, 2022, mta-sts.color ofchange.org/press_release/statement-from-rashad-robinson-president-of-color -of-change-on-passage-of-emmett-till-antilynching-act/.

57. Author's interview with Rep. James Clyburn, August 22, 2023.

58. "Remarks by President Biden on the Retirement of Supreme Court Justice Stephen Breyer," The White House, January 27, 2022, www.whitehouse.gov/briefing-room /speeches-remarks/2022/01/27/remarks-by-president-biden-on-the-retirement-of -supreme-court-justice-stephen-breyer/.

59. Timothy Bella, "Critics Slam Cruz for Saying Biden's Vow to Nominate First Black Woman to Supreme Court Is 'Offensive,'" *Washington Post*, February 1, 2022, www .washingtonpost.com/politics/2022/02/01/cruz-black-woman-biden-supreme -court/.

60. "Remarks by President Biden on his Nomination of Judge Ketanji Brown Jackson to Serve as Associate Justice of the U.S. Supreme Court," The White House, February 25, 2022, www.whitehouse.gov/briefing-room/speeches-remarks/2022/02/25 /remarks-by-president-biden-on-his-nomination-of-judge-ketanji-brown-jackson -to-serve-as-associate-justice-of-the-u-s-supreme-court/.

61. "Congratulations Judge Jackson!," Black Lives Matter, February 28, 2022, black livesmatter.com/congratulations-judge-jackson/.

62. Libby Cathey, "Highlights from Senate Vote to Confirm Ketanji Brown Jackson," ABC News, March 14, 2022, abcnews.go.com/Politics/live-updates/?id=8353215 1&offset=57.

63. Author's interview with Stacey Abrams, August 1, 2023.

64. "Remarks by President Biden, Vice President Harris, and Judge Ketanji Brown Jackson on the Senate's Historic, Bipartisan Confirmation of Judge Jackson to Be an Associate Justice of the Supreme Court," The White House, April 8, 2022, www.whitehouse.gov/briefing-room/speeches-remarks/2022/04/08/remarks -by-president-biden-vice-president-harris-and-judge-ketanji-brown-jackson-on -the-senates-historic-bipartisan-confirmation-of-judge-jackson-to-be-an-associate -justice-of-the-supreme-court/.

10: THE BLOWUP

1. Aaron Morrison, "New Black Lives Matter Tax Documents Show Foundation Is Tightening Its Belt, Has $30M in Assets," Associated Press, May 26, 2023, ap news.com/article/black-lives-matter-donations-george-floyd-protests-ddcf0d 21d130a5d46256aa6c5d145ea7.

2. Juliana Menasce Horowitz, Kiley Hurst, and Dana Braga, "Support for the Black Lives Matter Movement Has Dropped Considerably from Its Peak in 2020," Pew Research Center, June 14, 2023, www.pewresearch.org/social-trends/2023/06/14 /views-on-the-black-lives-matter-movement/.

3. Sam Levin, "Patrisse Cullors on 10 Years of Black Lives Matter: 'A Painful Reminder of What Hasn't Changed,'" *The Guardian*, February 5, 2023, www.theguardian .com/world/2023/feb/05/patrisse-cullors-black-lives-matter-keenan-anderson.

4. "A Conversation with Patrisse Cullors," *Into America*, MSNBC, May 16, 2022, www.msnbc.com/podcast/into-america/transcript-patrisse-cullors-making-mis takes-n1295454.

5. Hannah Hartig, Andrew Daniller, Scott Keeter, and Ted Van Green. "Demographic Profiles of Republican and Democratic Voters," Pew Research Center, July 12, 2023, www.pewresearch.org/politics/2023/07/12/demographic-profiles-of-repub lican-and-democratic-voters/.

6. Florida CS/HB 7, 2022, www.flsenate.gov/Committees/BillSummaries/2022 /html/2809.

7. Joana Williams, "A Brief History of Woke," *Spiked*, May 272022, www.spiked-on line.com/2022/05/27/a-brief-history-of-woke/.

8. Sam Dorman, "Chris Rufo Calls on Trump to End Critical Race Theory 'Cult Indoctrination' in Federal Government," *Tucker Carlson Tonight*, Fox News, September 1, 2020, www.foxnews.com/politics/chris-rufo-race-theory-cult-federal -government.

9. Benjamin Wallace-Wells, "How a Conservative Activist Invented the Conflict over Critical Race Theory," *The New Yorker*, June 18, 2021, www.newyorker.com/news /annals-of-inquiry/how-a-conservative-activist-invented-the-conflict-over-critical -race-theory.

10. Paul Kiernan, "Conservative Activist Grabbed Trump's Eye on Diversity Training,"

The Wall Street Journal, October 9, 2020, www.wsj.com/articles/conservative-ac
tivist-grabbed-trumps-eye-on-diversity-training-11602242287.

11. Daniel Golden, "Muzzled by DeSantis, Critical Race Theory Professors Cancel
Courses or Modify Their Teaching," *ProPublica*, June 3, 2023, www.propublica
.org/article/desantis-critical-race-theory-florida-college-professors.

12. Christopher Rufo, "The Courage of Our Convictions," *City Journal*, April 22,
2021, www.city-journal.org/article/the-courage-of-our-convictions.

13. twitter.com/realchrisrufo/status/1611406507815636993.

14. Moms for Liberty, www.momsforliberty.org/about/.

15. "Moms for Liberty," Southern Poverty Law Center, www.splcenter.org/fighting
-hate/extremist-files/group/moms-liberty.

16. Lisa Lerer and Patricia Mazzei, "Florida Sex Scandal Shakes Moms for Liberty, as
Group's Influence Wanes," *New York Times*, December 16, 2023, www.nytimes
.com/2023/12/16/us/politics/moms-for-liberty-sex-scandal.html.

17. "Youngkin Denounces Critical Race Theory, Promises to Restore 'Excellence' to
Virginia Schools," 1776Action, September 14, 2021, 1776action.org/2021/09/14
/transcript-youngkin-denounces-critical-race-theory-promises-to-restore-excel
lence-to-virginia-schools/.

18. Executive Order Number 1, "Ending the Use of Inherently Divisive Concepts, Including Critical Race Theory, and Restoring Excellence in K–12 Public Education
in the Commonwealth," January 15, 2022, www.governor.virginia.gov/executive
-actions/executive-ordersdirectives/executive-action-title-918432-en.html.

19. Gabriella Borter, Joseph Ax, and Joseph Tanfani, "School Boards Get Death
Threats Amid Rage over Race, Gender, Mask Policies," Reuters, February 15, 2022,
www.reuters.com/investigates/special-report/usa-education-threats/.

20. *Allen v. Milligan*, 599 U.S. 1 (2023), www.supremecourt.gov/opinions/22pdf/21
-1086_1co6.pdf.

21. Executive Order 10925—Establishing the President's Committee on Equal Em-
ployment Opportunity," March 6, 1961 www.presidency.ucsb.edu/documents
/executive-order-10925-establishing-the-presidents-committee-equal-employ
ment-opportunity.

22. Charlotte Steeh and Maria Krysan, "Affirmative Action and the Public, 1970–1995."
The Public Opinion Quarterly 60, no. 1 (Spring 1996): 128–58.

23. *Regents of Univ. of California v. Bakke*, 438 U.S. 265 (1978), supreme.justia.com
/cases/federal/us/438/265/.

24. *Grutter v. Bollinger*, 539 U.S. 306 (2003), supreme.justia.com/cases/federal
/us/539/306/.

25. David Moore, "Public: Only Merit Should Count in College Admissions," Gallup,
June 24, 2003, news.gallup.com/poll/8689/public-only-merit-should-count-col
lege-admissions.aspx.

26. *Students for Fair Admissions v. Harvard*, 600 U.S. 181 (2023), www.supremecourt
.gov/opinions/22pdf/20-1199_hgdj.pdf.

27. Ibid.

28. NAACP, "NAACP Condemns SCOTUS Ruling on Affirmative Action," June 29,
2023, https://naacp.org/articles/naacp-condemns-scotus-ruling-affirmative-action.

29. "Civil Rights Organizations Denounce SCOTUS Decision in Affirmative Action

Case," National Urban League, April 7, 2024, nul.org/news/civil-rights-organiza tions-announce-virtual-news-conference-on-scotus-affirmative-action-decision.

30. Color of Change Board Chairs, "Facing Challenges, Moving Forward," Color of Change, June 22, 2023, https://medium.com/@cocboardchairs/facing-challenges -moving-forward-a8b46547ab05.

31. Center for Antiracist Research, www.bu.edu/antiracism-center/.

32. Michelle Goldberg, "Ibram X. Kendi and the Problem of Celebrity Fund-Raising," *New York Times*, September 25, 2023, www.nytimes.com/2023/09/25/opinion/col umnists/kendi-center-antiracist-research.html.

33. twitter.com/realchrisrufo/status/1704877709061697969.

34. Devin Dwyer, "Justice Ketanji Brown Jackson Says 'Whole Truth' About Black History Must Be Taught," ABC News, September 15, 2023, abcnews.go.com/Politics /justice-ketanji-brown-jackson-truth-black-history-taught/story?id=103220003.

35. Frederick Douglass, "West India Emancipation," speech, August 3, 1857, www .blackpast.org/african-american-history/1857-frederick-douglass-if-there-no -struggle-there-no-progress/.

CONCLUSION

1. "Commencement Address at Howard University," The American Presidency Project, May 7, 2016, www.presidency.ucsb.edu/documents/commencement-address -howard-university-1.

2. Author's interview with Rev. Al Sharpton, May 9, 2022.

3. Author's interview with Rep. James Clyburn, August 22, 2023.

4. Author's interview with Ben Crump, June 21, 2023.

5. Author's interview with Dr. Wayne Frederick, September 28, 2023.

6. Jonathan Vespa, Lauren Medina, and David M. Armstrong, "Demographic Turning Points for the United States: Population Projections for 2020 to 2060," U.S. Census Bureau, March 2018, https://www.census.gov/content/dam/Census/library/publi cations/2020/demo/p25-1144.pdf.

7. "Americans Divided on Whether 'Woke' Is a Compliment or Insult," *USA Today/* Ipsos, March 8, 2023, www.ipsos.com/en-us/americans-divided-whether-woke -compliment-or-insult.

8. Author's interview with Wade Henderson, June 27, 2022.

9. Author's interview with Stacey Abrams, August 1, 2023.

10. Katherine Schaffer, "The Changing Face of Congress in 8 Charts," Pew Research Center, February 7, 2023, www.pewresearch.org/short-reads/2023/02/07/the -changing-face-of-congress/.

11. "Women Increasingly Outnumber Men at U.S. Colleges—But Why?," *The Feed*, Georgetown University, September 10, 2021, feed.georgetown.edu/access-afford ability/women-increasingly-outnumber-men-at-u-s-colleges-but-why/.

12. Erica Pandey, "The Rise of Interracial Marriage—And Its Approval Rating," *Axios*, September 6, 2022, www.axios.com/2022/09/07/approval-of-interracial-marriage -america.

13. Justin McCarthy, "U.S. Same-Sex Marriage Support Holds at 71% High," Gallup, June 5, 2023, news.gallup.com/poll/506636/sex-marriage-support-holds-high .aspx.

14. "World Migration Report, 2022," International Organization for Migration, United Nations, reliefweb.int/report/world/world-migration-report-2022?gad_source=1 &gclid=Cj0KCQjwiMmwBhDmARIsABeQ7xRn5ocubuoA9iLT-sWfRd0xsyM VZjk-w3Pzz5-ovJYXHYe2c3S42j8aAlbwEALw_wcB.

15. Author's interview with Stacey Abrams, August 1, 2023.

16. Author's interview with Marc Morial, October 15, 2023.

17. Author's interview with Stacey Abrams, August 1, 2023.

18. Author's interview with Patrick Gaspard, July 20, 2022.

19. "QuickFacts Wyoming," U.S. Census Bureau, July 1, 2023, www.census.gov /quickfacts/fact/table/WY/PST045223.

Index

Till, Emmett, 53–54, 187, 214. *see also*
Emmett Till Antilynching Act
Time magazine, 82–83, 106, 120, 130, 140
Tlaib, Rashida, 126, 129
Tometi, Opal, 65, 80, 81–82, 106,
131–132, 156
Trump, Donald, and administration
backlash against, 127, 140–141
and COVID-19 pandemic, 152
and events in Charlottesville, Va.,
113–115
false election claims, 133
impeachment trials of, 175
and January 6 insurrection, 170–173
on Colin Kaepernick, 100
and Barack Obama, 39, 41
Barack Obama on, 133
online posts of, 144145
on Pittsburgh killings, 125–126
and presidential campaign (2016),
85–87, 89–90, 99, 101, 103
and presidential election (2016),
104–105
and Republican Party, 207
responses to killings of Black men and
police, 99
and Russia, 117
Trump, Fred, 90
21 Savage, 132

Underwood, Lauren, 126
UnidosUS, 205
United States
demographic changes, 7, 10
as white-majority country, 216
"Unite the Right" rally, 112
University of California, Davis, 203
University of Massachusetts-Amherst, 11
University of North Carolina, 203
University of Pennsylvania, 57
University of Southern California, 175
University of Virginia, 112
Urban League, The, 205
USA Today, 64, 217
U.S.-Mexico border wall, 93, 118

VDARE (website), 112
Virginia, 199–200

voter suppression, 135–136. *see also* Black
voters
Voting Rights Act, 8, 135, 201

Waithe, Lena, 107
Walker, William, 175
Wallace, Chris, 165
Wall Street Journal, 93
Walt Disney Company, 198
Walters, Ron, 30
Warnock, Raphael, 44, 176–177
Warren, Elizabeth, 159
Washington Post, 40, 46, 57, 86–87, 99,
109, 110, 114, 181
Watts, Daniel J., 67
Welker, Kristen, 167
Wells, Ida B., 187
West, Cornel, 41
West, Kanye, 121
When They Call You a Terrorist (Cullors),
132
white backlash, among Trump supporters,
93
white evangelical voters, 12
White Fragility (DiAngelo), 131
White House Press Office, 45
white supremacy and supremacists, 89,
111, 113–114, 145, 170, 215
Wilson, Darren, 72–73, 81
Winfrey, Oprah, 136, 139
"woke" culture, 143, 196, 200, 217
women in Congress, 126
Women's March (2017), 130
Woodly, Deva, 155
World Migration Report, 218
Wray, Christopher, 145
Wright, Jeremiah, 33–34
Wyoming, 221

Yang, Andrew, 159
Young, Andrew, 30
Youngkin, Glenn, 199

Zarate, Jose Garcia, 84–85, 87
Ziegler, Bridget, 199
Ziegler, Christian, 199
Zimmerman, George, 50–51, 53, 55–57,
60–61, 64

About the Author

JUAN WILLIAMS is a prizewinning journalist and historian. He is the author of the best-selling civil rights history *Eyes on the Prize: America's Civil Rights Years 1954–1965*, which accompanied the PBS series of the same name. He also wrote the landmark biography of the first African American on the Supreme Court, *Thurgood Marshall: American Revolutionary*, as well as the *New York Times* best-sellers *Enough* and *Muzzled: The Assault on Honest Debate*. Williams worked for *The Washington Post* as a celebrated national political correspondent, White House correspondent, and editorial writer. His NPR talk show took ratings to a new high. He has written for *The New York Times*, *The Wall Street Journal*, *The New Yorker*, *The Atlantic*, and *Ebony*. He is currently senior political analyst for Fox News Channel and a columnist for *The Hill*.